T0304117

ROUTLEDGE LIBRARY EDITIONS:
THE ECONOMICS AND BUSINESS OF
TECHNOLOGY

Volume 41

THE MANAGEMENT IMPLICATIONS OF NEW INFORMATION TECHNOLOGY

THE MANAGEMENT IMPLICATIONS OF NEW INFORMATION TECHNOLOGY

Edited by
NIGEL F. PIERCY

LONDON AND NEW YORK

First published in 1984 by Croom Helm

This edition first published in 2018
by Routledge
2 Park Square, Milton Park, Abingdon, Oxon OX14 4RN

and by Routledge
711 Third Avenue, New York, NY 10017

Routledge is an imprint of the Taylor & Francis Group, an informa business

© 1984 N. Piercy

British Library Cataloguing in Publication Data
A catalogue record for this book is available from the British Library

ISBN: 978-1-138-50336-6 (Set)
ISBN: 978-1-351-06690-7 (Set) (ebk)
ISBN: 978-0-8153-5152-8 (Volume 41) (hbk)
ISBN: 978-1-351-14124-6 (Volume 41) (ebk)

Publisher's Note
The publisher has gone to great lengths to ensure the quality of this reprint but points out that some imperfections in the original copies may be apparent.

Disclaimer
The publisher has made every effort to trace copyright holders and would welcome correspondence from those they have been unable to trace.

THE MANAGEMENT IMPLICATIONS OF NEW INFORMATION TECHNOLOGY

EDITED BY
NIGEL PIERCY

CROOM HELM
London & Sydney
NICHOLS PUBLISHING COMPANY
New York

© 1984 N. Piercy
Croom Helm Ltd, Provident House, Burrell Row,
Beckenham, Kent BR3 1AT
Croom Helm Australia Pty Ltd, First Floor,
139 King Street, Sydney, NSW 2001, Australia

British Library Cataloguing in Publication Data

The Management implications of new
    information technology.
    1. Microelectronics   2. Industrial
    management
    I. Piercy, Nigel
    670'.68'4   HD45
    ISBN 0-7099-2073-3

First published in the United States of America 1984 by
Nichols Publishing Company, Post Office Box 96,
New York, NY 10024

Library of Congress Cataloging in Publication Data
Main entry under title:

The Management implications of new information technology.

    1. Management information systems.   2. Management
science. I. Piercy, Nigel.
T58.6.M335   1984   658.4   84-8260
ISBN 0-89397-201-0

Printed and bound in Great Britain

CONTENTS

LIST OF FIGURES

LIST OF TABLES

There is clearly wide recognition in the academic and popular literature that recent years have displayed all the signs of what may, without exaggeration, be regarded as a revolution in the general capacity to process information. Transformations in the ability to capture data, to manipulate and store them, and to disseminate and communicate information, and to apply these abilities in quite novel areas, have been radical and have occurred with escalating rapidity, frequency, and discontinuity.

While the widespread use of mainframe computers is a well-known and established fact of working life, it is the advent of newer technologies, and particularly microelectronics, which have raised the most fundamental and intractable issues. Indeed, it should be borne in mind that we continue to experience rapid, accelerating technological change, and it has been suggested, for example, that at the time of writing the microelectronics revolution is itself in danger of being overtaken by optics technology and other developments.

Indeed, it is the very pervasiveness and cheapness of new information technology, which generates a wide range of fundamental questions and increases the urgency of providing answers. The areas influenced by these issues in society at large are wideranging, but the particular focus in this book is the impact of new information technology on working life, and specifically its impact on business organisations and the managers and other employees within them.

It is clear that a great deal of attention has been devoted to the overt and observable impact of new information technology on business, in replacing earlier technologies. Most obvious, perhaps, are such examples as the micro or mini computer replacing the clerical handling of paperwork (or replacing the mainframe computer terminal) and the word processor replacing the typewriter in the office, or the automation of production processes through the use of computer controlled machines and robots. Even on this level, there have been some signs that such transitions have been far from straightforward, and change has been accompanied by unanticipated and often dysfunctional side-effects. For example, in upgrading management information systems through new technology, it has quickly become apparent that our understanding of how managers use information to make decisions is somewhat limited, and our ability to anticipate and cope with the organisational aspects of information systems change is even more constrained.

However, what is even more disturbing is that with continued innovation in information technology there are accompanying changes in organisational functioning and management processes, which are furthered by, as well as being implemented by, new technology. Our understanding, for instance, of the impact of new technology on management control to date may be considered as yet rudimentary, and yet of fundamental significance to organisational participants.

The suggestion, therefore, is that attention should be focussed, with some urgency, not simply on the problems of implementing new technology, but on the issues involved in adapting organisations and management to cope with a very different working situation. It is to this somewhat ambitious endeavour that this present volume is dedicated.

Perhaps the central point of the ideas and issues expounded here is that the technology exists and is largely in-place, with effects which have yet to be fully analysed. The implication is that the response required from management should be strategic and proactive and not merely an ad hoc reaction to implementation problems.

While the contributions put forward in this book are relatively wide-ranging, reflecting considerable variation in the background expertise and areas of specialisation of the authors, their common thread is the analysis of the importance of new information technology for management.

This first volume in the new UWIST/Croom Helm Series: Management and New Information Technology, aims to take a fairly general overview of the field, but it is to be followed by more specialised volumes on particular topics such as industrial relations, management control and organisational structure, and management information systems, among others.

The target readership for this current volume falls into two main areas: firstly, the business school, where management teachers, researchers and business students are faced with the problems of analysing, and preparing for work in the new technology environment; and secondly, the business manager, who is already unavoidably immersed in that environment. It is intended that the papers included here will be of interest and value to both groups, and to those with general and functional management responsibilities, in a wide range of industries.

The majority of the chapters in this book started life as papers presented at a symposium run by the Department of Business Administration and Accountancy at UWIST, in September 1983, and therefore thanks are owed to all those who played a role in organising and participating in the symposium, as well as especially to the authors of the work presented in this book. In particular, Professor Roger Mansfield is at least as responsible for the symposium taking place and this volume being produced, as is the editor. Additionally, Dr. Catherine Bailey undertook the proof-reading task, for which gratitude should be expressed, as also to Miss Kath Hollister for invaluable help in the final preparation of the manuscript.

Lastly, very special mention should be made and thanks extended to Miss Stevie Burges at UWIST, for her efforts in handling the administrative burdens of the symposium, for producing the copy of all the papers produced in this book, under the usual unfair pressures, and for assisting in indexing the book.

This said, the residual shortcomings in this volume remain inevitably the responsibility of the editor.

Nigel Piercy
UWIST, January 1984

Chapter 1

MANAGEMENT AND NEW INFORMATION
TECHNOLOGY

Nigel Piercy

INTRODUCTION

A fitting starting point in an exercise of the type represented
by this volume would seem to be to attempt at least a working
definition of 'new information technology', even though others
later in the book note the ambiguity and lack of precision in
the term. One such attempt is provided in the statement:

> 'Information Technology (IT) is the coming together of the
> existing computing, communication and control engineering
> technologies. It affects the way we live, work and enjoy
> ourselves and our future ability to compete in the
> "information society".' (Department of Industry, 1982)

While such a definition may be considered, in technical
terms, ingenuous to the point of being simplistic, it is none
the less suggestive of two factors of central importance: the
convergence of previously separate technologies, and a broad
and pervasive impact on society.
The 'new' in this present context of new information technology arises from a third, similarly fundamental, characteristic: simply the rapidity of shared technological change, as
illustrated recently by Pelton (1981). Pelton notes of the
convergence of the telecommunications, information processing
and energy sectors that:

> 'These industries will be increasingly using common
> technology, derivative of today's silicon chip
> microprocessors, photovoltaic cells, robotic devices and
> space electronics.' (Pelton, 1981)

Pelton is led to the term 'telecomputerenergetics' as a
way of describing such technological convergence, based on the
disappearance of boundaries between telecommunications, information processing and energy, and their overlapping or common
reliance on the same technological base. His concept is of a

worldwide information network, allowing for 'global talk' between communities of different kinds (Pelton, 1981).

This said, the present discussion is concerned not with
the technology itself - in its accelerating rate of change or
the convergence of its components - nor even directly with its
broad impact on society at large.   Rather the interest here is
with the implications of new information technology for one
major sector of society - those managing at various levels in
both commercial and public organisations.   Clearly, such organisations are dependent on their various environments - for resources, markets, social legitimacy, and so on - so the implications of new information technology for management are to some
extent inseparable from the broader effects on society.

In this sense, the first goal pursued by this present work
is to facilitate the analysis and understanding of the new
environment for management - both within and outwith the organisation itself.

Over and above the analysis of the impact of environmental
change, however, a second goal is to examine the more active
managerial choices faced and the types of responses implied.
The availability of the concrete output of the microelectronic
technological revolution is indisputably with us, together with
the related and increasingly sophisticated software.

This suggests firstly that attention be devoted to the
process of technological innovation in organisations.   In this
context, one researcher has noted of his work that:

'The research shows that popular predictions about the
radical and automatic advantages of new technologies are
exaggerated... management has a choice of means and ends
in the use of new technology; these choices can and should
be identified and evaluated in advance of change.'
(Buchanan, 1982)

While this provides what is perhaps the central focus for
this book - choice and managerial discretion in the management
of the new technology - even then, only a start has been made
in making explicit those managerial choices faced, in the sense
that while operational implementation is of vital interest, the
technology impact is potentially far greater than simply adding
peripherals like word processors and leaving it at that.   The
new information technology potentially impacts on such diverse
and fundamental issues as: the degree and type of control
exercised by management in organisations, and hence through
management style on organisational climate; the structure of
organisations - since structure may be represented as information flow - and thus on the relationships and the roles played
within the structure; the pattern of jobs - and thereby at the
individual level on motivation, satisfaction, performance, and
at the macrolevel on employment and educational requirements;
the relationships between organisations, and on the tendency

towards 'quasi-integration' (Blois, 1977) through information networking and mutual dependency between previously apparently independent organisations; and so on.

In each such issue there are both strategic and tactical or operating decisions faced, and it is intended that this present work should aid in making explicit the fundamental choices involved.

Having stated the goals pursued here, this chapter offers some brief introductory commentary on the nature of the change associated with new information technology - by way of justifying and explicating the goals pursued and hopefully to provide at least an initial point of reference; and then discusses the nature of the managerial response implied by such changes. Finally, the chapter discusses the coverage and scope of the contributions to the book, in relation to the goals pursued.

THE IMPACT OF NEW INFORMATION TECHNOLOGY

At one level new information technology might be regarded as no more than simply a way of upgrading existing processes in organisations, and the products and services they provide - computerised data processing is faster, cheaper and more widely available; electro-mechanical control devices in all manner of machines are replaced with more sophisticated electronics; word processors replace typewriters; microcomputers replace filing systems; and so on. Indeed, in some situations such a view is valid, at least in the short term.

However, what is becoming increasingly apparent is that new information technology has potentially a somewhat more fundamental impact within organisations, and in the relationships between organisations, and that there are distinct phases or stages in microtechnological change, which vary in their nature.

To demonstrate this point, consider, for instance, how Handy (1980) threw down the challenge of generally reevaluating certain of the traditional assumptions about industrial society and the nature of the business organisations within it, in a way which is directly relevant to the present trends in new information technology.

Handy drew attention to the discontinuity of change in the modern environment, where 'the assumptions we have been working with as a society and in organizations are no longer necessarily true', and discussed as 'fading assumptions' those relating to what causes eficiency, what constitutes work, and the value of organisational hierarchy.

First, Handy pointed to the pursuit of scale by companies and their consequent problems of integration as the root cause for the demotivation of the technical specialists who were created by the processes of concentration and specialisation. Drawing on possible alternative assumptions, Handy pictured the 'contractual' organisation based on the payment of fees for work done rather than wages for time expended. Second, he noted the assumption that labour is a cost paid for the commodity of work, leading to the conclusion that if costs increase then we should seek to reduce the amount of the commodity used and paid for. Instead, Handy suggests viewing labour as an asset to be applied by a responsible management wherever opportunities exist:

> 'Instead of finding labor to do the work that is needed management will be urged to find work to fill the hands available. "If tires don't sell anymore", the laid-off workers said as Dunlop closed its tire factory at Liverpool in 1979, "management ought to find something for us to make that will sell." If, after all, management has always regarded its physical assets as capital in search of an outlet, why not its human assets as well?' (Handy, 1980)

As Handy further notes, such a revision in underlying assumptions would have a revolutionary impact on the strategic planning of many organisations - perhaps most obviously in the light of the various predictions for labour shedding discussed later in the book.

Third, he challenged the assumption that hierarchy is the natural form for organising economic activies in modern society - an assumption he suggests relies on an obediance ethos which may no longer persist, and which anyway confuses level with role in organisations. Instead, he points to the possibility of the organisation as a community, based on consultation and democratic principles in decision-making.

The point is that in each of the issues raised by Handy, the new information technology is potentially an enormously powerful catalyst. In the first instance, we have for example, the concept of the 'devolved corporation', where small units are linked by electronic networking rather than geographically or through formal integration mechanisms, and there are already operating examples of companies where workers and managers work in geographically diverse locations, linked by terminals accessing a computer system and a shared data base (see, for instance, the discussion in Chapter 6). In the second instance, it is apparent that the displacement of labour by the new technology is a major contemporary issue, suggesting various scenarios for the future - some optimistic, some less so (see for example, Chapters 7 and 8). Similarly, the control and structural issues discussed in Chapters 12 and 13 demonstrate the changing nature of organisational hierarchies, while Warner and Davies (Chapters 9 and 10) highlight the potential and actual position regarding the use of new information technology to share data for consultation and joint decision-making.

In each case what emerges is that the decisions faced by

management, and the choices which must be made, are of strategic importance - a point developed further in the next section of this chapter.

However, this question of the nature of the change engendered by new information technology should not be left without noting another theme which recurs throughout the book - that there are both optimistic and pessimistic views of the future for organisations.

For example, one recent commentator (Doll, 1981) concerned with the socioeconomic impact of new information technology, drew attention to such unplanned consequences of the technology as: a decrease in the number of small businesses and companies, because they will be less able to fully exploit new information technology; the increased growth of multinational corporations with a greater ability to control resources and in some cases to supplant the nation-state; and the development of a 'technological elite' in information access and control.

Doll's view may be contrasted with the rather more optimistic, and contradictory, thesis advanced by Halal (1982), who sees new information technology 'transforming business into a more mature and enlightened institution', including a 'new flowering of individual enterprises' - perhaps in the type of corporation discussed as prototypical in Chapter 8. Halal points to the total reorientation in the style and practice of management, in what he stylises as 'democratic free enterprise'. He forecasts the growth of 'organic networks and multidimensional matrices combining rigorous accountability with autonomous operations'.

Such differences in viewpoint and optimism or otherwise for the future of business may reflect different calculations and extrapolations, different time scales and assumptions about human reactions to technological change, or indeed different value-judgements. This said, they also demonstrate different assumptions about the choices that will actually be made by managers in organisations (and other related institutions). At the end of the day, this present analysis, and the research and theory it reports, is largely dedicated to making such choices explicit and informed.

THE MANAGERIAL RESPONSE TO NEW INFORMATION TECHNOLOGY

The suggestion made earlier is that while the initial interest in the management of new information technology is likely to be in the short term problems of implementing the technology and overcoming the inevitable problems of resistance and dislocation, over and above this operational question there is the issue of the longer term. One need becoming increasingly apparent is for a strategic response from management which reflects the fundamental nature of the changes faced as a result of new information technology.

While many definitions of strategy have been advanced,

consider for present purposes the hierarchy offered by Hofer and Schendel (1978), which suggests that strategy should be seen as a composite consisting of: (a) enterprise strategy, (b) corporate strategy, (c) business strategy, and (d) functional strategy. This provides at least a crude vehicle for considering the type of managerial response called for at the strategic level.

At the level of enterprise strategy, the managerial concern is essentially with the social legitimacy of the organisation and its role in society, in the light of the uncontrollable and sociopolitical aspects of the environment. It has been noted by one authority that:

'during the past twenty years, a major escalation of environmental turbulence has taken place. For the firm it has meant a change from a familiar world of marketing and production to an unfamiliar world of strange technologies, strange competitors, new consumer attitudes new dimensions of social control and, above all, a questioning of the firm's role in society.' (Ansoff, 1979)

In the present context, this throws up such questions as those relating to the responsibilities of organisations for providing employment, the quality of the working lives of those employed, the types of controls placed on organisations by governments and other institutions, and generally the expectations that society has for organisational management. Ansoff (1979) suggests, for example, that while the managerial focus in the middle of the twentieth century has tended to be on developing strategies and structures to achieve production and marketing effectiveness, in the later stages of the century, the preoccupation will increasingly be with such factors as adaptation to environmental turbulence and discontinuity, the redesign of internal organisational climate and work structures, and coping with constraints like resource scarcity, the limits to growth, and external sociopolitical initiatives.

In this sense, new information technology cannot be separated from the search for social legitimacy and the positioning of an organisation in the broader social framework. On the other hand, at the level of corporate strategy, the issue at stake is far more to do with the impact of new technology on a particular industry's prospects than the question of institutional legitimacy. None the less, from what has already been said (and what is discussed further in Chapters 13 and 15) it is clear that the impact of new technology at the industry level may be considerable. When turning to business and functional strategies, the issues are far more concerned with the problems of integration and coordination, and management control over operations, and the potential impact here of new technology is undeniable - in upgrading information systems, the ability to monitor work, the capacity for centralising previously decentralised decision-making, and so on.

Given such impact at the various levels of strategy, it would seem unavoidable to conclude that there is a need for a managerial response at a similar level.

This case has been argued elsewhere by the present writer, but is represented most clearly in this volume by Chapter 11, in Michael Earl's consideration of emerging trends in the management of new technologies.

With some introduction to the goals of the book, and the emphasis to be placed on managerial rather than technological issues, it is timely to examine the coverage and structuring of the book as a whole.

COVERAGE AND SCOPE OF THE BOOK

The work contributed to the book has been structured into four main groups, each of which is described briefly below. Part I is concerned with the impact of the new technology on production systems; Part II turns to employment issues; Part III examines the implications for industrial relations in the institutional sense; while Part IV emphasises the question of managing new technology and the implications for control and organisational design and for environmental relationships in external marketing systems.

Of the four sections of the book, Part I is probably the most optimistic, representing the view of three specialists in production technology and robotics in manufacturing. Towill is concerned primarily with making clear the impact already being made by new technology on manufacturing methods and hence inevitably on manufacturing management. He describes the possibilities for computer aided planning and computer aided design in manufacturing, as well as illustrating the problems faced in implementing such methods in companies, and highlights the trend towards the automatic factory, although placing some emphasis on the situational question of choosing the most appropriate level of automation for a particular company at a particular time. Towill concludes that the disappearance of the traditional distinctions between design, computing, and production management is creating the need for a new specialist — the manufacturing professional — who links these specialisms.

The other contributions to Part I are somewhat different in character to Towill's review, and are complementary in nature. Drazan describes his view of the central role of the engineer in society, and the type of problems and the design philosophy involved in the design of the pioneering Placemate robot. He then puts forward an engineer's view of the contribution being made by new technology, in such areas as the automation of menial and degrading work, and the benefits of increased manufacturing efficiency in economic growth. He examines the need for better engineering education and research funding, stressing the need for a systems approach to developing from the flexible manufacturing concept.

The interest in robotics and automation is maintained in Batchelor and Cotter's examination and illustration of the potential impact of intelligent sensors in developing machine vision and artificial intelligence. This chapter demonstrates the power of high level computer languages, developed in artificial intelligence research, for reasoning and drawing conclusions and ultimately making decisions. The authors continue to describe the use of intelligent sensory devices - robots with 'vision' - in flexible manufacturing systems. They conclude with a review of the direction which this aspect of the technology is taking, the need for companies to plan in ways which accommodate the realities of robotics and the automated factory, and the decision-making power of computer systems.

Part II, on the other hand, turns to the question of the various employment implications of new information technology, generally taking a markedly less optimistic view than that put forward by the technologists.

Land's chapter is concerned firstly with the question of the enhancement of the ability of organisations to exert social control using the new information technology. By social control he refers to the measurement of performance, the restriction of the way individuals perform tasks, the collation of information about individuals, and the impact on careers at the individual level. He discusses in this context some of the organisational implications of new information technology, and the need for new approaches to systems design. He concludes his review of the literature and the preliminary results of a major European Community sponsored research study, with a list of the factors identified which contribute to the way in which technology is introduced in organisations and how it is perceived by members of the organisation, suggesting the need for a contingency approach to this question.

Long is concerned with a somewhat more specialised employment issue - that of the use of microelectronics in the office, drawing on both Canadian and British research. He draws attention to the implications, in the later phases of the microelectronics revolution in the office, to the impact on communications and thus on decision-making. He is then involved in examining such related issues as the impact on hierarchies in organisations, the development of flexibility in work places and work times, and the effects on lower level employees. In the particular context of electronic word processing, Long reviews the somewhat confused findings about the employment effects of the technology, together with the question of possible effects on employee health, the impact on job design for the office of the future, and the issues associated with the greater facility for computer monitoring of work. He concludes that microelectronics may affect the quality of working life in the ofice in ways which may be either favourable or unfavourable, depending on a variety of situational factors.

The next chapter in Part II, by Blyton, considers the impact of new information technology more generally on work patterns for the future, and he is led to consider the possibilities for reducing working hours and for work sharing as responses to labour displacement, making a number of international comparisons and considering the obstacles which exist to making major reductions in working time. He concludes that even in considering only the quantitative impact of new information technology on jobs - setting aside the quality of working life issue - there is growing pessimism regarding the scale of labour displacement, and differentiation between groups, compared to the development of mechanisms to cope with this by-product of the technology.

Part III turns to the institutional aspects of labour relations. First, Poole provides a review of the theoretical analysis of the implications of technology for industrial relations, contrasting the US and Japanese situations. He then presents a case study of a 'Silicon Valley' company in the US, which he suggests may be prototypical and illustrative of changing management/union relationships. His conclusions concern the emergence of significant changes in control and autonomy in the work place, conflict and the accomodation of interests, the levels and styles of bargaining, and the possibility of collective bargaining being replaced by other regulatory mechanisms, and he emphasises the various strategic choices faced by different groups and the consequent impact of the values they seek to apply.

Warner, on the other hand, is more concerned with the impact of new information technology on such matters as the autonomy/discretion left to the individual worker or workgroup in organisational decision-making. Given the possibility with the new technology of information processing for the greater decentralisation of decision-making, Warner considers the possible impact on participation, and the choices which are faced between the extremes of 'Taylorism' and industrial democracy.

Closely related to the issue raised by Warner of the trade union response and role in the new information technology revolution, is Davies' study of the introduction of new technology in one particular industry. Her empirical work leads her to conclude that in the industry studied, the major emphasis in introducing new technology was that of increased managerial control (which may be compared to a similar empirical finding reported by Sawers in Chapter 14), and that other possible benefits were by-products rather than major goals. While management/union conflict was found, Davies questions the degree of real influence achieved by the trade unions, and the size of its impact.

Part IV is concerned with a number of general management questions inherent in new information technology.

To begin, in what may be the centrepiece of the book, Earl presents a detailed analysis of the trends emerging in the management of new information technology in major corporations. He discusses and illustrates the multiplicity, the dispersal, the acceleration of, and the pervasiveness of information technologies, and then presents some empirical findings relating to how such major organisations are developing a coherent managerial response to information technology. He concludes with a management agenda, suggesting that information management must be 'normalised', information technology strategies must be formulated, information technology infrastructures must be constructed, the information technology executive must be elevated, that there should be greater attention to behavioural factors, and that the various realities of new technologies should be recognised by decision makers.

Next, Mansfield considers the relationship between new information technology and organisational design and managerial control. He highlights the controversy surrounding the impact of technology on structure, and the related question of the level and type of management control exercised. His view of the organisation of the future suggests inevitably higher levels of automation in manufacturing with the accompanying displacement of labour, increasing reliance on computer support in design and development, with a managerial role involving more supervision of information functions and the need for enhanced leadership skills to offset the demotivating effect of automation. The top management role, he predicts, will involve greater conceptual input to management of the total system and greater emphasis on coping with external relationships.

In considering similar issues, Nicholas is more concerned with the specific question of relating together organisational structure and managerial control philosophy in technological change, and discusses the manufacturing context for this debate. He argues that the most important organisational elements associated with new information technology are thus control and structure, but also identity - in terms of the form and maturity of the industry and the product concerned. He concludes that effective innovation relies on the appropriateness of the management strategy adopted, but that the subsequent success and development of the innovation depends on the technological infrastructure of the firm.

Chapter 14 is rather different in context, in reporting an empirical study of microtechnological innovation in a retail firm. Sawers found that the major positive effects of new technology at the retail point-of-sale were increased managerial control together with certain increases in operating efficiency, but that those gains have to be placed in the context of problems of evaluation, resistance, and dislocation.

Finally, Chapter 15 considers the question of the broader

impact of new information technology on marketing systems. Attention is devoted first to changes in the market environments faced by firms, the potential for commercial failure with technological innovations, and the consequent need for coherent corporate product-market strategies, in addition to changes in the operational management of marketing programmes. Secondly, the administrative systems of marketing management - information and organisation structure - are considered in terms of the potential for developing macro-marketing information systems which transcend the organisational boundary, and the need for an information strategy in marketing. The related changes in the organisation of marketing - in both its organisational positioning and internal structuring, imply the parallel need for an organisational strategy for marketing, which accepts the realities of the new information technology.

CONCLUDING REMARKS

While the goals of this work are clearly ambitious - and are unlikely to be fully realised in a single volume - it is hoped that the contributions made here will be of value both to analysts and researchers exploring this field, and management teachers concerned with the preparation of material which relates to the real environment for management, and decison makers in organisations who are currently involved with this area. At the end of the day, it seems clear that none of the traditional academic or functional specialisms can cope individually with the totality of this area of technological change, so it may be that the type of multidisciplinary approach taken here is the best that can be offered at present. Certainly, having mentioned the recurring themes through the chapters here of the existence of choices which have to be made, and the alternative views of what the future holds for organisations, this brief introduction closes by noting the third theme, which is the need for the emergence of a new type of management specialist who is trained and prepared to deal with the continuing implications of the microtechnological revolution.

REFERENCES

Ansoff, H.I. (1979) 'The Changing Shape of the Strategic Problem' in Schendel, D.E. and Hofer, C.W. (eds.) Strategic Management: A New View of Business Policy and Planning, Little Brown, Boston

Blois, K.J. (1977) 'Problems in Applying Organizational Theory to Industrial Marketing', Industrial Marketing Management, 6, 273-80

Buchanan, D.A. (1982) 'Using the New Technology: Management Objectives and Organizational Choices', European Journal of Management, 1(2), 70-79

Department of Industry (1982) Information Technology: A Bibliography, Department of Industry, London

Doll, R. (1981) 'Information Technology and Its Socioeconomic and Academic Impact', Online Review, 5(1), 37-46

Halal, W.E. (1982) 'Information Technology and the Flowering of Enterprise', European Journal of Mangement, 1(2), 65-9

Handy, C. (1980) 'Through the Organizational Looking Glass', Harvard Business Review, January/February, 115-121

Hofer, C.W. and Schendel, D. (19780 Strategy Formulation: Analytical Concepts, West, St. Paul, Minnesota

Pelton, J.N. (1981) Global Talk: The Marriage of the Computer, World Telecommunications and Man, Harvester, Brighton

PART I

THE NEW INFORMATION TECHNOLOGY
AND PRODUCTION SYSTEMS

Chapter 2

Information Technology in Engineering Production
and Production Management

Denis R. Towill

INTRODUCTION

Information technology (IT) is the modern name for the means by
which we collect, store, process, and use information
(Zorkoczy, 1982). Furthermore, it is not confined to hardware
and software, but involves man in target setting and assessment
criteria. It is built around the scientific, technological,
engineering, and management disciplines used in information
handling and processing, and at the present time is generally
regarded as relating to computers and the interaction between
man and machine. However, many of the basic ingredients
needed within IT pre-date the microelectronic revolution. For
many years effective management of manufacturing engineering
has required the collection, generation, communication, recording, manipulation, and exploitation of information. A motivating factor in the new IT is the hope that the principles,
practice, and terminology of information handling can be
treated in a united, systematic way.
     Engineering production and production management are con-
cerned with the effective use of people, products, plant and
processes in modern manufacturing industry. This, in turn, is
achieved by the proper selection and implementation of policies
and plans. However, all six factors interact with each other,
which partially explains the operational complexity which
presently seems unavoidable. As we shall see, it is assisting
the introduction of an integrated systems approach to problem
solving in modern manufacturing industry which makes IT such a
potentially powerful production management tool.
     The interaction problem can be best illustrated via the
Venn diagram shown in Figure 2.1, in the type of display origi-
nated by Bestwick and Lockyer (1982). IT can help make each of
the six cells independently more effective, but it is in the
interactive zone where by far the biggest contribution may be
expected. There are particular problems in the 'people' area,
which are receiving exhaustive study under the heading of
'dialogue engineering' (Sime and Coombe, 1983).

Figure 2.1: Interactions Between Major Factors in Engineering Production and Production Management

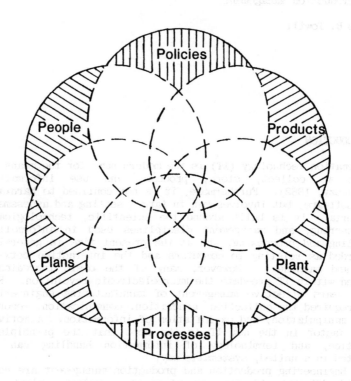

Source: Adapted by the author from Bestwick and Lockyer (1982)

The history of computer usage in problem solving has three distinct stages. Stage 1 was where computers were necessarily used by specialist technicians; Stage 2 allowed a much wider range of users to access computers but via specialist technicians; Stage 3, which is already partly with us, is where the computer is designed to be 'user friendly' from the outset. Thus, the goal is for a business or manufacturing professional to access the computer directly in 'user' language, in which dialogue relates directly to the relevant knowledge base (Gaines, 1979).

16

Table 2.1: How the Major Factors in Engineering Production
and Production Management Relate to the Use of
Computers in Industry

PRODUCTION FACTORS	DEGREE OF COMPUTERISATION			
	COMPUTER AIDED PLANNING	COMPUTER AIDED DESIGN	COMPUTER AIDED MANUFAC-TURE	COMPUTER AIDED ENGIN-EERING
People	0	0	0	0
Plant		*	0	0
Processes		*	0	0
Policies	0			0
Plans	0	0	0	0
Products	*	0	0	0

0 Constituent Factors
* for Data Base construction only

If we now return to Figure 2.1, it is possible to define
how the interactions relate to the three specific routes
through which IT has already been applied within manufacturing
industry. Table 2.1 shows these relationships. Computer Aided
Planning (CAP), Computer Aided Design (CAD), and Computer Aided
Manufacture (CAM), have quite separate origins, but together
form Computer Aided Engineering (CAE) with the ultimate goal of
achieving the automatic factory covering activities from
automatic parts ordering right through to automatic warehousing
of finished goods.

It is the purpose of this paper to review CAP, CAM and
CAD. To do so, we shall need to distinguish between the
tactical use of IT in planning, and its strategic use for
corporate policy decision-making. The importance of sensor
development, especially 'intelligent' instrumentation, will
also be highlighted.

COMPUTER AIDED PLANNING (CAP)

The oldest IT use in CAP is at the level of management
information systems. Computers make it much easier (when
proper data collection discipline is applied) to keep
production management aware of the situation regarding orders,
finished stocks, work-in-progress, and costs. Clearly, such
information is of immediate tactical use in production
planning, production scheduling, raw material purchasing,
delivery date forecasting, and so on. One example of a
comprehensive programme is that developed by the United States
Steel Corporation (Luther and Kupfner, 1982). This
computerised system is now being adapted to suit all the major

facilities in US Steel plants for preventative maintenance, maintenance planning and materials control. The timespan between requirements definition and total implementation for all plants is approximately three years.

There are at least seventy six software packages available in the UK at the time of writing, with up to seven modules contained within each package. Table 2.2 summarises the modules available, and it can be seen that they are all at the tactical level, i.e. they relieve the workload on clerks, buyers, progress chasers, and foremen, once the strategic policy has been agreed.

Table 2.2: Common Characteristics of Microcomputer-Based Production Scheduling and Control Systems

---

1. **Bill of Materials Module.** Data base with details of every part used in the factory. Details include code number; description; supplier(s); cost; lead time; related assemblies.
2. **Stock/Inventory Data Module.** Tracking of parts movements and stock levels throughout the factory.
3. **Requirements Planning Module.** Plans and adjusts stock levels necesary to maintain minimum stock levels and improved customer services.
4. **Sales Order Control Module.** Records and controls progress of each sales order from receipt to despatch.
5. **Shop Floor Control Module.** Sequences work orders so as to minimise delays, highlight potential delays.
6. **Factory Documentation Module.** Describes route cards, job cards, and materials requisitions.
7. **Purchase Module.** Deals with processing and expediting of orders.

Source: Synopsis of 76 software packages listed in Production Management and Control, October, 1983, and based on material first published in Which Computer?

However, as Graham (1983) has pointed out, the acquisition of these packages does not, in itself, lead to improvements in company performance unless accompanied by the right motivation and data collection discipline. He quotes as an example the case where data are only 95 per cent complete and 95 per cent accurate, leading to disaster if the production manager is not aware of this uncertainty. The difficulty of coping with a hybrid manual-computerised production control system has been graphically illustrated in a case study by Edghill and Cresswell (1983), in which performance standards were claimed in white consumer goods manufacture that could not possibly be substantiated by cross-checking against the materials drawn from stock.

One solution, for successful CAP implementation under these circumstances, is to provide a shopfloor network of factory data collection terminals, which feed into a local computer or controller (Smith, 1983). Such terminals need to be robust to withstand adverse environmental conditions, and user friendly to factory personnel. Ideally, there should be a cross-check facility within the computer to interrogate the users, should unexplained discrepancies be observed between materials-in and goods-out, thus picking up immediately the stocktaking problems identified by Edghill and Cresswell (1983).

The next stage in automation here is to directly monitor each stage of the manufacturing process. This is particularly important where there are combinations of high output rates and high machine utilisation, leading to line stoppages being very costly. An example of a successful system is the BL Transfer Line Monitoring System (TLMS) described by Yeoh et al (1983). TLMS monitors the 0.5 km long automated machinery transfer line producing 80 cylinder blocks per hour. There are 18 transfer machines, 2 boring machines, 2 honing machines, 2 leak-testing machines, 2 washing machines, and 2 automatic assembly machines. All machines are linked together by automatic conveyors and pick-and-place material handling units.

The objectives of TMLS design are conveniently summarised in Table 2.3. The resulting design has 178 optically isolated data acquisition interfaces, with a multiplexer capable of scanning all the inputs once per second. Two Z80 microprocessors (with RAM and PROM) accumulate the data ready to transmit to a 32K microcomputer for analysis. The microcomputer accepts data at a speed of 4800 baud formatted in ASC11 code. Long term data storage is via two floppy discs. A matrix printer provides written reports, whilst a CRT is used for on-line enquiries and updating certain files. TLMS success has been spectacular and well-publicised in the literature, as a technique for reducing production line downtime. At the same time, only one foreman is now required to supervise the line in place of the four needed prior to TLMS being installed. Major contributions to increased productivity have been achieved by predicting tool wear ahead of quality reduction, and fault isolation so that the appropriate repair gang can be called up in the event of failure.

Whilst TLMS is a good example of IT 'closing the loop' for maintenance of a highly automated production line, it is the loop closing principle which is the important feature (Deis, 1983). This is because irrespective of the nature of the production business, IT can become the means whereby top management monitors all the performance criteria, provided the feedback data are made available at the correct sampling rate.

Table 2.3: Design Requirements for Transfer Line Monitoring
            System (TLMS)

Acquisition of Data Directly from Multiple Sources
Transmission of Data at High Speed
Filtering of Noisy Data
Statistical Analysis
Data Trend Detection
Presentation of Manipulated Data in Summary Form
Data Recording for Post Mortem and System Updating
Report Communicated to Right Personnel in Form for Immediate
    Action
TLMS to Repay Cost over Realistic Period

Source: Yeoh et al (1983)

COMPUTER AIDED STRATEGIC PLANNING

We have so far concentrated on the tactical level of
applications of IT to CAP. At the strategic (policy making)
level, there are a number of ways in which IT can help via
interactive simulation. Two differing approaches to policy
formulation have been developed. The first (Holloway and
Pearce, 1982) is based on classical operations research
techniques of linear programming (Moore and Thomas, 1978). A
'static' simulation model is used to explore and compare
feasibility plans for short term (one year) and medium term
(five years) on the basis of such features as debt/equity
ratio. In contrast, management dynamics (variously called
systems dynamics and industrial dynamics) is concerned with
establishing dynamic simulation models of the firm (Roberts,
1978). Here, the purpose is to explore the improvement in
performance which can result from particular management
policies relating to the marketing, production, storage, and
distribution functions of a company. The simulation model is
composed of a structural representation of the organisation,
such as shown in Figure 2.2, which is for a production-
distribution system. There are three levels of inventory:
warehouse; distributor; and retailers. The circled numbers
refer to the delays in weeks for each of the appropriate
manufacturing, clerical, storage, and transit actions. Full
lines represent the flow of finished goods, and dotted lines
represent the flow of orders. Note that there is no feedback
except between adjacent echelons in the system, a modus
operandi with potentially disasterous results, as a later
example will confirm.

Figure 2.2:   Organisation of Production-Distribution System

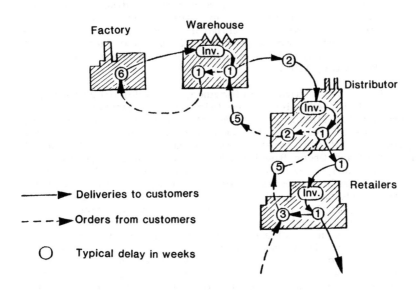

——▶ Deliveries to customers

– – –▶ Orders from customers

○   Typical delay in weeks

Source: Adapted by the Author from Forrester (1958)

Special simulation packages (DYNAMO, DYSMAP) have been designed to simplify the simulation problem, and hence produce sample results as shown in Figure 2.3, which are for an assumed step change in demand rate of 10 per cent.   In the words of Forrester (1958), the spectacular phenomena shown can be explained in the following way:

> 'Because of accounting, purchasing, and mailing delays, the increase in distributors' orders from retailers lags about a month in reaching the 10% level. The rise does not stop at 10%, but reaches a peak of 18% at the eleventh week because of the new orders that have been added at the retail level (a) to increase inventories somewhat, and (b) to raise the level of orders and goods in transit in the supply pipeline by 10%. These inventory and pipeline increments occur as "transient" conditions. Factory warehouse orders show an even bigger swing because incoming-order level at the distributors persists above retail sales for more than 4 months, and is mistaken for

an increase in business volume. Distributors' orders to
the factory therefore include not only the 18% increase in
orders they receive, but also a corresponding increase for
distributor inventories and for orders and goods in
transit between distributor and factory.   The
manufacturing orders peak by 51%, and the factory output
peaks by 45%, all in response to a 10% change in sales.'
(Forrester, 1958)

In order to improve performance, the model parameters must
be adjusted (reduction of certain delays, addition of extra
communication lines, etc.).   Unfortunately, this must be done,
even interactively, in an ad hoc manner, since only a few
general solutions exist.   One example is the design of
Inventory and Order Based Production Control Systems (IOBPCS)
(Towill, 1983).   Otherwise, the effective use of management
dynamics simulation packages is very much an art to be acquired
from 'hands-on' experience.   It therefore follows that
strategic planning is a potential area of application for one
of the most advanced IT concepts - the Expert System (Gevarter,
1983).   By using a suitable Expert System, policy improvements
would be obtained much more readily via a structured
interactive dialogue with the eventual user.   Such a
development was forecast years before IT became commonplace,
when Forrester (1958) looked forward to the day when the
simulation would be undertaken by a line manager and not a
staff specialist. Such a massive step forward is now feasible
using the 'If.....then' characteristics of Expert Systems.   For
example, in the large scale problem of medical diagnosis, MYCIN
is one such package, and incorporates some 450 rules, to aid
the physician in arriving at a conclusion.   Another IT approach
is to use artificial intelligence techniques to solve problems
when conflict occurs, such as assigning jobs to machines.
Bullers et al (1980) have proposed such a system, and concluded
that there is a need for the development of a more English-like
problem statement language.   There would appear to be scope
here to link with problem descriptions defined by DYNAMO and
DYSMAP.

COMPUTER AIDED DESIGN

The next IT application area in manufacturing industry to be
considered is Computer Aided Design (CAD), in which computers
plus graphics terminals are used as tools in both conceptual
and detail design phases of a new product, as suggested in
Figure 2.4.   CAD allows designers and draughtsmen to spend the
maximum amount of time on creative work, leaving much drudgery
to the computer.   The outcome of CAD is a set of working
drawings produced much more quickly and consistently than would
be the case of manual means.   Drawing office productivity
increases of as much as 4:1 have been reported.   Speed is also

Figure 2.3:   Response of a Production-Distribution System
to a 10% Step Increase in Sales Rate As
Predicted From Industrial Dynamics Simulation
Package

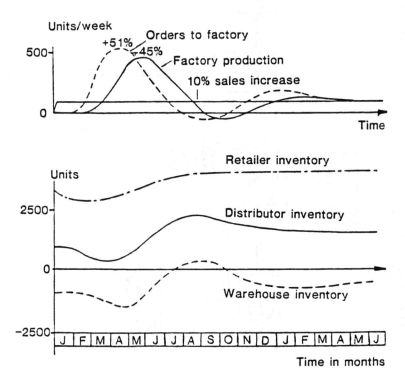

Source: Forrester (1958)

an important factor at the project feasibility stage, when the
company is tendering for new orders. Here again, CAD has a big
part to play, especially when three-dimensional sketches of the
product are required.   Since the CAD output is of the form
needed for CAM, there is now much pressure to develop CAD/CAM

Figure 2.4: Basic Concept of Computer Aided Design System Using Interactive Graphics

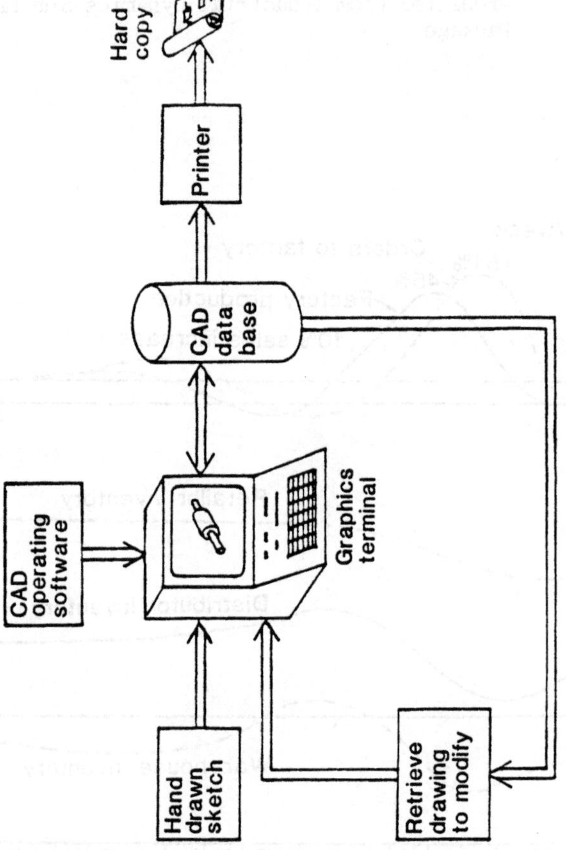

systems in which the product can be manufactured on computer-controlled machines directly from the CAD data base (Simons, 1982). CAD/CAM is presently a costly exercise, but has the additional virtue that mistakes are found in the drawing office

24

(where they are relatively cheap), compared with making them on the factory floor (where they are very expensive!). Thus, the goal is to use CAD modules which include graphics facilities to check the planned path of each cutting tool, so as to predict potential collisions (Rosenbaum, 1983).

There is a long history of CAD applied to the solution of control engineering problems, especially in the aerospace industry. However, CACSD (Computer Aided Control System Design) as typified by Wieslander (1973), Mobley and Paddison (1973), Allen and Atkinson (1973), Rosenbrock (1975), and Ashworth and Towill (1981), refers to the selection of major components parts and control algorithms to meet the dynamic performance specification of the system. Inevitably, CACSD has involved compromises, or 'trade-offs' between different goals. In sophisticated CACSD packages, the 'trade-off' is achieved by setting up a 'performance index' which combines the various goals into a mathematical function, the optimum value of which defines the 'best' system available. CACSD packages then proceed interactively with the human designer to iterate

Figure 2.5:   An Example of Drawing Trends in the Design of US
               Navy Systems

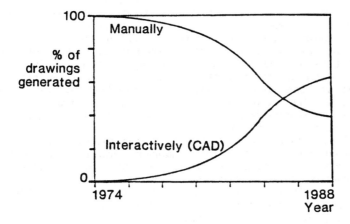

Source: Wang and Jurica (1981)

from an initial design to the 'best' one. In at least one case, the design technique has gone as far as computer selection of individual stock items needed to assemble the complete product (Chubb, 1969).

Nowadays, CAD is taken to especially refer to the computerised preparation of all working drawings needed to manufacture new components. The 'detailing' stage in the draughting of such drawings is particularly boring, and onerous to cross-check in the case of complex assemblies. For these reasons CAD is sometimes referred to as 'Computer Aided Draughting', so as to emphasise the provision of computer aids to remove a great deal of the drudgery, leaving the designer more time to spend on creative work. Figure 2.5 is an example of how the new technology will increasingly affect the draftsman's way of life. For the complex product concerned, (a US naval defence system), the expectation is that 50 per cent of all drawings will be produced via the CAD system by 1985 (Wang and Jurica, 1981).

One of the best known UK CAD systems is the Ferranti-Cetec CAM-X based on a DEC VAX 11/780 computer. A short description of this system will suffice as an introduction to CAD hardware and software, and is based on that given in Simons (1982). Each workstation (with the ultimate aim of one per designer), is equipped with a graphics visual display unit which can display all or part of a stored drawing. It can also supply orthographic, perspective, and sectioned views of a stored model. Workstations have alphanumeric displays and keyboards to display messages for operator guidance, data base communication, and for drawing construction. Plotting facilities are provided for the production of working drawings and all associated data needed for manufacture. Assembly, installation, numerical control tool path locus and maintenance information can also be added. An essential feature of CAD system is the need to 'capture' design information in a comprehensive data base listing shapes, dimensions, material, part number, supplier, etc.

In the CAM-X system, the three-dimensional geometry is generated automatically in a manner familiar to skilled draftsmen. A section through one half of a part is drawn and then rotated through 360 degrees. By using volumetric or solid geometry, CAM-X avoids the need for using artificial conventions in the representation of component shapes. In this way, some of the disadvantages of earlier 3D systems can be overcome. The older systems used a wire-frame technique in which the 3D model was generated from information on its edges, which in turn necessitated additional interactive inputs from the designer.

In some application areas, CAD is now incorporating iterative optimisation techniques similar to the CACSD philosophy, so that a drawing, once created by the designer, will be the 'best' at satisfying the particular functional specification, instead of merely being adequate – i.e. the first satisfactory solution to the problem to emerge from the creative process. For example, the General Motors 'Optimum Shape Generation' package (Bennett and Botkin, 1983), incorporates a finite element modelling subroutine, which permits the evaluation of stress contours in the component, for a given structural loading pattern. As it is important to save weight in automotive components, this CAD system iterates until a configuration of minimum mass is obtained. This configuration will result in some maximum stresses in the component being near the permitted limit. An example is shown in Figure 2.6, being the VDU portraits at four points during an iterative design requiring some 60 steps. From step 0 to step 60 the reduction in weight is from some 0.28 kg to 0.12 kg. This improvement has been achieved without the need to provide a stress engineer as part of the back-up resources to support the creative designer. Instead the stress engineer has himself acted as a designer when working on the subroutines incorporated in the optimisation package.

HOW TO SUCCEED AT FAILING, OR HOW NOT TO IMPLEMENT A CAD SYSTEM!

As with all computer-based systems, there have obviously been disasters following the introduction of CAD. The usual horror stories concerning lack of proper planning and specification prior to acquisition, inadequate management and technical infrastructure to support the system, and the NIH (not invented here) syndrome have emerged. Dellenbach (1983) has humorously illustrated the certain route to failure; his concluding remarks are a particular reminder of how not to do it:

'Several months after the CAD arrived, and training was completed, a manager is selected. He wasn't a member of the original team, but everyone up the line feels he'll do a splendid job. He comes highly recommended because: one upper manager owed another manager a favour: he's the administrative type - knows nothing about engineering and less about CAD. Was he the one who made some comment that CAD was just another expensive engineering toy? Or: you can't trust those damn computers; or what's wrong with drafting boards? We've been doing it this way for 50 years.' (Dellenbach, 1983)

Dellenbach emphasises that new technology cannot be bought-in to a company in isolation. The proper procedures and planning must be designed-in at the outset with regard to equipment selection and acquisition, facility preparation, training, maintenance and management. Otherwise he predicts 'how to succeed at failing, or how not to implement a CAD system' will become a reality.

Figure 2.6:   Iterative CAD Procedure for Minimising Mass of
             Automotive Component Subject to Structural
             Loading

(Intensity of shading shows approach of stress levels towards
acceptable maximum)

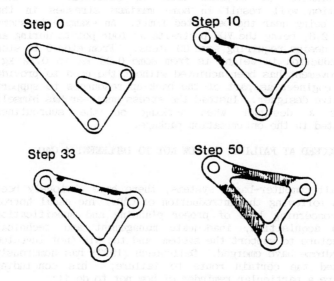

Source: Bennett and Botkin (1983)

COMPUTER AIDED MANUFACTURE

The origins of computer aided manufacture are to be found in certain areas of industrial automation, and especially those which carry over from the process industry. In contrast to Detroit type automation, with fixed aids (usually mechanical handling devices) to increase productivity, the process industry has a long history of automation via flexible means which includes a large battery of sensors for monitoring and recording important variables. These measurements are also fed into computers to control operations via feedforward and feedback strategies which can be extremely complex, but usually include at least a (proportional + integral + derivative) term. In simple physical terms, this three term controller, often abbreviated to PID control, is operating on a weighted combination of information relating to the instantaneous error, time history of the error, and future predicted error, where the error refers to the difference between the target and actual values of plant variables.

The analogy of process control with 'management-by-exception' is therefore obvious. Forrester (1964) first drew attention to the lessons which discrete production management might absorb from the well-established concepts in use in the process industry. One reason for the early progress in automation in the process industry was the ready availability of analogue computers developed during World War II, which provided a cheap and reliable means for closing local feedback loops (Smith, 1972). As the same author showed, by virtue of an extensive case study, the digital computer, when first introduced into the process industry, was used as a hierarchical controller to update target values for the local analogue loops. The equivalent, but later, development in discrete manufacturing industry consisted of local analogue control of contouring lathes which reproduced components by following a physical model (Kusic, 1980), and numerical control (NC) lathes which reproduced components by following a mathematical model stored on tape (either paper or magnetic) (Pressman and Williams, 1977).

IT has changed this modus operandi in discrete manufacturing industry in two ways. The first development is the provision of cheap communication and computing devices which permit a number of NC machines to be grouped together to form the next stage of vertical integration in IT automation, and controlled by a single supervisory computer. Figure 2.7 shows such a configuration, with six NC machines linked to the computer, and bulk memory storage of NC programmers to form a CNC manufacturing cell. Sometimes it is advantageous to adopt a hierarchical control configuration (Groover, 1980), with satellite computers interposed between the central (managing) computer and groups of NC machines, depending on the data acquisition and processing rates required. One commercial CNC

Figure 2.7: Communication Lines for Direct Numerical Control
of a Cell of Machine Tools

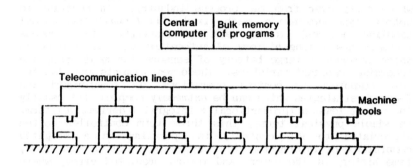

Source: Groover (1983)

system boosts a capability of controlling up to 256 machine
tools. Advantages which are claimed for CNC are reduction of
component programming errors; avoidance of tape damage at
shopfloor level; enhanced reliability, since punch tape
readers tend to breakdown frequently; ease of incorporating
improvements in manufacturing system design; and ready
presentation to management of machine utilisation data etc.;
thus making full use of the two-way flow of information within
the system.

The second effect of IT at the local level in discrete
manufacture is in improved control of machinery and processes.
This is largely due to microprocessors being available for
implementing linear or non-linear feedback control algorithms
(again a carry-over from the process industry) for hierarchical
control within a machine, or for data processing within a
control loop (Kochar and Burns, 1983). One example which
illustrates the new opportunities made available at this level
by IT is shown in Figure 2.8. Here the optical signal from
the seam tracking camera is processed using the seam extraction
algorithm, and used to 'fine-tune' the position of the robot
welder so as to reduce errors in arc welding. The system shown
compensates for errors, whether they originate from data base
inaccuracies or poorly located workpieces (Villers, 1982). In
general the robot itself is likely to include microprocessor
control, and is thus also a product of the new IT era. Drazan
and Jeffery (1978) note that the IT involvement is self-evident
once the computational requirements for the microprocessors in

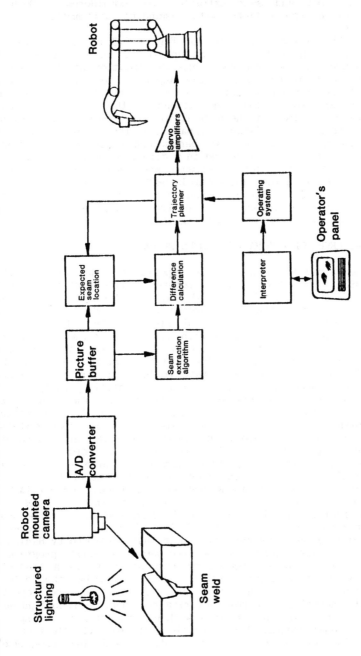

Figure 2.8: Robovision Arc Welding Robot With Automatic Seam Tracking Source: Villers (1982)

both robot and seam extractor are considered. Both are real-time applications with demanding arithmetic execution rates.

The Robovision system of Figure 2.8 scans an area 4 cm ahead of the weld at speeds up to 100 cm per minute. It measures on the observed image the location of the centre of the seam to be welded, the apparent seam width, and the distance from the workpiece to the sensor. This information is then used to establish deviations of the actual seam beyond pre-set limits from the nominal, or expected value predicted by the data base. Command signals are then sent to the robot servo system several times per second to reduce the error in the elevation direction and in a direction perpendicular to the path. All these data processing and command calculations are performed with the same Motorola 68000 microprocessor. Because the robot is usually purchased as a stand-alone device, it will have separate microprocessor control to implement any internal control algorithm or decoupling of axis motions.

WHAT LEVEL OF AUTOMATION SHOULD WE HAVE?

A good review of automation opportunities appears in Schehr (1983), who distinguishes between those pertinent to the manufacture of machined products, and those for non-machined products, as shown diagrammatically in Figure 2.9. For machined products, the dedicated machine line (Detroit automation) is associated with very high volume, followed as the volume decreases, by special NC machines, FMS, cells, and then standard machines. The system shown in Figure 2.7 is a cell, although generally there would be a mixture of machine types, grouped according to certain scientific principles, such as materials flow control (Burbidge, 1982). There is a rather blurred distinction between an FMS (flexible manufacturing system), and a cell, and a review paper by Dupont-Gatelmand (1983) provides helpful background material and categorises three types of FMS. For the purpose of this chapter, the demarcation adopted by the US Bureau of Standards is adequate, and will be illustrated later in the context of the automatic factory. Whether automation is via a cell or an FMS, an important consideration especially with 'in-house' design of the facility is the provision of an adequate networking system for communicating between all its elements. An interesting example of an 'in-house' system is that developed by Hanlon and Weston (1982), which combines the use of satellite programmable controllers and microcomputers communicating via a trunk-line of 3000 metres maximum length. Their system has the following advantages: each item or machine can be operated independently; the manufacturing cell can be reconfigured to meet new production demands without extensive re-wiring; an individual programmable controller failure will affect only one machine or element in the cell; and any programmable

Figure 2.9:   Relationship Between High and Low Volume
              Manufacturing Methods for Minimum Production
              Cost

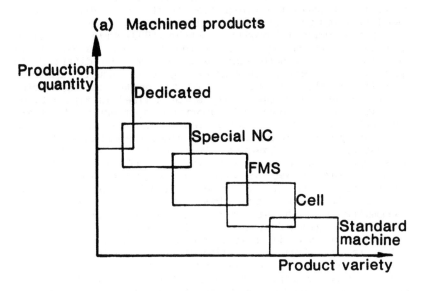

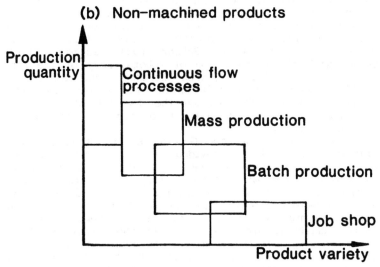

Source: Schehr (1983)

controller can be modified without disturbing other machines.

The demonstration system includes a pick-and-place robot and a rotary transfer drilling machine as the main functional units. A further advantage of the scheme is that the networking permits the integration of the robot directly with CAM facilities such as GRASP (Heginbotham et al, 1979).

For non-machined products, Schehr (1983) shows that volume affects the scheduling policy on the shopfloor, as Figure 2.9 confirms. It is here that automation may be difficult to justify on economic grounds according to the usual industrial pay-off criteria. He suggests that the production engineering department uses the opportunity space defined in Figure 2.10, to establish the level of automation appropriate to their company's manufacturing activities. The further into the opportunity space is the company located, the easier will it be to justify partial automation. However, in IT terms, the three axes represent quite different species! If order quantity is high, Detroit automation would be acceptable, with the IT contribution being in performance monitoring (for example, as in the TLMS of BL Cars discussed earlier). If product commonality is high, at least an FMS will be used, probably with computer aided design of the plant layout (Groover, 1980). The order repeatability axis is the most interesting. Batching policy is a strategic application of IT, but on the other hand, the massive use of IT implied by FMS would permit the 'batch-of-one' concept, that is by optimum scheduling of a load of different products, the floor-to-floor time would still be comparable with that achieved by Detroit automation.

As we saw earlier, Dellenbach (1981) had some horror tales to tell concerning the potential hazards following the introduction of CAD. Whilst Schehr (1983) was particularly concerned with the introduction of robots, many of the same lessons apply. Specifically, when introducing automation, the right IT infrastructure must be established at the same time. An inoperable robot often causes the downtime of the whole manufacturing system, of which the robot forms a tiny fraction of the capital cost.

We saw earlier that the General Motors 'Optimum Shape Generation' CAD package provided on-line stress analysis support to the creative designer. This builds the human operator into an IT-dominated design loop. In a similar way, a new philosophy to NC part-preparation has been developed at UMIST in an endeavour to keep the machine operator as the human in the programming loop (Boon et al, 1980). Now, for a wide range of industrial parts, it has been shown that the lathe operator can programme the NC machine to make a batch of parts, simply by manufacturing the first item in the batch, and then making the machine repeat his operations automatically to make the rest. Where the UMIST scheme improves on this practice is to use a computer interface. The operator then carries out the

Figure 2.10:   Automation Opportunity Space
              (The further away from origin, the easier it is
              to justify automation on payback, although FMS
              seeks to reduce to a 'batch of one'.)

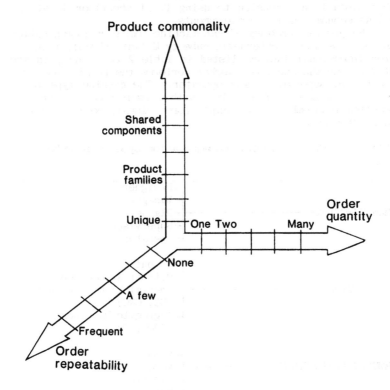

programming via conversational interaction with a microcomputer, with the interface attached to the guard of the lathe. Operating experience suggests this is a more efficient means of programming compared with the alternative off-line approach. Machine utilisation is believed to be increased, and operator job satisfaction improves. There is thus a job satisfaction dimension to using IT at shopfloor level, as well as economic and other arguments.

The general problem of man-machine-computer communication has been posed as a cybernetic cube by Milacic (1982), with the three-dimensional factors listed in Table 2.4. Thus, in the UMIST scheme the shopfloor worker performs the triple functions of planner, supervisor, and operator. The machine type being NC is therefore special, but with computerised interface. Communications embrace, in simple form, visual, vocal, tactile, and written methods.

Table 2.4: The Man-Machine-Communication Cybernetic Cube

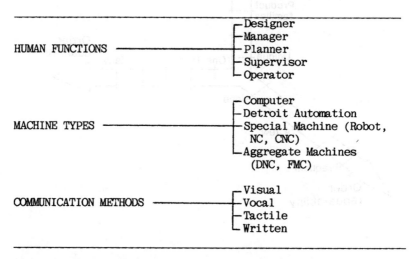

HUMAN FUNCTIONS	Designer Manager Planner Supervisor Operator
MACHINE TYPES	Computer Detroit Automation Special Machine (Robot, NC, CNC) Aggregate Machines (DNC, FMC)
COMMUNICATION METHODS	Visual Vocal Tactile Written

Source: Milacic (1982)

EFFECT OF IT ON SENSOR DEVELOPMENT FOR AUTOMATION

The Robovision system described earlier is one example of local automation made possible by IT developments involving microprocessors. It is typical of the new breed of 'smart' sensors which are essential to many new application areas. Bollinger and Duffle (1983) describe a range of low cost, small size, microelectronic sensors capable of measuring such physical quantitites as flow rates and dew points. These 'smart' sensors have microprocessor-based calibration, computational, and decision-making power built into them. They

Figure 2.11:   Information Flow Sensors in Robot Cell Control
Hierarchy

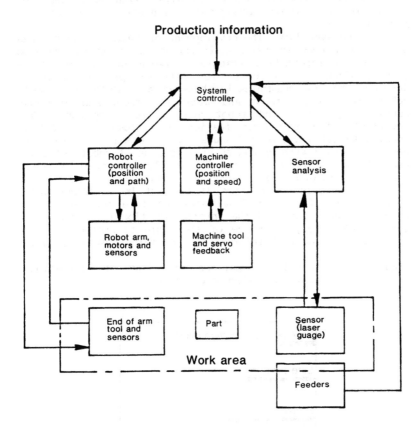

Source: Thomas (1983)

greatly enhance measurement quality, especially those made by inherently non-linear devices. The control computer therefore receives more readily usable signals, with much improved signal-to-noise ratios, making automation not only easier, but more effective.

At the same time, the development of 'smart' sensors lags behind their need in robot applications, where there are also problems in information transfer between system components (Nagel, 1983). He calls for standard procedures to be developed to ease communication between manipulator and robot; robot and robot; robot and machine; robot and materials handling system; and robot and control computer. The importance of sensor communication for automatic control in local automation has been discussed by Thomas (1983), in which he is concerned with extending applications of robot cells via provision of adequate sensors. The resulting control hierarchy and flow of information is shown in Figure 2.11.

In successful automation there must be a proper match between the information flow rates feasible for the device under consideration, and the information flow rates needed to achieve adequate performance of the complete system. Figure 2.12 compares the 1981 information flow rates associated with:

Figure 2.12: Flow Rate Comparison for a Range of Information Handling System Components

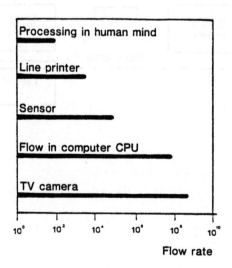

Source: Milacic (1982)

processing in the human mind; a line printer; a typical
sensor; flow in computer CPU; and in a TV camera, although
clearly, some of these figures will change greatly with
advancing technology. Thus, although the TV camera information
flow rate is impressive, the quantity of information sometimes
needed to make judgements in closed loop control is
sufficiently high for the camera to be one limiting factor.
Hence, Coulon and Nougaret (1983) found that the memory effect
of the TV tube could be a limiting factor in performance. To
overcome this deficiency, either the patterns sought by the
camera had to be made larger (hence permitting the threshold to
be recognised at high speed), or the system had to be slowed
down to a speed at which the existing pattern could be
detected. Clearly, TV camera controlled systems (Villers,
1982) are already operating commercially. There is also much
current worldwide research (including some at UWIST - Batchelor
et al, 1982) aimed at rapidly increasing the application of
these systems.

COMPUTER AIDED ENGINEERING - OR TOWARDS THE AUTOMATIC
FACTORY

The previous sections have outlined the contributions which IT
can make towards improving production engineering and
production management performance via CAD and CAM. As the
boundaries between CAD and CAM become more blurred, via
improved data capture and data base design, the automatic
factory becomes an increasingly available option for
industrialists to consider, initially as a way of operating
expensive machinery, for the third (or night) shift, which is
difficult to man anyway. For example, as Dorf (1983) has
reported, there is a Fanuc plant in Fuiji, Japan, producing
spark-erosion machine tools and robots, which has been
operating in this way. The plant has 29 automated workstations
connected by unmanned, optically-guided vehicles, and materials
and finished products are stored in automatic warehouses.
During the day shifts, 19 workers are in the machining section,
making up the pallets that carry the parts, and 63 are in the
nonautomated assembly section. At night the assembly section
stops work and the machining section continues operating with
the pallets made during the day. A single worker monitors
operations via TV.
       One of the best publicly documented automated
manufacturing research facilities is that at the US National
Bureau of Standards (McLean et al, 1983). This system has been
conceptually designed as shown in Figure 2.13. There are five
control levels arranged in hierarchical fashion operating on
the feedback outputs of sensors which observe the states of
each machine and component. Table 2.5 lists the functions
performed at each level of the system. Space restrictions
limit the information to keywords - the original reference

discusses each level in considerable detail. It is interesting to note that Figure 2.13 is couched by the authors in IT terminology, in which cross-talk and feedback data move along a 'broadcasting' system. At the individual equipment level (5)

Table 2.5   Function Levels in National Bureau of Standard
            Automated Manufacturing Research Facility

Level	Description	Function
1	Facility	Information Management Manufacturing Engineering Production Management
2	Shop	Task scheduling Resource allocation
3	"Virtual" Cell	Task analysis Batch management Scheduling Dispatching Monitoring
4	Work Station	Machine set-up Issue equipment commands Machine take-down
5	Individual Equipment	Machining Measurement Part and tool handling Transport Storage

Source: McLean <u>et al</u> 1983)

in Figure 2.13, the sensors required will be of the type already discussed.

However, the industrialist can make progress towards the level of automation appropriate to his business without making a drastic change at any particular point in time. The well-run company will reach this level by evolution, not revolution. Only in this way will the professional resources for equipment and software selection, implementation, and support be available at the inevitable critical times. Taylor (1983) has summarised the evolutionary approach in Figure 2.14 as a business moves from individual machines to the microcosm of the fully automatic factory. He forecasts that by 1990, 20 per cent of all machine tools being manufactured will have unmanned

Figure 2.13: Block Diagram Representation of US National Bureau of Standards Automated Manufacturing Facility. Source: McLean et al (1983)

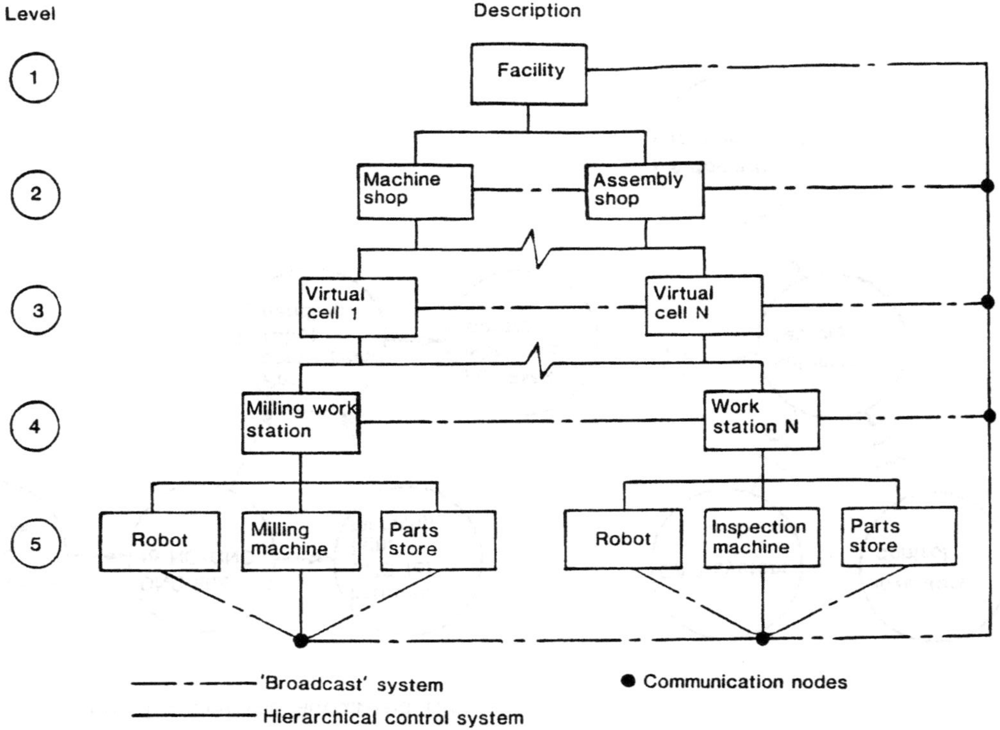

Figure 2.14: Evolutionary Steps Towards the Automated Factory

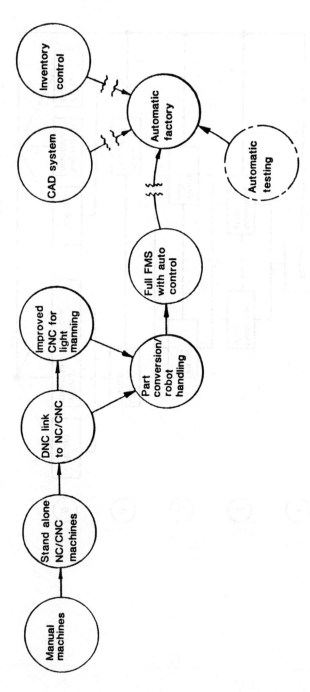

Source: Adapted by the Author from Taylor (1983)

operating capabilities. It would therefore seem highly appropriate for all machine tool users to plan for some movement in this direction.

Finally, in considering CAE, we must not forget the impact of IT on product testing. This is particularly important in aerospace and military systems, in which a particular piece of equipment may be tested in several stages during manufacture, on leaving the factory (for certification purposes), on installation in the field, and at periodic intervals thereafter. It is obviously convenient if the same test set can be used at all levels, and even for new prototype testing (Dabney, 1982). By including sophisticated software packages, the results may be used by management for many purposes, including sensor selection, test sequence design, process trend detection, and product health monitoring (Williams, 1977). Recently, this methodology has been successfully applied to white consumer goods manufacture using fully flexible microprocessor-based test stations for quality audit (Rowlands, 1983). This additional route to the automatic factory is shown in dotted lines in Figure 2.14.

CONCLUSIONS

We have seen that Information Technology is already making a profound impact on manufacturing methods and manufacturing management. The principles needed for successful introduction of IT into manufacturing industry remain the same as for any other new development. The company must invest in planning and selection procedures for equipment, software, and personnel. These matters cannot be delegated to an outside consultant, who will have little or no responsibility for keeping the plant operating at a proper level of efficiency. The support staff and technology must be available for system maintenance, updating, and most importantly, looking ahead and preparing for the application of next generation IT ideas, so as to further increase company performance. Management must see that IT can regularly save direct labour costs only by investing a fraction of these savings in in-house technical expertise. Also, the traditional boundaries between functional design, design for manufacture, software development, planning control, and production processes are fast disappearing. The result will be the generation of a new breed of 'manufacturing professionals' - the systems experts who can link all these specialisms together to reduce lead time, reduce costs, and improve product quality simultaneously.

REFERENCES

Ashworth, M.J. and Towill, D.R. (1981) 'Computer Aided Design of Tracking Systems', Radio and Electrical Engineer, 48(10), 479-492

Allen, A.J. and Atkinson, P. (1973) 'Interactive Design of Sample-Data Control Systems', IEE Conference Publication, No. 96, 141-148

Batchelor, B.G., Cotter, S.M., Heywood, P.W. and Mott, D.H. (1982) 'Recent Advances in Automated Visual Inspection', Proceedings 2nd International Conference on Robot Vision and Sensory Controls, Stuttgart, 307-326

Bennett, J. and Botkin, M. (1983) 'The Optimum Shape', High Technology, 3(8), 26-27

Bestwick, P.F. and Lockyer, K. (1982) Quantitative Production Management, Pitman and London

Bollinger, J.G. and Duffle, N.A. (1983) 'Sensors and Actuators: New Sensors Do More', IEE Spectrum, 20(5), 70-73

Boon, J., Satine, L., Hinduja, S. and Vale, G., (1980) 'Back to Operator Control', Numerical Engineering, 1(2), 27-29

Bullers, W.I., Nof, S.Y. and Whinston, A.B. (1980) 'Artificial Intelligence in Manufacturing Planning and Control', AIIE Transactions, 12(4), 351-363

Burbridge, J.L. (1982) 'The Simplification of Material Flow Systems', International Journal of Production Research, 20(3), 339-347

Chubb, B.A. (1969) Computer Aided Optimization of Non-Linear Servo-Mechanisms Employing a Directed Search of Multi Parameter Component Libraries and Statistical Tolerancing, Michigan State University, Ph.D thesis

Coulton, P.Y. and Nougaret, M. (1983) 'Use of a TV Camera System in Closed-Loop Position Control of Mechanisms' in A. Pugh (ed.), Robot Vision. IFS Publications, London

Drazan, P.J. and Jeffery, M.F. (1978) 'Some Aspects of an Electro-Pneumatic Industrial Manipulator', 8th International Symposium on Industrial Robots, 1, 396-405

Dabney, I. (1982) 'Computer-Aided Engineering: the Integrated approach to Design Test and Manufacture', Automotive Engineer, 7(5), 66-67

Dupont-Gatelmand, C. (1983) 'A Survey of Flexible Manufacturing Systems', Journal of Manufacturing Systems, 1(1), 1-16

Dellenbach, K.K. (1981) 'How to Succeed at Failing, or How Not to Implement a CAD System', Proceedings of the 3rd Symposium on Automation Technology in Engineering Data Handling, Monterey, California, September, 57-60

Deis, P. (1983) Production and Inventory Management in the Technological Age, Prentice-Hall, Englewood Cliffs, New Jersey

Dorf, R.C. (1983) Robotics and Automated Manufacturing, Prentice-Hall, Reston, Virginia

Edghill, J. and Cresswell, C. (1983) 'The Design of a Microcomputer System for Integrated Job Shop Materials Control', Proceedings Annual Industrial Engineering Conference and Exposition, Louisville, Kentucky, 587-599

Forrester, J.W. (1958) 'Industrial Dynamics: A Major Breakthrough for Decision Makers?' Harvard Business Review, 36(4), 37-66

Forrester, J.W. (1964) 'Common Foundations Underlying Engineering and Management', IEEE Spectrum, 1(9), 66-77

Games, B.R. (1979) 'Logical Foundations of Database Systems', International Journal of Man-Machine Studies, 11(4), 481-500

Gevarter, W.B. (1983) 'Expert Systems: Limited But Powerful', IEEE Spectrum, 20(8) 39-45

Graham, S.H. (1983) 'Computerise? It's the Last Thing You Should DO!', Production Management and Control, 11(4-5) 25-26

Groover, M.P. (1980) Automation, Production Systems, and Computer-Aided Manufacturing, Prentice-Hall, Englewood Clilffs, New Jersey

Hanlon, P.D., and Weston, R.H. (1982) 'Use of Local Area Networks Within Manufacturing Systems', Microprocessors and Microsystems, 6(8) 425-42

Heginbotham, W.B., Dooner, M., and Case, K. (1979) 'Rapid Assessment of Industrial Robot Performance, by Interactive Graphics', Proceedings 9th International Symposium Industrial Robots, Washington, USA, 78-83

Holloway, C. and Pearce, J.A. (1982) 'Computer Assisted Strategic Planning', Long Range Planning, 15(4) 55-63

Kochar, A.R. and Burns, N.D. (1983) Microprocessors and Their Manufacturing Applications, Edward Arnold, London

Kusic, G.L. (1980) 'Feedback Design of Closed Control Servomechanisms', IEEE Transactions 1A-16 (4), 547-551

Luther, R.D. and Kupfner, J.W. (1983) 'Maintenance Information Management Systems for the 80's', Proceedings of AIEE Annual Conference, New Orleans, 227-230

McLean, C., Mitchell, M. and Barkmeyer, E. (1983) 'A Computer Architecture for Small-Batch Manufacturing', IEEE Spectrum, 20(5) 519-64

Moore, P.G. and Thomas, H. (1978) The Anatomy of Decisions, Penguin, Harmondsworth

Mobley, D.J. and Paddison, M.A.M. (1973) 'Design of a Missile Autopilot by the use of Nonlinear Programming Technique', IEE Conference Publication, No. 96, 29-35

Milacic, V.R. (1982) 'Computer-Based Informatisation of Manufacturing Engineering Activities', International Journal of Production Research, 20 (3), 369-408

Nagel, R.N. (1983) 'Robots: Not Yet Smart Enough', IEE Spectrum, 20(5) 78-83

Naylor, C.R. (1983) Build Your Own Expert System, Sigma Technical Press, Wilmslow

Pressman, R.S. and Williams, J.E. (1977) Numerical Control and Computer Aided Engineering, Wiley, New York

Roberts, E.B. (1978) Managerial Applications of System Dynamics, MIT Press, Cambridge, Mass.

Rosenbaum, J.D. (1983) 'A Propitious Marriage: CAD and Manufacturing', IEEE Spectrum, 20(5) 49-52

Rosenbrock, H.H. (1975) Computer-Aided Control System Design, Academic Press, New York

Rowlands, H. (1983) Low Cost Flexible Automatic Test System for Sequential Electromechanical Device Testing, M.Eng. thesis, Department of Mechanical Engineering and Engineering Production, UWIST, Cardiff

Schehr, L.H. (1983) 'Is Robotics For You, Now?', Proceedings of AIIE Annual Conference, Kentucky, 3-7

Sime, M.E. and Coombe, M.J. (1983) Designing for Human-Computer Communication, Academic Press, New York

Simons, G.L. (1982) Computers in Engineering and Manufacture, NCC, Manchester

Smith, W.A. (1983) 'Source Data Automation - The Key to Shop-Floor Control', Production Management and Control, 11(4-5), 1-11

Smith, C.L. (1972) Digital Computer Process Control, International Textbook, Scranton, Ohio

Taylor, I. (1983) 'How to Realise the Benefits of FMS', The Production Engineer, 62(10), 44-48

Thomas, R. (1983) 'Sensing Devices Extend Applications of Robotic Cells', Industrial Engineering, 15(3), 24-32

Towill, D.R. (1982) 'Dynamic Analysis of an Inventory and Order Based Production Control System', International Journal Production Research, 20(6) , 671-687

Villers, P. (1982) 'CAD-CAM Link May Make Robot Use Practical in High-Precision Production Tasks', Production Engineering, 14(4), 22-28

Wang, P.C.C. and Jurica, L.J. (1981) 'A Modernisation Plan in Engineering Data Repository Studies of Naval Ship Weapons Systems Engineering Station', Proceedings of the 3rd Symposium on Automation Technology in Engineering Data Handling, Monterey, California, 290-314

Wieslander, J. (1973) 'Interactive Programs for Computer Aided Design', IEE Conference Publications, 96, 1-7

Williams, J.H. (1977) Probabilistic Models for Quality Assurance, Ph.D Thesis, UWIST, Cardiff

Yeoh, O.B., Wilcock, F.A. and Franks, I.T. L(1983) 'Monitoring of Automated Manufacturing Systems', Chartered Mechanical Engineer, 30(5), 52-53

Zorkoczy, P. (1982) Information Technology: An Introduction, Pitman, Bath

Chapter 3

THE IMPACT OF ROBOTS ON MANUFACTURING PROCESSES AND
SOCIETY AT LARGE

Paul Drazan

INTRODUCTION

The purpose of this paper is to present a technologist's view,
rather than a manager's, and some of the points made are
somewhat controversial. In the post-war period a large effort
was spent in automating process industry, such as: chemical
plants, refineries, water treatment plants, gas distribution,
power stations, and so on, even though this was frequently
unseen from outside.

In automating these processes, attempts were usually made
to approach them as complete plants. This happened naturally,
partly because the processes were connected to complete plants
by pipelines handling the processed fluids, and partly because
the processes were themselves continuous by nature. Control
research followed the trend and developed multivariable
state-space theory to deal with complex plant situations.

Most manufacturing processes are, on the contrary, discrete by nature, producing quantities of discrete components.
In manufacturing, the major effort was aimed at developing
advanced machine tools, (for example, numerical control) and at
developing the individual manufacturing processes, still treat-
ing them in isolation. Handling and transport of components
between the tools was not considered an integral part of the
production system. Only relatively recently, when the first
attempts were made to automate the production process in total,
was it realised that a major link was missing in the production
chain, that is, a machine which would deal automatically with
the required handling operations - the industrial robot. The
industrial robot has thus become a necessary element in flexible manufacturing systems, essentially providing mechanical
arms to link machines in the process.

It should be realised that manipulation forms a substantial part of any production operation as it forms a substantial
part of overall human activity, like walking, writing, house-
work, etc.

The point is that once the robot has arrived on the industrial scene, it will stay. However, its function should complement that of man, and not compete with it. For example, while machines are more dedicated and faster than man, man is more universal but slower. Similarly, the robot is more limited in its handling skills than man. Robots are still very clumsy and much improvement in their handling capacity has to be made before they can compete with man.

Essentially the function of the robot is not comprehensive but should be seen as dealing with jobs which are, for example, repetitive, degrading, unhealthy and hazardous – indeed, the jobs for which it may be difficult to recruit human labour. Even in the production environment, particularly in cases of automatic assembly, many jobs will still have to be carried out manually because the robot handling capabilities are too limited for such tasks. Or, these processes have to be redesigned in such a way that the handling tasks are broken down to simpler modules which can be handled by robots. Cost considerations imply that machines will remain task-specific.

ENGINEERING ACTIVITY

A central point to this writer's thesis is that there is a considerable difference between science and engineering. Science enhances our understanding of nature and is concerned mainly with passive studies of the environment. Engineering, on the other hand, is a creative activity, applying scientific knowledge to the design of new machines. Engineering is an art which tries to simplify theories in order to make them applicable and usable.

Indeed, looking at the engineering scene makes us realise that we live in very challenging times when engineering is undergoing a major change. The effect is due to convergence between, for instance, mechanical engineering, electrical engineering, computer science, mathematics, design, and so on. In effect, engineering is acquiring new powerful tools which can considerably enhance the design of engineering systems. The tools I have in mind are particularly computers and micro-computers, new advanced sensors like vision, lasers, ultra-sonics and the availability of solid state, in general influencing the design of the interface, which plays a very important role in all engineering systems.

As a result engineering design requires a true systems approach, as it deals with many variables and factors influencing the result of the engineer's work. As processes become more and more automated, control becomes not only an integral part of design but is a very important component allowing the engineer to synthesise the system.

Control theories have been developed by mathematicians who do not necessarily appreciate design goals, and some of them have gone somewhat astray, becoming self-perpetuating, or too complicated generally, and too formalised for use by engineers.

Naturally, engineers strive to keep up with the new technological developments, in order to incorporate them into their designs, since their primary purpose is to maintain the competitiveness of the product by modernising it and, at the same time, by retaining a cost-effective edge on the market.

I shall try to illustrate some of the challenges faced by describing the design and philosophy approach which we used when designing the Placemate robot (Figure 3.1).

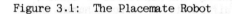

Figure 3.1: The Placemate Robot

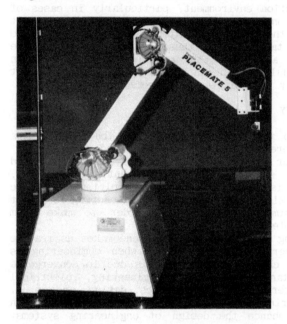

THE PLACEMATE ROBOT

Allow me to return first to the advent of microcomputers. It became evident to us in 1972, that engineers would have at their disposal a flexible, powerful and cost-effective tool: a 'brain' for their systems, in the form of the microcomputer. In the 1960s we struggled to realise relatively simple mathematical functions, such as multipliers or square-roots, by designing special mechanisms. Nowadays we instead develop software which will generate such functions. We are experiencing a shift from mechanisms to microelectronics and software. The wristwatch is just one example where a highly mechanical chain of gears is replaced by digital dividers, the hands of the watch are replaced by digital displays and the mechanical watch movement is replaced by the crystal. The motto of our robotic work became: shift the complexity from hardware to software and thus increase reliability and achieve savings. This meant in practice aiming at the simplest possible mechanical solution which would meet the specification and capture the right market.

As robotics is a multi-disciplinary activity, the success of design depends on maintaining the right balance between the individual disciplines, that is, mechanical design, electronics, software and sensory devices. An understanding of control theory is necessary and the appreciation of some of the related aspects of biological systems is an advantage. Back in 1974 we carried out a brief but intensive market survey which revealed then that there was a lack of robots, of a point-to-point type, in the lower price bracket below £15,000. These are robots which can transfer objects between specified locations in space, but which do not need to follow a particular path between these locations. As these point-to-point robots cater for up to 80 per cent of the whole market it was worthwhile, in our view, looking for new solutions. Apart from searching for suitable mechanisms we were particularly interested in investigating the use of the microcomputer for direct 'on-line' control, that is, using it directly in the control loop (Figure 3.2). As mentioned previously, particular emphasis was placed on designing an advanced system at a competitive market price. While there is no doubt that advanced systems can be designed when no cost

Figure 3.2: The Microcomputer for On-Line Control

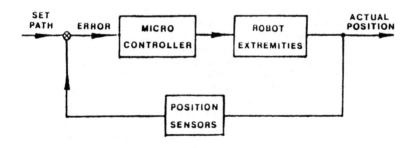

restraints have to be applied, it is much more challenging to design a modern system to a competitive cost, and new approaches may sometimes offer more elegant and effective solutions, which could not be realised by the use of classical methods.

THE BENEFITS REAPED FROM ENGINEERING

Society at large benefits considerably from engineering activity. It enjoys the comforts, but unfortunately does not give recognition to the wealth creators, but complains about pollution. The man in the street does not appreciate how much engineers have created. He does not see necessarily that he would not have water on tap, gas in his house, the electricity network, the motor car, or fast air transport, just to mention a few recent gains. He is concerned about the loss of jobs through automation and does not see that automation would mainly replace men in jobs which are repetitive and therefore degrading, tiring, dirty and unhealthy. If automation is applied properly it should allow us to lift ourselves to better and more interesting jobs, give us time to read, to educate ourselves and to have more leisure. Sociologists complain about these effects instead of blaming themselves for not being able to plan a proper restructuring of society, and pressurising politicians to look further ahead, instead of catering for short term policies.

In fact, there are many direct advantages to be reaped from automation. When a job is done manually by a worker, because of his inherent flexibility and adaptability, he can cope with the situation occurring on the production line. The production engineer does not then usually learn about the problems the worker is facing and tackling. There is a general lack of information concerning production activity. When, on the other hand, the production line is automated by robots or other types of flexible automation, every work place, work station and process has to be thoroughly analysed and understood, so that the machine fits in its place completely and is linked appropriately into the process. Nowadays, production and other processes are continuously improved, adapted, changed, modernised, and so on. The R & D element in competitive industry becomes a major part of the overall production involvement, if competitiveness and market share is to be maintained. Flexible automation offers particular advantages because it makes the change of production runs much easier. Programmable automation supported by computers can be used more extensively, and consequently more changes can be accommodated by changing mainly the software. Hence, because of the reduction in hardware changes, overall costs can be reduced.

ENGINEERING RESEARCH AND DEVELOPMENT

Because of the increased need for research and development the national infrastructure of R & D has become critical for the manufacturing base in the UK to survive. Large commercial enterprises usually have their own research and development centres capable of supporting new developments. Small and medium sized companies, on the other hand, find it more and more difficult to staff development projects, as they require specialist knowledge. This knowledge cannot be absorbed by a few individuals, but requires larger teams. I, therefore, strongly believe that there is a need for grouping smaller companies and providing for them access to research establishments. The Fraunhofer Institute network in Germany provides one example of such an R & D network. In Belgium, on the other hand, a company has access to a university, usually the one nearest to the company, and can use the equipment and the staff expertise, and in return makes a contribution to university research funding which is related to the company profits. In this way universities can be well-equipped and have a direct incentive to research areas relevant to industrial needs. The situation in the UK is slowly improving. The Science and Engineering Research Council jointly with the Department of Industry coordinates and organises collaborative work between universities and companies. However, one disadvantage in the UK is that companies generally are not accustomed to such collaboration, and indeed when managers do approach universities, they often do not appreciate the complexity of the technical problems involved. This type of initiative is relatively recent in the UK, whilst on the continent and in the United States the practice is well established.

There are, of course, difficulties in the university/ industry relationship. In cases of collaborative research and development work, for example, policies concerning publishing have to be carefully observed in order to protect developments critical to the industry. Universities have to gain experience in the areas of patents and licensing so as to arrange mutually acceptable agreements with industry. Patents become very important and have to be applied for, and universities have to appoint staff capable of giving professional advice in these areas. At the moment in UK universities, little emphasis is put on such special requirements, which occur largely in engineering departments. The educational system has been established mainly for non-technological education, for example in the arts, and has not adjusted to more recent developments within the university system.

ENGINEERING EDUCATION

Engineering education is not academic but vocational. Indeed, there are some good reasons for separating high technical education from the general university system. This separation was made in central Europe a long time ago, and my own high technical school was founded in 1707. The high technical educational system in Europe is usually divided into two stages: normally a four year course consists of two years establishing the foundations of engineering science, and a second two years dealing with vocational subjects, which are pursued in much greater detail than in the UK . We, in the UK, have some advantage in developing more specialised knowledge at the 'A' level period, but also a disadvantage in narrowing education at too early a stage and running the danger of developing narrow-minded technocrats instead of rounded intellectuals.

In engineering, we still do not recruit the most gifted youngsters. This is largely due to the ignorance of headmasters about what engineering entails, thus turning youngsters away from a very challenging and creative profession, into areas where they will not necessarily generate much wealth for the nation in the future. We run plenty of refresher courses for engineers, but these should be compulsory courses for the headmasters dealing with, among other topics, the marketability of their students.

The situation has improved slightly in the last few years. However, there is another danger emerging from the recent upsurge of interest in microelectronics and software engineering. This interest seems to be related to disinterest in the design of hardware. It is essential that we maintain balanced attitudes towards both software and hardware engineering and ensure that we produce engineers who are capable of designing complete systems. One can argue that mechanical engineering is even more challenging than the software engineering, as the hardware and the materials we use are not inherently as flexible as software.

THE ECONOMIC CLIMATE IN THE UK

It is quite clear that the only way to reduce unemployment is to get a bigger share of the world market. This can only happen if Britain manufactures products which are in demand internationally. It seems to me that, although Britain always excelled in high technology, it never really developed large volume engineering production for consumer markets, and in addition it has been losing markets for products like machine tools, motor cars, etc.

Since the war Europeans have consciously and systematically developed their new markets by providing selective, centrally planned incentives and guidance. Britain, on the other hand, left it to chance called the 'free market'. In my view, it would be very useful if the government looked carefully at some of the European approaches, instead of too often drawing comparisons with the USA and more recently with Japan. Both of these countries are placed in a rather different economic framework and the parallels drawn can be very wrong.

However, we can certainly use some examples from these

countries which could help us to improve our manufacturing situation. One such telling example is that top Japanese directors from large industrial concerns retire to banks to advise
them on financing policies required by industry. We do suffer
consequences from adopting short term policies in the UK. For
example, we have far the lowest utilisation of railways in
Europe for transporting goods. We now have one of the lowest
number of students in higher education per capita of all the
developed countries. One of the results in the engineering
industry is that we have a very low number of graduates in
middle-management.

BRITISH MANAGEMENT

The management we often still see in British industry is
amateurish, dealing mainly with trouble-shooting and fire-
fighting, instead of with planned, conceptual schemes. Too
often these managers pride themselves in developing their
experience by starting from the shopfloor. Unfortunately, too
often they do not go on any professional managerial courses, in
order to learn about fundamental tools used in systematic
management. There appears to be a gap between the
middle management and top management who very often do not have
sufficient understanding of engineering, because they consist
mainly of accountants, lawyers, etc. who deal with the
financial side of the enterprise but who do not relate it to
product problems. They are solely concerned with the financial
state of the company but have no interest in product
development.
     Fortunately, the arrival of the flexible manufacturing
concept is going to force us into a complete reappraisal of
production and make us treat it as a complete system. The
large sums of money involved in setting up FMS will hopefully
also make us assess carefully the production methods, product
ranges, and their marketability, before the commitment is
made.

Chapter 4

INTELLIGENT SENSORS

Bruce Batchelor and Simon Cotter

HUMAN AND MACHINE INTELLIGENCE

Until a few years ago, the word 'intelligence' would never have
been associated with a machine, but was reserved for people,
and the higher animals. Nowadays, the concept of intelligence
in machines is widely accepted, although it must be admitted
that we cannot sensibly measure the 'IQ' (Intelligence
Quotient) of a machine and thereby compare it with a person.
Calculators, chess-playing machines, and home computers with
question-answer dialogues programmed into them, are all
commonplace. When connected to appropriate sensors, such
machines are able to perform some interesting and useful tasks,
and ones which eventually will have an enormous impact on
society, as we hope to show in this chapter. Machines already
exist which can, to a limited extent, perform such tasks as:
recognising a speaker (from a given group of individuals who
are known to the system); recognising spoken words; diagnosing
faults in engines from their acoustic emissions; recognising
typed or printed text (optical character recognition); guiding
a robot visually;   and detecting faults in manufactured
objects, such as bottles, stampings or mouldings.

It is a fact, though not immediately obvious perhaps, that
perception necessarily involves intelligent reasoning. In this
chapter, we shall explain the present level of understanding of
intelligent sensory devices. First, we describe an intelligent
question-answer dialogue by which it is possible for a person
to 'discuss' friendships, family relationships, etc. with a
computer. Then, we outline the possibilities for basing man-
computer dialogues on speech. The chapter concludes with a
discussion of machine-vision systems for industrial inspection
and robot control.

INTELLIGENT DIALOGUES BETWEEN MAN AND MACHINES

Three topics are discussed in this section: (a) artificial
intelligence (AI) and dialogues between a person and a computer

(using a conventional terminal/VDU);   (b) speech recognition, by which a person may speak to a machine;   and (c) speech synthesis, by which a person can hear messages 'spoken' by a machine.   These are, of course, the three fundamental components of a verbal conversation.

Prolog (Clocksin and Mellish, 1981) is a specialised computer language, quite unlike Fortran, Basic, Pascal, etc., and is an example of a language devised especially for AI research. There are others, including Lisp and Poplog, while any other language which can handle sets, trees, lists, graphs, can be used for AI purposes.   Using Prolog, it is easy to describe the 'world', as Table 4.1 shows.   Here, the family and friends of one of the authors are described.   This seemingly trivial example was chosen to illustrate how easily an AI language, such as Prolog, can be used to describe the 'world', without introducing other concepts which distract the reader from appreciating the power of the AI language.

The essential features of AI are illustrated in this simple example:

1.   There is a collection of facts (specific to the author, his family and friends).

2.   There is a general set of rules by which the knowledge base may effectively be extended by deductive reasoning.

3.   The computer accepts questions which cause it to try and match the various parts of a question to the known facts or other deducible but undeclared truths.

4.   When there is a partial match, the unproven part is investigated by the Prolog system to see if it matches some other known fact or deducible truth, derived by applying the rules to the facts.   This process effectively expands the knowledge base and is repeated recursively until the veracity of the question can be established.

5.   A question such as '? - friend (bruce, john).' can have two answers 'yes' or 'not proved' (which Prolog abbreviates to 'no'.)

6.   A question such as '? - pal (X, bruce).' can have the answers 'not proved' or 'yes, if X = ...'.   A conditional affirmation like this is common in everyday speech.

In the simple example given in Table 4.1, the format of the questions posed is clumsy.   By extending the programming, it is possible to produce a user-friendly dialogue in which such questions as 'Are peter and sue likely to know each other?' or 'Where does the father of david work?' are posed by the user of the computing system.

Using an AI language, like Prolog, it is possible to perform the dialogue in English, albeit with a somewhat stilted style, rather than the cryptic form shown in Table 4.1.   These then are the basic elements of an AI dialogue.   Later in this section, we describe a more serious application where a manager wishes to interrogate a computer-based information system, in which there are stored facts about such features as: stock levels in stores, machines out of use, and key operators who are ill or on leave.

It is not difficult to imagine the system guiding the manager to certain critical areas, where, for example, a certain

Table 4.1: A Simple Prolog Description of Batchelor's Family
and Friends

A series of facts (a) is given and a collection of rules (b) is
used to interpret them and draw conclusions in response to a
set a questions (c).

(a) facts

Prolog	Explanation
friend (bruce, peter).	bruce has a friend called peter.
friend (bruce, john).	(notice that there is no
friend (bruce, douglas).	specifiation of that thing called
friend (meryl, bruce).	'bruce' (or 'peter') and that
friend (eleanor, pauline).	'friend' is defined to be a
friend (kath, eleanor).	relationship existing between
friend (sue, eleanor).	'bruce' and 'peter'. Such a
	definition is unidirectional.)
husband (bruce, eleanor).	bruce is the husband of eleanor
father (bruce, helen).	bruce is the father of helen
father (bruce, david).	

(b) rules

Prolog	Explanation
buddy (X,Y): - friend (X,Y); friend (Y,X).	X is a buddy of Y if X has a friend called peter or Y has a friend called X. The above rule is then ORed with that following:
buddy (X,Y):- (husband (X,Z); husband (Z,X)), (friend (Z,Y); friend (Y,Z)).	X is a buddy of Y if (X is the husband of Z or Z is the husband of X) and (Z has a friend called Y and Y has a friend called Z).
pal (X,Y): - (buddy (X,Y),	X is a pal of Y if X is a buddy of X
son (X,Y): - father (Y,X), male (X)	X is the son of Y if Y is the father of X and X is male
son (X,Y): - father (Z,X), husband (Z,Y), male (X)	X is the son of Y if Z is the father of X and Z is the husband of Y and X is male. (Z is the mother of X.)
may know (X,Y): - pal (X,Z), pal (Z,Y).	X may know Y if X has a pal Z and Z has a pal Y.
may know (X,Y): - son (X,Z), son (Z,Y).	X may know Y if X is the son of Z and Z is a pal of Y

may know (X,Y): - son (Z,X),	X may know Y if Z is the son of X and
pal (Z,Y).	Z is a pal of Y

(c) questions

Prolog user types	Interpretation	System types in reponse
? - son (david, bruce).	Is david the son of bruce?	yes
? - son (helen, bruce).	Is helen the son of bruce?	no (i.e. 'not proven'
? - son (X, bruce).	Who (i.e. X) is the son of bruce?	
? - son (david, eleanor).	Is david the son of eleanor?	
? - buddy (bruce, meryl).	Does bruce have a buddy called meryl?	yes
? - pal (meryl, eleanor).	Does meryl have a pal called eleanor? (Notice that meryl and eleanor are not stated as having any direct relationships in the facts)	yes
? - pal (X, bruce).	Who is/are bruce's pals?	X=peter, john, douglas, meryl, pauline, kath, sue
? - may know (X, sue).	Who may know sue?	X=kath, sue, peter, john, douglas, meryl, pauline

product line is needed urgently and the machines /operatives needed to make them are unavailable. The potential of AI dialogues is truly enormous in such situations. The benefit of the AI component in the dialogue is that it can amplify the manager's own 'native wit' by discriminating between simple straightforward situations, which the system can manage unaided, and other more critical cases which deserve his attention. In the future, we shall no doubt see many management functions being replaced by intelligent machines. At the moment, the AI system can merely augment the manager, by acting like a diligent PA/secretary. It cannot replace the manager. People, particularly those who are untrained in its use, are much less adept at giving commands via a keyboard than by speaking. For this reason, there has been a great deal of research on the recognition of speech by machine and on the synthesis of speech from a computer-like device. Using a speech-recognition system, a human being is able to communicate with a computer in a natural way, leaving both hands and eyes completely free for other activities. (Indeed, the user of a speech based system could be both blind and quadraplegic.) As a result, speech-based dialogues between man and machine are far less tiring for the user and are likely to be faster, more reliable and less frustrating than using a keyboard-based VDU. However, there are problems because speech recognition by machine is not yet as cheap and reliable as we would wish; speech recognition systems are not yet refined enough to accommodate very large vocabularies, large numbers of different speakers, and/or heavy accents/speech impediments, such as stammering. To overcome this deficiency, we might choose one of several options: (a) use an expensive machine to achieve good results; (b) use a cheaper machine which can accommodate only one known speaker and/or a limited vocabulary; (c) use visual or acoustic feedback to check /modify the system's response to a spoken phrase, since feedback is tedious for the user, or (d) use an intelligent analysis program within the machine to decide, in advance, what are the most likely responses by the user to a given question. In a dialogue on chess, for example, we can limit the vocabulary by letting the machine ask questions, to each of which there are likely to be fewer than a dozen possible responses.

Speech recognition research is continuing apace, as there is a huge potential market for such systems. Within the next few years, we may well find such machines replacing audio-typists, data-entry operators and theatre/airline ticket booking personnel. Considering these developments, taken together with AI programming, we can confidently anticipate a rapid increase in the acceptability and effective power of computers for ordinary (i.e. untrained) people. To complete the picture, speech synthesis, which is already well advanced, allows the user to receive messages from a computer, without turning his head or diverting his eyes.

To illustrate the points we have made in this paragraph, imagine a factory manager talking to a computer like this:

Man	Machine
'Hello! Bruce Batchelor here' (user 'signing in', fixed format)	'Hello Bruce' (giving confirmation of identity of the speaker)
'What is the news today?'	'Small fire in the paint shop during the night. No serious damage. Difficulties in finding reliable supplies of steel wire', etc.
'How many staff are ill?'	'37. No serious problems though'
'Have I got any appointments today?'	'Lunch with MD at noon'
'Who else is going?'	'I don't know. I will find out and report back later' (System now interrogates the MD's secretary/file and responds in a few minutes).
'What was last week's prod- uction of size 7 widgets?'	'2® million. That is _ million fewer than the‾ previous week'
'What was the cause'	'Difficulties in getting the correct grade of steel wire'
'Get me John Smith on the telephone' (John Smith is the Production Manager and is now about to receive a query/prompt about last week's low production level)	Will do! Do you want me to record the con- versation?' (System now dials John Smith)

'No!'

'Sorry John Smith is
out now. Do you want me
to try again in a few
minutes?'
'Nobody else is coming
to lunch with MD'
(System responding from
earlier question)

'No! I am going out now'

'Goodbye, but don't
forget the lunch at noon
with the MD'.

(Manager exits, muttering
under his breath)

'Sorry I cannot under-
stand'

Such a dialogue is no mere flight of fancy, although such
a system, able to respond intelligently using speech as a
man-machine communication medium, would at the moment be
prohibitively expensive. To be really effective, such an
information system would need to have a wide range of
data-entry points and other sensors, as illustrated in Figure
4.1.

It is worth mentioning a few of the other man-machine
communication developments which have taken place recently and
which will all have an impact on such management-centred
activities. These include such innovations as: large
format/high resolution VDUs (for drawings, plans, etc.);
displays for grey-scale and colour images (discussed below);
laser discs for video storage (i.e. archiving of pictures);
signature validation (for security, time-keeping, etc.);
touch-sensitive screens for modifying/editing pictures and
text; miniature and flat-screen displays of text; and
low-bandwidth television for easy transmission of images around
a factory or office complex.

Let us now turn our attention to automated inspection and
the sensing methods which might be used for component handling.
We shall concentrate on machine vision systems, although other
sensors, e.g. electrical, acoustic, magnetic, optical, are of
equal importance.

ROBOT CONTROL, FLEXIBLE MANUFACTURING AND MACHINE VISION

To illustrate the principles of automated manufacturing and the
intelligent sensory devices needed for it, consider a bakery.
Our task will be to take a tray out of an oven; place it on a
cooling table; wait; pick up the tray and place it on another
table; pick up the cakes on it, one at a time; inspect each
cake (discard malformed and discoloured ones); place a cherry
on it; inspect the cherry placing; pack the cake in a box (6

Figure 4.1: A Corporate Computer Network of the Future

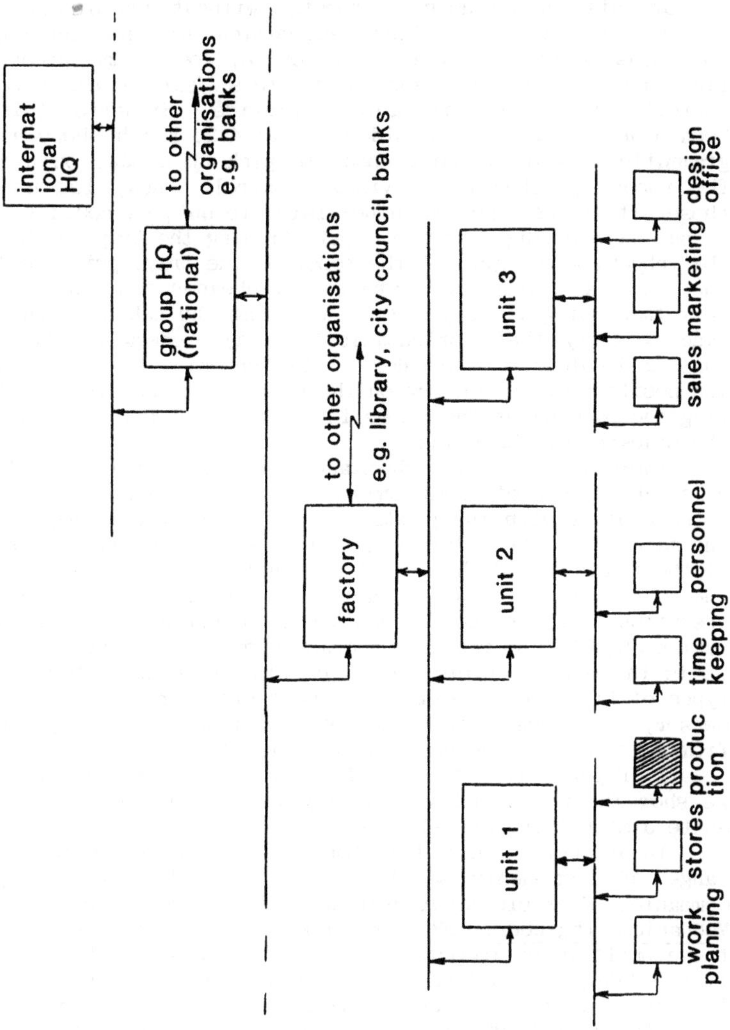

cakes/box); stack the boxes; wrap and stack the box-packages. All of this can be done by robots, without any direct human intervention, but as 'blind' automation is very unreliable, good sensors are essential. Of course, low volume production lines need flexibility and it is this feature which modern 'intelligent' sensors are able to provide. Hitherto, this has been done by people. Consider Figure 4.2, which shows a dia-grammatic view of a robot about to pick up a cake on a tray. The robot operates under visual control. Now, let us list those situations where machine-vision techniques could be used in our cake-making exercise: (a) finding the tray in the oven (b) checking the grip of the robot on the tray, prior to lift-ing it, (although there are easier/cheaper methods of doing this than using vision); (c) locating the cakes on the tray (and possibly their orientation); (d) checking the size, shape and colour of the cakes; (e) checking the size, colour and position of the cherry on the cake; (f) checking/ control-ling the packing of the cakes in the boxes; and (g) checking the stacking of the boxes.

There are several advantages of using vision which, in cake making, are of great importance: it is clean, since there is no contact with the product; it is very versatile, because one machine can (with re-programming) satisfy most, if not all, of the tasks listed above; it does not damage the cakes, since there is no physical contact with them; it is fast in operation; it is safe, consistent, reliable and capable of taking objective quantitative measurements; in many instances, it is the only feasible method of examining cakes for certain types of fault, (e.g. placing of soft cream or icing); and the sensor, being remote from the point of inspection, is protected from being damaged by heat, dirt, oil, etc.

In Figures 4.3, 4.4 and 4.5 (at the end of the chapter), we show the power and versatility of machine vision on three quite distinct industrial tasks.

In another case, a flat toroidal object is typical of the range of components which are made in the 600 Group of Companies' flexible manufacturing cell, called SCAMP (Chartered Mechanical Engineer, 1983; Heywood, 1983). The orientation of these parts is so important that the development of SCAMP was, at one time, threatened by the lack of an appropriate sensor. The parts could be positioned mechanically but the wide variety of parts which SCAMP makes, renders mechanical orientation sen-sors impractical. Vision was studied as one possible means of determining orientation in a series of laboratory tests. Following this, a machine using two cameras, two turntables, a robot and a computer (to control the vision system and mechani-cal handling) was designed and built by British Robotic Systems Ltd. New (i.e. previously unseen) parts are regularly pre-sented to the SCAMP vision machine. One sample of each new component class is used to 'teach' it. The 'teach' phase takes under two minutes and can be performed by an operator with

Figure 4.2: Robotics in the Bakery

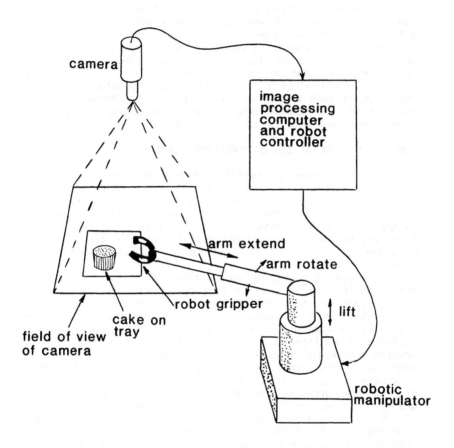

minimal training; the machine guides the operator throughout the 'teach' operation. Thereafter, the machine automatically recognises parts representative of the classes it has seen before and orientates them to within 0.5 degrees. The machine can accommodate a repertoire of fifty classes and is robust enough to operate with wet, shiny (bare metal or painted) or dull (metaloxide) surfaces.

In another project, a robot is used to grab similar parts out of a bin in which they are stacked. The vision system then fixes orientation and position (to lie within fairly tightly defined limits). Clearly, human operators could do this type of task but it is boring, physically demanding work. Machines can now release human beings from such tasks and allow them to do other more interesting things.

CONCLUSIONS: SOCIAL AND ECONOMIC IMPLICATIONS

Intelligent devices are rapidly gaining acceptance on account of their versatility and ease of use. Moreover, they frequently provide a marked reduction in the cost of performing a given job. The examples illustrated here are, of course, examples of factory automation. In the future, office automation will become equally important. We can list the following developments which will have a significant effect on office working practices.

1. Optical character recognition (OCR) - an OCR machine reads printed, typed text or (carefully printed) handwriting. A typed page can be coded in electronic form and then stored/ manipulated inside a computer. Thus, documents which were not originally intended for electronic processing can be read, analysed or modified and then reprinted. The production of braille text would be greatly facilitated by the use of OCR, as would the filing/archiving of letters, memos, etc. when they originate on paper. Bar-code readers are already in widespread use and banks have used magnetic ink character recognition for nearly a decade, and OCR is a more recent innovation.

2. Electronic mail, publishing, etc. - although electronic mail is not strictly within the scope of this chapter, it is interesting to note the possibility of an intelligent program, perhaps based on Prolog, which sorts the incoming (electronic) mail according to its priority and recovers any relevant (electronic) files from the achive, ready for a manager to read. This is, of course, no more than what a good secretary does, but the electronic system should be faster, more reliable and cheaper. An intelligent program can also compensate for a poor secretary.

3. Data entry devices - apart from OCR there are such novel devices for data entry as pressure-sensitive pads, which allow a person to draw or write data directly into a computer. Intelligent programs can then interpret these data in a variety of ways, e.g. 'clean-up' sketches, recognise drawing symbols

(e.g. for electronic circuit diagrams), or recognise signatures of people as they try to gain access to secure buildings.

Touch sensitive VDU screens are particularly appropriate for indicating preferences from a list provided by a computer. They are useful therefore for administering computer-based questionnaries (e.g. on an inspector's checklist).

4. Image plus text displays - there are numerous occasions when a picture plus a portion of text are required together. Electronic displays of both are now possible. Figures 4.4 to 4.5 are photographs from one such display. In addition, laser printers/engravers can produce hard copy on paper, plastic or metal surfaces. Estate agents, car sales offices, personnel offices, publishers, advertisers, etc. are likely to benefit from these developments.

An awareness programme, called 'Information Technology Year' was held in the UK during 1982. By contrast, the Chinese refer to 1983 as 'The Year of the Pig'! However, the following year is more sinister; George Orwell's book 1984, predicted a totalitarian regime able to monitor and thereby control its population. The technology exists to do far more than Orwell predicted! Non-technical readers should be under no illusions about the reality of this, and we must all be diligent to ensure that Orwell's book remains mere fantasy. The advance of modern technology has become so rapid that any organisation must plan its approach to it with very great care. However, the subject cannot be ignored - your competitors won't ignore it!

Figure 4.3: Machine Vision - An Electrical Plug

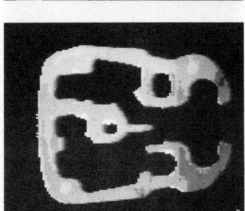

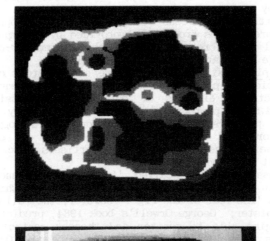

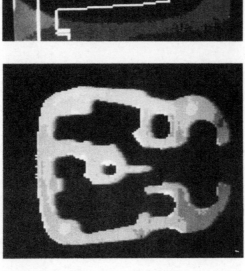

(a) In this image, the height of the surface of the moulding is indicated by the intensity. This is called a 'depth map', in this case of an electrical plug.

(b) A height/intensity profile plotted for the cross section indicated by the horizontal white line.

(c) The plug base and cap depth maps have been superimposed to show how they mate together.

Figure 4.4: Machine Vision - Steel Sheets

(a) A laser scanner was used to obtain this image of bright sheet steel, which shows a scratch about 10mm long.

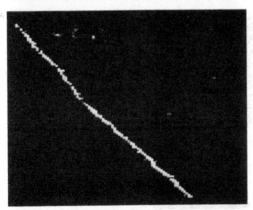

(b) After electronic filtering and noise reduction, the scratch is enhanced.

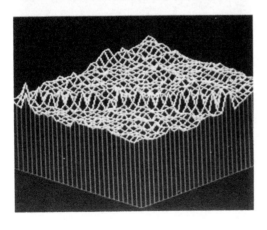

(c) A so-called 'surface plot' of (a) shows the scratch as a raised ridge.

Figure 4.4: Machine Vision - Steel Sheets (continued)

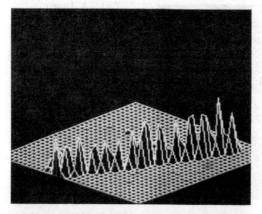

(d) After filtering, the surface plot of (b) shows the scratch more prominently.

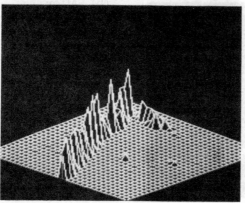

(e) A better angle of view of the surface plot in (b), also showing a second scratch to the right of the first.

Figure 4.5:   Machine Vision – Cakes

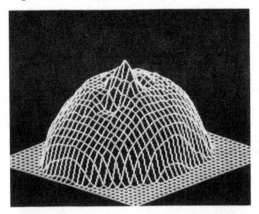

(a) A surface plot derived from a depth map of an iced cake with a cherry on top.

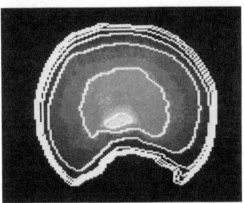

(b) A depth map of a defective cake, with a bite out of it. Height contours have been superimposed.

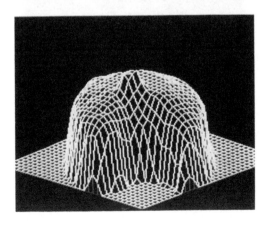

(c) A surface plot of the cake in (b) showing the bite.

REFERENCES

Chartered Mechanical Engineer (1983) 'SCAMP - The Latest in
Flexible Manufacturing', The Chartered Mechanical Engineer,
January

Clocksin, W.F., Mellish, C.S. (1981) Programming in Prolog,
Springer Verlag, Berlin

Heywood, P. (1983), 'Vision Sensing for FMS - the SCAMP
Project', in Proc. Industrial Applications of Image Analysis
IRSIA/IWONL and CETA, Antwerp 1983

PART II

MANAGEMENT IMPLICATIONS –
EMPLOYMENT ISSUES

Chapter 5

THE IMPACT OF INFORMATION TECHNOLOGY
ON THE WORK PLACE

Frank Land

INTRODUCTION

This chapter is based on the UK contribution to a three nation
study - in Denmark, the Federal Republic of Germany, and the UK
- sponsored by the European Community (Dehning and Schonberg,
1982). The study investigated the extent to which the introduction of information technology imposed (or was perceived to
impose) social control on the individuals who worked with the
new technology.

The project took the form of some general observations of
the issues raised, based on a study of research carried out in
the UK, on relevant technical literature and on discussion with
experts. This was followed by a more detailed exploration of
the topic of social control based on a number of case studies
carried out as part of this project, and finished with an
analysis of the mechanisms, which, in the UK, influence the
degree to which technology imposes social control.

The context of the study is that the last decade has seen
an enormous increase in the use of computers for company data
processing in Europe. This has resulted in a four-fold
increase in computers in business enterprises over the decade.

The technology has become more visible. No longer is the
computer hidden behind the doors of the EDP department. The
spread of microcomputers and on-line systems means that
computing facilities are seen in all departments, and form a
part of the office equipment of each clerk. And the technology
has spread throughout industry and commerce, even into the
smallest business.

TYPES OF SOCIAL CONTROL

The study looked at a number of ways in which information technology could impose control on employees, which are listed
below.

1. The technology could be used to measure the performance of individuals or groups of employees. At a management

level, computer based budgeting systems could be used to evaluate the performance of a manager. At the level of an operator, for instance, the technology could be used to count, record, and report the average number of key strokes of a word processing operator during each working day.

2. The technology could restrict the way an employee carried out his (or her) task. At one level, the computer could take away some of the decision-making functions of a middle manager, by, for example, automating the function of calculating order quantities for a buyer. At another level, it could indicate the sequence and timing of the operations of a computer terminal operator.

3. The technology could be used to collate information about employees from different sources without the knowledge or acquiescence of the employees, thus infringing their privacy rights. Personnel systems might hold information about employees and be used in decisions about their promotion without their knowledge.

4. The technology could have an effect on employees promotion prospects and career paths. Employees who could 'cope' with the technology might advance at the expense of employees who are made dispensable or whose jobs are deskilled by the new system, or who are deemed not to be able to 'cope'.

PROBLEMS OF RESEARCH

Despite the amount of discussion generated, in the recent past, regarding the impact of information technology, serious research is very limited. With only a few exceptions, practitioners and users have not described and published details of systems objectives or of designs, or of implementation experience. Few enterprises have put on record the outcome of their investment in information technology, except in the broadest of terms. There are many reasons for this: (a) the fear of giving away commercially confidential information; (b) the fear that published details of, for example, reductions in employment will increase trade union and employee resistance; (c) the sheer lack of time of the busy executive; (d) the reluctance to admit failure in cases of systems which have not been successful; and (e) the lack of knowledge of what the outcomes of the project were.

Where case studies have been published they are often oversimplifications of the real situation, or represent post hoc attempts at justification or rationalisation of decisions taken. Case studies too, tend to stress methods rather than effects.

Empirical research into the effects of information technology is also limited in extent. Although a study of the literature and research in this area, such as the 1982 study by the Science Policy Unit at Sussex University (Arnold et al, 1981) found a considerable number of references, many of them were of limited value, even in the context of the study, which was mainly concerned with effects on employment.

Empirical research into the impact of information technology on enterprises and their workers bristles with methodological difficulties. Observed effects may be the consequence of a number of things affecting the organisation at the same time. In a dynamic, turbulent environment, cause and effect relationships are almost impossible to disentangle in the absence of laboratory conditions. Few researchers have sufficient resources to take adequate samples, and controlled experiments are not possible. Organisations which provide information to researchers may not have kept relevant records, reliance on memory is fallible, and executives are constrained by problems of commercial confidentiality. The researcher is caught between the need to have a representative sample, and the need to study a very few cases in great detail.

The only satisfactory method of case study based research is the longitudinal study, observing the impact of an application of information technology through all the stages of development and operation. But even studies of this kind present acute difficulties. It is often impossible to sort out cause and effect relationships in circumstances where many kinds of changes are taking place in the same time period - some planned, but others unplanned. Such studies are expensive and few organisations are prepared to act as hosts to a research team for a prolonged period. We have not found a single published case of a longitudinal study into the impact of the new technology in the UK. It is not surprising that most research takes the form of snapshots, and that most of the reported research is anecdotal, relying heavily on 'folk-lore', and that results reported are often largely conjectures. Case studies on their own are inadequate for measuring the extent of any impact. They would have to be combined, for example, with surveys of the number of employees displaced and their destinations, whether it be to the pool of unemployed or to new jobs.

AWARENESS OF THE PROBLEM

In any case, the issue of new technology and social control has not until recently been regarded as a topic of major significance in the UK. The social problems associated with the introduction of new technology have been seen (and investigated) in terms primarily of effects on employment and the labour market, and, also, but to a much lesser extent, as problems associated with the health and comfort of employees using the new technology.

At the level of the systems manager, or within user management, there is little indication of awareness that the impact of information technology on human behaviour is an important design variable, except in the limited sense of

designing for 'user-friendliness'. It is recognised that poor
screen layouts, for example, can result in user resistance, and
inefficient use of a new system. There is, thus, considerable
research and a fast-growing literature into aspects of 'user
friendliness', such as the design of man-machine dialogues
(Mehlmann, 1981). In a sense 'user friendliness' is treated as
a technical design problem. There is, however, a growing diss-
atisfaction with the conventional design and implementation
methodologies, reflected in a search for new techniques and
tools. This had led individual systems managers to experiment
with different approaches, including methods which permit a
high degree of user participation in the design of systems
(Mumford et al, 1978), and which attempt to reconcile
technical/economic requirements with social objectives of the
workforce, such as the enhancement of job satisfaction
(Mumford, 1981b). Most of these attempts have been on an individual project basis and have had little impact on the overall
strategy of the organisation for the application of information
technology.

In practice, the major impact on social factors appears to
have been achieved through the employment effect of the technology. It is the displacement of labour by information technology which has led to the restructuring of work, with the
attendant changes in job content, rather than the use of the
technology to meet explicit objectives to change patterns.
The overall impact of using the technology to save costs may
well have been to reduce the level of skills needed, and rather
than making jobs more interesting, as has frequently been
claimed by computer experts, to have made jobs more
monotonous.

At the trade union level the dominant concern has been,
and still is, with the employment effects of the new technology, with a secondary concern for the health and safety implications of the installations. Not surprisingly, in a period of
rising unemployment, questions of social impacts tend to be
regarded as of a lesser importance. This also reflects the
more traditional concerns of trade unions in the UK, who have
generally concerned themselves with work practices only to the
extent that they affect the rate of pay or affect issues of
health and safety. However, there is a growing awareness in
trade union circles that the proposed introduction of new technology could provide a lever to exercise power in their negotiations with employers. This had led some trade unions in
recent years to permit the installation of new technology only
after management has been prepared to sign a Technology Agreement. Trade unions are beginning to recognise that the impact
of information technology on work practices is an area of legitimate concern in their negotiations with employers.

A third group which might be expected to concern
itself with the impact of information technology on social control is the academic community. In the UK, the discipline

most likely to be researching into information technology is that of computer science. Computer scientists have shown little interest in the issues of social control. They recognise problems in the implementation of computer systems, but see the solution in terms of improvements in software engineering practice, including within that the problem of 'user friendliness'. A few academics, coming in general from social science or ergonomics faculties, have taken up the issues of the social impact of information technology, and have played a leading part in the development of new approaches to the design and implementation referred to above (Damordaran, 1980; Mumford, 1981b).

A number of university based research units have been set up in recent years, which carry out empirical research into the impact of technology, including information technology. These include the Science Policy Research Unit (SPRU) at Sussex University, the Technology Policy Unit at Aston University, and the Technical Change Centre in London. Loughborough University has the long established Human Science and Advanced Technology Unit (HUSAT), which has pioneered ergonomics research in information technology in the UK, and another pioneering group has been the MRC Unit at Sheffield University.

The work of these units is beginning to provide a better (and more firmly based) picture of the effects that the new technology is having on the national economy, on employment and industrial enterprises, and on the employee and his/her job. However, in no sense, can the research to date, and the published case studies, be regarded as constituting a fair or representative sample to help measure the impact of the new technology. Studies in progress, or which are being planned, will throw more light on the issues which were the subject of our research project. It is clear, however, that 1982 was a little too early to see the major impact of the new technology. Many enterprises are still only beginning to understand the applications which are now feasible, and the next few years will see the effects on a much larger scale.

Despite the generally low level of attention paid to these issues in the past, and the lack of prior studies concentrating on issues other than employment, we discovered in our discussions with trade union officials, user managers, EDP managers, and academic researchers, a surprising degree of interest and willingness to collaborate in the project. We approached ten organisations from a range of UK industries, with a view to their letting us examine computer applications in detail, including interviewing staff at all levels. The organisations selected were, in the main, known to the study team from previous contacts or studies. All but two organisations welcomed our approach, thought that the issues raised were of interest to management, and agreed to collaborate in the study. Most people contacted agreed that the issue of social control was relevant, but had not been studied within their organisation, and that our study could provide them with significant information for use in future applications. Similarly, trade union officials were helpful and understanding. Discussions with academics from the USA, and Australia, suggested that a similar interest would be shown in other countries. Indeed, some academics suggested the possibility that a larger collaborative project should follow our study.

ORGANISATIONAL ISSUES

This section examines the most important variables which affect the impact of information technology on organisations, and on the people who work in them. The variables, discussed are: (a) the motivation and objectives which lead enterprises to change information systems by the use of information technology; (b) the approaches and methods used to design and implement changes in information systems; and (c) the technology available, and the technology used.

Hedberg (1980) suggested a model of the way organisations use computers. He suggested that when organisations first started to use computers for data processing (Phase 1), the designers of the information systems attempted to increase the efficiency with which data processing tasks were carried out. The introduction of computer based systems had not been intended to change the organisation, and if there were impacts on the organisation, these were largely unforeseen, often dysfunctional, and surprised both designers and users. Alternatively, systems were carefully designed to avoid organisational change (Phase 2). It is only in Phase 3 that systems designers attempt to use the technology to shape an organisation's structure so that the organisation becomes more effective.

The majority of computer users in the UK are still in Phase 1 and Phase 2 of the Hedberg model. Most systems were designed to achieve rather limited objectives concerned initially with cost savings, and later with objectives such as improvements in customer service, or coping with growing workloads, and the provision of extra or new services without increasing establishments. Few applications attempted to alter the decision processes of senior management, although many organisations used computer systems to improve the timeliness and form of management reports such as sales analyses. At lower levels in the organisation, computer systems were designed to replace the decision-making tasks of employees. Many stock control systems, for example, included automatic ordering facilities, thus replacing the function of a buyer. The British Shoe Corporation in the late 1960s developed a system for the automatic replenishment of its retail shoe shops, taking the job of ordering from the branch manager. This application was typical of many in the distributive trades and was typical in that the principal impact in terms of task structure was on junior management, whose responsibilities were simplified, routinised and hence diminished.

The more detailed case studies carried out for this project reinforce this view of development in the UK. Two of the cases relate to new systems designed and implemented in the past two years. In each case the enterprises concerned are long-standing users of information technology, in the case of one company (in the oil industry) dating back to the mid-1950's. Both are major companies in their industries. Yet, the applications the study team was invited to look at are typical of Phase 1 or Phase 2 of the Hedberg model. In neither case did the designers of the system or the users look for organisational impacts beyond the more efficient operation of the units in question.

The objectives of systems change have nearly always been related to the technical and economic goals of the enterprise. It is only in exceptional cases that managers or designers have seen a relationship between the social needs of employees, measured in terms of job satisfaction or the quality of working life, and technical and economic goals measured in terms of operating efficiency and ultimately profitability. If such relationships have been recognised, and have affected the actual design of the system, they have rarely been described or documented. It is therefore interesting to note that the problem of low job satisfaction had been one of the main motivating forces in considering systems change in one of the case studies (a medical insurance firm) even though it had not appeared explicitly in any statement of requirements, and was not evaluated in the feasibility study. In one of the other case studies (in engineering manufacturing) the problems associated with the proposed change in work practice were sufficiently realised for the designers to seek a way of offsetting the workforce's loss of control over production reporting, by making the new system provide a very fast feedback to machine operators, plus the possibility of higher bonus payments. There are a small number of cases reported (Mumford and Henshall, 1978; Mumford 1981b) in which management and designers chose an approach to design which enabled them to identify some of the social objectives of the workforce and design the system to achieve both these and the technical/economic goals of the enterprise.

DEVELOPMENT APPROACHES

A key element in the potential impact of information technology is the approach taken to development, by those responsible for the design and implementation of the information system, and in the vast majority of UK enterprises the methods used have been derived from methods of software engineering. The design approach is oriented towards the optimum use of the technology, and designers and implementors are judged more on the technical excellence of the design than on its long run organisational consequences. If the system is not successful, it is often the user who is blamed.

Studies (Hedberg and Mumford, 1975) have shown, too, that the kind of people who are attracted to work with computers have values associated with scientific rationalism and find the concepts of scientific management satisfying.

The conventional design approach, reinforced by the values of its practitioners, has certain severe limitations: (a) the approach does not pay attention to work design, and work design methods are not taught to trainee systems analysts, so as a result, the work design component of an information system is neglected, and work systems tend to be copies of the previous system; (b) the dominant emphasis in the design of the technical (computer) part of the system, accentuates the concentration on the formal, structured features of the system; (c) the conventional approach views the process of analysis, design and implementation as a predefined sequence of activities in which requirements are elicited at the beginning of the process, and a system is designed, constructed and implemented on the basis of those requirements.

In the last few years a number of alternative approaches have been formulated, and have begun to be discussed. Two in particular are relevant to this study: first, the participative, socio-technical approach pioneered in the UK by Enid Mumford (1981a); and second, the experimental approach to the design of information systems which rejects the concept of a sequential deterministic systems life cycle (Brittan, 1980).

A system may exert social control over those who have to work with it because the designers intended it - for example, by including performance measurement features in the design - or by accident, as when a system is designed to help a manager by providing him with a budget system, but which he feels limits his freedom of action (Dew and Gee, 1973). The use of an experimental approach can help to reduce the accidental, and often dysfunctional, impacts of the technology. But the approach can also result in a change in design if the experiments reveal unexpected adverse reactions to design features, such as the collection of performance data and their storage in a personnel record.

The growth of the centralised EDP function up to the mid 1970s was based, in part, on the technical properties of computer technology. Significant economies of scale could be obtained from large mainframe computers, and this factor encouraged the trend towards centralisation. In many organisations this represented a major shift in power from those responsible for the wealth creating activities of the organisation, to those who understood (could programme) computers, and who were therefore capable of developing the information systems the wealth creators needed. In time, many line managers began to resent their loss of control over their own information systems and their own data, and resented the fact that they had to wait upon the convenience of the EDP department before changes in data processing systems could be made, or new systems developed. A number of studies such as that carried out by the British Computer Society (1978) indicate the tension that had often built up between user departments and the EDP department. Perhaps the best articulated type of social control is that which resulted from the shift in power to the EDP professional, and of which the line manager felt himself to be the victim. The new technology, epitomised by the microcomputer, is perceived by line management to provide an escape from the trap, and to give him the possibility of regaining lost power.

The impact of the new technology on management thinking has raised important questions regarding the future role (if any?) of EDP departments and computer professionals in user organisations. Management has seen the microcomputer and office technology as an opportunity to escape from the tyranny and control of the traditional type of EDP department (Land, 1979). There is evidence that in a growing number of companies, even companies with a long history of computing, and with strong and successful EDP departments, individual line managers have begun to acquire microcomputers which are intended to provide local processing facilities, often independent of the company's data processing service. In some companies, for example a major paper manufacturer, the traditional EDP department has been dispersed and made responsible to local user management, retaining a small, but high level EDP staff to promulgate standards and to offer an advisory service.

ALTERNATIVE VIEWS AND PERSPECTIVES

Only slowly is it dawning on systems designers that the success of a computer system cannot be assured if it is not acceptable to its users (see Arnold (1982) for a discussion of 'usability'). Important work in this direction is carried out by the Human Sciences and Advanced Technology Unit (HUSAT) at Loughborough University of Technology. However, this work begins with an ergonomic approach, starting with the relation between a single user and a terminal, and radiating from there to his working environment, which includes relations with other people.

The approach of Fitter and Sime (1980) is quite different. The system's designer must work on the assumption that 'a computer is not, and should not, be capable of interacting with its user on an equal footing. The computer is a conceptual tool and the user should always be its master.' They quote C.A.R. Hoare as saying 'such a one-sided communication should probably not be called a dialogue, in which you expect a human partner to give essentially uncontrolled and even unpredictable responses and take responsibility for them.'

The well-known work of Enid Mumford (1981b) together with others (Land et al, 1980) advocates a method of participative design of information systems. By involving the users at every stage in the design process, they believe, it is possible consciously to aim to improve working conditions, and in so doing to ensure the efficient working of the resulting system. Furthermore, the work of this school presents some of the few available detailed case studies on the introduction of computer systems in the UK.

The work of Rosenbrock (1976; 1977; 1982) on this question has stressed that two opposite paths of development are possible for the new technology.

Although discussions of the impact of information technology have concentrated on the possible loss of jobs, some surveys in the field of office work have also examined changes in job satisfaction.

Wynne and Otway (1982) concentrate on the impact of computer based information systems on upper and middle management. In their review of the management literature they note the importance of the informal system, in successful organisations. At the same time they observe the tendency of information systems 'engineers' to rely on a deterministic, rationalistic model of managerial behaviour:

> 'if the information system is based on a false model of
> authority and organisation (or, even worse if it has been
> intentionally designed to force the organisation to become
> more 'rational'...), then the constructive functioning of
> the real information network in the informal social
> system... can be damaged or destroyed... this can
> accelerate the process of deskilling and alienation.'
> (Wynne and Otway, 1982)

The authors deny that technology and its application 'embody intrinsic forces which predetermine organisational degradation.' It is a question of design concepts and the values and ideologies upon which they are based.

From the review of the literature, it is apparent that the evidence available is too scant for commentators to find common ground. It is clear that most of the judgements made by authors are based on their own preconceptions, and their forecasts of the future are of doubtful value. This view is supported by Sorge et al:

> 'A great number of studies have been carried out, which
> deal with microelectronics as a general phenomenon and try
> to determine economic and social consequences. However,
> no reliable assessment of the impact has been possible.'
> (Sorge et al, 1982).

Hard facts await further study. And, in the UK, funding for such studies is very limited.

MECHANISMS OF SOCIAL CONTROL

There seem to be two schools of thought regarding the social impact of information technology. The first school, whose views are articulated very clearly by writers like Cooley (1980), see the diffusion of information technology as a continuous process of rationalisation and very much a part of the industrial revolution. Whereas the first industrial revolution replaced muscle by machines, the new industrial revolution replaces mind by machines. The first industrial revolution was characterised by the factory system which resulted in the control of the workforce by the employers. The system culminated in the almost complete abdication of control over his job by the worker on the assembly line, under Taylor's principle of scientific management. The only way the worker could maintain a position approaching equality was by organising into unions and taking an opposing stance to management.

Those who belong to the first school believe that the same process is now overtaking white-collar management, and professional workers. The school is divided into optimists and pessimists. The optimists believe, like Cooley, that technology is neutral, but that the capitalist system has to maintain the process. Because the technology is neutral, they believe it is possible to organise workers (via the unions) to choose alternative, humanistic ways of using the technology, thus achieving both social and technical goals.

The pessimists (Braverman, 1971) believe that the process is deterministic: social controls are bound to increase and will result in a progressive degradation of work. Some believe too, that there is a technological imperative whereby the proper utilisation of the technology demands increased control over the actions of the worker (Noble, 1979).

The second school takes a contingency approach. It notes the enormous variation in experience and outcomes, and suggests that a wide range of factors underlie these experiences. Sorge from Germany and Warner from England put these views very clearly:

'The impact of new information technology depends on where and how it is used. The wide range of application leads to a similarly wide range of effects, many of which may be in different directions. We would argue.... that the consistent references to microelectronics having 'effects' is not helpful' (Sorge et al, 1982).

The work of our recent study lends support to the contingency approach and helps to identify some of the factors which contribute to the way technology is introduced and how it is perceived. These factors are as follows:

1. The extent to which those who work in the organisation share in its goals and values. This can even vary within an organisation as is illustrated by the engineering production company we studied. Where values are shared there is a better chance of the new technology being accepted, and for the workers to get satisfaction from improved efficiency. At the same time, shared values imply that management gets satisfaction from seeing the technology used in a humanistic way. Evidence from the case studies and work reported elsewhere (Bird, 1980) provide support for this conjecture. The contrary case - where goals and values are not shared - has an opposite effect. Change is resisted, and counterimplementation strategies employed (Keen, 1981). Workers regard the introduction as an opportunity to demonstrate their independence and, where possible, their power. They get satisfaction from winning battles against management. Management seeks to overcome resistance by increasing control over the work situation.

The extent of shared values is itself contingent on other factors. These factors include: (a) The industrial relations climate prevailing in the country, the industry, or the workshop. Historical, economic and personal factors determine what the climate is like at any moment. Evidence from the case studies demonstrates that industrial relations can range from excellent to catastrophic, even in one enterprise. It should be noted that in contrast to the case reported in this study, (Sorge et al, 1982) claim:

> 'Industrial relations differences between Britain and Germany were not central to greater or lesser success of NC adoption and use. Consequently, we did not stress collection of industrial relations information.' (Sorge et al, 1982)

(b) Management style. An authoritarian style militates against shared goals. On the other hand, both paternalistic and democratic styles can encourage it. (c) Personal relations. Good personal relations within a department can encourage shared goals as evidenced by our medical insurance case in the Birmingham branch. Poor relations, even where the general industrial relations climate is good, can reduce the perception of shared goals. (d) Management distance. A remote management, either physically remote, but more importantly one which erects barriers between itself and its employees, is less likely to achieve shared goals than a management which attempts to avoid barriers. UK management, perhaps because of the existing class structure, is reputed to erect more barriers than management in other industrial countries. The success of Japan is often ascribed to conformity, and certainly Japanese management attempts to avoid the appearance of remoteness. (e) Management goals. Where management goals are narrowly defined in economic terms, and where information technology is introduced primarily to reduce the workforce, shared goals, even if they existed beforehand, will cease to be shared. (f) Cultural and political factors. Different cultures have different behavioural norms and expectations. In some societies deference to authority is the norm, and an authoritarian style is expected and hence accepted. In other societies it is expected that those who have authority seek a consensus with those in subordinate positions. In other societies those who have authority seek to ensure a shared ideology and hence shared values, by a process of conditioning starting at an early age, and any dissent from the prevailing ideology is discouraged by harsh teatment of the dissenter.

2.   The approach chosen for the introduction of the technology.   Earlier a number of design approaches were reviewed which attempt to avoid creating conflict, or dysfunctional design decisions, and which thereby reduce the incidence of social control.   Participative and experimental design approaches were selected as most likely to lead to the introduction of satisfactory systems. It should, however, be pointed out that Kraft (1979) has criticised the participative approach as merely manipulative, and other critics, as Hirschheim reports (1982), throw some doubts on the effectiveness of the approach.   Against that, there is strong evidence that the more conventional approaches are based on inadequate models of organisational realities (Land et al, 1980) and can result in the introduction of degrading systems.

3.   The philosophy or principles which underlie the way systems are expected to operate.   If the design is based on an explicit acceptance of the principles of scientific management, social controls will be maximised. Most designers and managers in the UK are not philosophically inclined, and prefer to use a pragmatic approach. An interesting discussion of these issues is printed in the Journal of Applied Systems Analysis (1981). Even at the management level many of the earlier management information systems were designed to be prescriptive. As such they were intended to take over the decision-making tasks of managers, and were designed on a rationalistic model of decision-making. In recent years an alternative strategy has been formulated, which is based on the realisation that management decision processes, in many situations, cannot be predetermined. On the other hand, it is possible to provide the decision maker with a variety of aids, such as query languages to interrogate a data base, simulation facilities etc., which the decision maker is free to use (or not to use) as he pleases. The concept of decision support systems (DSS), provides a systems philosophy which avoids social control. Examples used at different levels in enterprises are provided by Keen and Scott-Morton (1978) and Hurrion (1976).

4.   The extent to which the organisation is used to technological and organisational change. An organisation which is used to change is more likely to assimilate changes, stemm-

ing from the introduction of new information technology, without creating adverse reactions to the idea of change, than is an organisation which is less used to a dynamic environment. Because the people working at all levels in such an organisation may be less good at dealing with the uncertainties resulting from proposals to introduce new systems, it may be felt necessary to exert more pressure and control to get the new systems implemented.

5. Economic factors can have a stong influence on the way new systems are introduced. Economic factors play a key role in the selection of goals. The condition of an enterprise's balance sheet, or movements in the market share of its products, may dominate the choice of application and the method of implementation. Efficiency and cost saving goals may become paramount and overshadow any consideration of other factors. Short term considerations may be allowed to dominate the design process, leading to the design of anti-social systems. At times of high unemployment the ability of the workforce to resist such changes is severely reduced.

6. Government regulations and legislation could have an important influence on the extent to which the technology is permitted to exert social control. There are three areas of possible government action, which are relevant: (a) Privacy regulations. In the UK a number of government appointed committees have produced reports (Younger, 1972; Lindop, 1978) suggesting that there is a need for legislation to protect the public's privacy rights. The present government has published a White Paper detailing its response to the committee report and proposing legislation. This includes the setting up of a privacy authority, responsible for the establishment of codes of conduct relevant to different situations. (b) Industrial democracy legislation. Although all the major political parties discussed the need for more industrial democracy in their election manifestos, no action has been taken, nor is it likely that legislation will be tabled in the near future. (c) Trade union legislation. The government, in power at the time of writing, has passed legislation restricting the rights of unions in some respects, and is expected to table further measures to control the unions. There is no evidence that the legislation to date has reduced the power of the unions in relation to the introduction of information technology.

7. The power of the unions to make conditions relating to the introduction of information technology. The main vehicle for laying down conditions has since 1978 been the Technology Agreement. Since that time a considerable number of such agreements have been signed, but, after an initial surge, the number of new agreements is now declining. This could be due to the severe depression reducing the bargaining power of the unions. Nevertheless, Peltu (1980) suggests that the Technology Agreement 'will be the major factor in the way new technology is accepted in the 1980s' and Williams and Mosely have

analysed over one hundred Technology Agreements (1982).

It is interesting to note that, in the UK, the CBI (the most important employers' organisation) has rejected the TUC suggestion for a joint approach towards technological change. Williams and Mosely see this:

'as a reminder that these changes may not be introduced on an equitable and consensual basis. Policies for the management of change have great significance in determining whether a consensual or conflict-based approach develops.' (Williams and Moseley, 1982)

Their analysis shows that nearly all the Technology Agreements cover white-collar workers only, and that only 24 of the 146 unions affiliated to the TUC have been able to sign agreements. Although most of the agreements permit the unions to discuss the changes before they are introduced, many fewer give the unions the right of negotiation, and only ten give the unions an equal right in the negotiations. Of 105 agreements studied, only 14 included any standards for job satisfaction and 22 had standards for task allocation. As against that, 40 agreements set up standards for VDU health and safety regulations. Overall the impression left by the analysis is that the impact of Technology Agreements on issues of social control will be very slight, even for white-collar workers. For other workers union influence on social control will be even less, though actual negotiations over pay and conditions may raise issues related to social control.

This list of contingency factors does not pretend to be exhaustive, but it probably highlights the most important issues. Of course, these are interdependent, and the actual outcome in any situation will be determined by a mixture of factors. It is that mixture which makes any forecasting difficult, and makes it important to continue with further studies of the issues.

SOME RESULTS FROM THE OTHER COUNTRIES

Finally, there is some value in comparing the UK position with the (mainly legislative) responses to the issue, in the other countries involved in the European Community sponsored research.

Denmark

In all Scandinavian countries, co-determination in the change of working conditions is regulated by Work Environment acts with the intention that there can be no change without improvements for the workforce.

These laws aim mainly at improving physical health and security at workplaces, but refer nevertheless to a so-called 'extended health concept', concerned with long term effects which are not, however, clearly defined. The principles of the laws are: (a) issues connected with the work environment shall be solved on a cooperative basis between employers, managers and employees; (b) in the design of future work-places, a satisfactory work environment should be taken into account in an early stage in the planning process; (c) employees shall be involved from the earliest planning phase.

The impact of these laws cannot be clearly evaluated yet, but there is evidence which suggests that the current economic climate imposes severe constraints on the interpretation of the extended health concept.

Apart from the legislative rules there are 'technical committees' who try to regulate company EDP operations by technology agreements at a national level. These can, however, be modified by local agreements.

Trade unions are seriously interested, and very much involved, in evaluating and attempting to control technological developments. They have been involved in attempts to increase their own knowledge about the technology and in analysing consequences of system solutions and suggesting alternative designs. The unions have had significant impact on influencing legislation, though their demands are generally resisted by employers. Empirical research has shown that in negotiations the union side is hampered by lack of information, and in general their representatives are badly informed.

Federal Republic of Germany
The introduction of new technologies comes under the authority of the Works Constitution Act. Co-determination is concerned in particular with technology which can control behaviour and performance. The Works Council of an organisation has the right of co-determination for special projects, and can enforce technology agreements. The new technology or working procedure can only be operated when the agreement is signed.

More recently, many conflicts have arisen as a result of the development of personal information systems which are outside the field of co-determination, provided the systems do not store performance data. However, the usage of personal data is regulated by the privacy protection law. Each company has a data protection representative, who is responsible for data processing and data transmission. The catalogue of data elements which can be stored in the personnel system must be agreed with the works council.

The efficiency of legal regulations appears to depend on the activity and interests of the employee representatives. Because of a lack of cooperation between the industrial partners, the rights of employees must often be resolved by the Labour Court.

CONCLUDING REMARKS

At the end of this present exercise we are left with the
pervasiveness of the potential for new information technology
to impose social control on employees, and the empirical
research problems discussed. It is to be hoped, however, that
the study may contribute to increased awareness of this
enduring characteristic of new technology, both as a general
phenomenon and as one which raises very specific organisational
issues relating to information systems development, and the
success of organisations in exploiting the technology.
Specifically, this study supports a contingency approach, where
it is possible to identify those factors significant to the
introduction of new technology under different conditions.
These identified factors may be compared with the management
agenda and strategic managerial response to technological
change discussed elsewhere in this volume.

REFERENCES

Arnold, E. (1982) 'Information Technology in the Home: The Failure of PRESTEL' in Bjorn-Andersen, N., Earl, M., Holst, O. and Mumford, E. (eds.), Information Society: For Richer, For Poorer, North Holland, Amsterdam

Arnold, E., Birke, L., and Faulkner, W. (1981) 'Women and Microelectronics: The Case of Word Processors', Women's Studies International Quarterly, 4 (3), 321-40

Bird, E. (1980) Information Technology in the Office: The Impact on Women's Jobs, Equal Opportunities Commission, Manchester

Braverman, H. (1971) 'Labor and Monopoly Capital: The Degradation of Work in the Twentieth Century', Monthly Review Press, New York

Brittan, J. (1980) 'Design for a Changing Environment', The Computer Journal, 23(1), 13-19

British Computer Society (1979) User Requirements in Data Processing, Hayden, London

Cooley, M.J.E. (1980)   Architect or Bee, Langley Technical Services, Slough

Damordaran, L., Simpson, A. and Wilson, P. (1980)   Designing Systems for People, NCC, Manchester

Dehning, W. and Schonberg, G. (1982)   New Technology and Social Control, EIFIP, Frankfurt

Dew, R.B. and Gee, K.P. (1973)   Management Control and Information, MacMillan, New York

Fitter, M.J. and Sime, M.E. (1980) 'Creating Responsive Computers: Responsibility and Shared Decision-Making' in Smith, H.T. and Green, T.R.G. (eds.) Human Interaction with Computers, Academic Press, London

Hedberg, B. (1980) 'The Design and Impact of Real-Time Computer Systems: A Case Study of a Swedish Commercial Bank' in Bjorn-Andersen, N., Hedberg, B., Mercer, D., Mumford, E. and Sole A. (eds.), The Impact of System Change in Organisations, Sijtoff and Noordhoff, Alphen Aan Den Rijn, Netherlands

Hedberg, B. and Mumford, E. (1975)   'The Design of Computer Based Systems: Man's Vision of Man as an Integral Part of the Systems Design Process', in Mumford, E. and Sackman, H. (eds.), Human Choice and Computers, North Holland, Amsterdam

Hirschheim, R. (1982) 'Participative Systems Design: Some Conclusions from an Exploratory Study', London School of Economics Working Paper, December

Hurrion, R.M. (1976) The Design, Use and Required Facilities of an Interactive Visual Computer Simulation Language to Explore Production Planning, Ph.D thesis, London University

Journal of Applied Systems Analysis, (1981), 8 April, whole issue

Keen, P.G.W. (1981) 'Information Systems and Organisational Change', Communications of the ACM, 24(1), 24-33

Keen, P. and Scott-Morton, M. (1978) Decision Support Systems, Addison-Wesley, Reading, Mass.

Kraft, P (1979) 'Challenging the Mumford Democrats at Derby Works', Computing, August 2nd

Land, F., Hawgood, J., and Mumford, E. (1980) 'Training the Systems Analyst of the 1980's: Four New Design Tools to Assist the Design Process' in Lucas, H., Land, F., Lincoln, T. and Supper, K. (eds.), The Information Systems Environment, North Holland, Amsterdam

Land, F. (1979) 'Organisational Problems in Implementing Distributed Systems, in Moseley, D. (ed.) Managing the Distribution of DP, Infotech State of the Art Report

Lindop, Sir N. (1978) (Chairman), Report of the Committee on Data Protection, CMND 7341, HMSO

Mehlmann, M. (1981) When People Use Computers, Prentice Hall, New York

Mumford, E. (1981a) Values, Technology and Work, Martinus Nijhoff, Amsterdam

Mumford, E. (1981b) 'Participative Systems Design: Structure and Method', Systems, Objectives, Solutions, 1,(1), 5-19

Mumford, E. and Henshall, D. (1978) A Participative Approach to the Design of Computer Systems, Associated Business Press, London

Mumford, E., Land, F. and Hawgood, J. (1978) 'A Participative Approach to the Design of Computer Systems', Impact of Science on Society, 28 (3), 251-72

Noble, D. (1979) 'Social Choice in Machine Design: The Case of Automatically Controlled Machine Tools', in Timbalist, A. (ed.) Case Studies in the Labor Process, Monthly Review Press, New York

Peltu, M. (1980) 'New Technology without Strife', International Management, November, 49-51

Rosenbrock, H. (1966) 'The Future of Control', Automatica, 13(4), 389-92

Rosenbrock, H. (1977) Interactive Computing: A New Opportunity, Report No. 388, UMIST

Rosenbrock, H., (1982) 'Technology Policies and Options', in Bjorn-Andersen, N., Earl, M., Holst, O. and Mumford, E. (eds.) Information Society: For Richer, For Poorer, North Holland, Amsterdam

Sorge, A., Hartmann, G., Warner, M. and Nicholas, I. (1982) 'Technology, Organisation and Manpower', in Bjorn-Andersen, N., Earl, M., Holst, O. and Mumford, E. (eds.), Information Society: For Richer, For Poorer, North Holland, Amsterdam

Williams, R. and Moseley, R. (1982) 'The Trade Union Response to Information Technology: Technology Agreements', in Bjorn-Andersen, M., Earl, M., Holst, O. and Mumford, E. (eds.), Information Society: For Richer, For Poorer, North Holland, Amsterdam

Wynne, B. and Otway, H.J. (1982) 'Information Technology, Power and Managers', in Bjorn-Andersen, N., Earl, M., Holst, O. and Mumford, E. (eds.), Information Society: For Richer, For Poorer, North Holland, Amsterdam

Younger, K., (1972) (Chairman) Report on Computers and Privacy, CMND 5012, HMSO, July

Chapter 6

THE APPLICATION OF MICROELECTRONICS
TO THE OFFICE: ORGANISATIONAL AND
HUMAN IMPLICATIONS

Richard J. Long

INTRODUCTION

That the application of microelectronics technology to the
office will have major and even revolutionary effects on the
work organisation and its members is not a point that would be
argued by many.   However, what the precise effects of this
technology will be is a subject of wide disagreement.   Some
envisage a future that includes happy productive workers freed
from the need to perform menial and repetitive tasks, working
in jobs which allow high discretion and full use of their
abilities and skills.   Others see a future where most people
will either be unemployed or working as adjuncts to machines,
under tight control by an organisation in which only the top
few have any power to make decisions.

The purpose of this paper is to examine the organisational
and human implications of electronic office technology, with a
special emphasis on issues relating to the quality of working
life.   These issues include implications for job and
organisational design, communication and decision-making,
physical and mental health, and employment levels.   Specific
implications for management policy will also be discussed.

Before proceeding, however, it is useful to make several
distinctions.   First it should be noted that there are at least
two distinct phases to the so-called office automation
'revolution', the implications of which vary considerably.   Up
to this time, the main impact of the new technology has been
simply to facilitate office operations as they are now being
carried out.   For example, the word processor replaces the
typewriter and the microcomputer replaces the filing cabinet.
While significant, these innovations simply increase the
efficiency of work as it is now done.

However, a second phase of application is now beginning,
which portends revolutionary changes to the organisation.   This
stage involves the outright elimination of many intermediary
functions and has been brought about by the convergence of the
three technologies of electronic data processing, telecommuni-

cations, and office machines (Tapscott, 1982). To illustrate, take the example of a firm where field sales personnel need to frequently telephone the central office for pricing and product information. Phase 1 automation would be illustrated by the adoption of microcomputers for storing this information, and the provision of video display terminals to the clerks answering the phone calls from the sales force. In contrast, phase 2 would involve provision of portable terminals to the sales force, or even, conceivably, to the customer, thus eliminating the clerks and even some of the sales personnel. Similarly, managers would communicate directly with one another through 'electronic mail' and interconnected data banks.

Menzies (1981; 1982) has developed a useful distinction between two basic types of office worker. The first is the 'information worker' who is involved in the routine entry, recording, storage and transmission of information. These include typists, secretaries, clerks and data entry personnel and are primarily female. The second group consists of those who analyse and utilise this information. These are known as 'knowledge workers', and are primarily male. Phase 1 of the microelectronic revolution affects only the 'information workers', while phase 2 will affect the 'knowledge workers' as well.

Thus far most of the experience has been with the phase 1 type of application of microelectronics and some empirical evidence exists on the effects of this. On the other hand, widespread application of the phase 2 technology is in its infancy, so little empirical evidence is available to inform the debate about its effects. The balance of this paper will reflect this dichotomy. After assessing the extent of application of microelectronics in British offices, this chapter will next discuss the organisational and human implications of microelectronics over the medium run, while the final section will illustrate some of the concerns of the phase 1 revolution by examining perhaps the most widespread form of office automation - word processing.

MICROELECTRONICS IN BRITISH OFFICES

What is the actual extent to which various types of microelectronic office technology are being applied in Britain? Although precise information on this is difficult to obtain several surveys have recently been conducted. In 1982 Steffens (1983) surveyed 231 British organisations that were known to be using some type of computer system. These organisations ranged in size from under 200 employees (29%) to over 5000 employees (20%) with the median size being about 500 employees. The most common type of microelectronic office equipment (excluding photocopiers and electronic typewriters) was the microcomputer, used by 79%, followed by microfilm/fiche (64%), word processors

(62%), facsimile machines (39%), executive terminals or work stations (29%), and viewdata/videotex (19%). Electronic mail was used by only 12 per cent of respondents.

In order to assess the future rate of adoption of each type of office technology, the researchers asked respondents to indicate whether they expected to increase expenditures next year (1983) in comparison to the previous year. Excluding word processors, which the researchers inexplicably did not include here, the greatest number of firms (70%) indicated increased expenditures for microcomputers, followed by executive terminals/work stations (52%), electronic mail (30%), microfilm/fiche (20%), facsimile machines (17%), and viewdata/videotex (13%). A study of 200 British managers by Nexos (1982), who asked them to project increases in expenditures for 1982, also found microcomputers at the top of the list with 71% of the respondents projecting increased expenditure. Next come word processors (66%), followed by executive terminals/work stations (44%), microfilm/fiche (39%), electronic mail and viewdata/videotex (both at 23%), with facsimile machines last (17%).

These results suggest that the application of microcomputers and word processors will continue to expand rapidly for some time, but also that usage of executive terminals/work stations and electronic mail is beginning to take off. The other types of technology will continue to grow in a limited kind of way. However, it should be noted that neither of these two samples is representative of British industry as a whole. These samples represent primarily 'leading edge' users, and for the typical firm these usage patterns cannot be expected for several years at least. It should also be noted that although many smaller organisations, as well as larger ones, are adopting microcomputers and word processing, other developments such as executive work stations and electronic mail will likely be adopted primarily in larger companies.

The use of the fully integrated office technology necessary for the second phase of microelectronic revolution can be expected to lag even further behind. In his survey, Steffens (1983) found that only 34 per cent of his respondents viewed their investment in word processors as a first step towards large scale office automation, and that only 25 per cent were fully committed to developing extensive electronic office systems.

MEDIUM AND LONGER TERM IMPLICATIONS

This section will discuss the organisational and human implications in the medium to longer term, a period when phase 2 of the microelectronic revolution should be taking place in a more substantial way. These implications will fall under four categories - communication and decision-making, the hierarchy and managers, flexibility of work time and place, and effects on lower level personnel. Two important implications that are more properly related to the phase 1 revolution - computer monitoring and pacing, and physical and mental health - will be treated in a later section which deals specifically with word processors.

Communication and Decision-making

What will happen to communication and decision-making processes within the organisation? Will the efficiency with which information can be transmitted to key decision makers lead to a centralised organisation structure, where all but the top few people in the organisation will become information gatherers and order followers? Or will this same ease of transmitting information enable decisions to be made and discretion to be applied at lower organisational levels than hitherto possible?

An optimistic view is held by Taylor (1982a; 1982b; 1982c) who believes that there are two forces at work in society. The first, based on older 'mainframe' computer technology, is pushing towards centralisation. The second process, based on microcomputers, leads toward what he calls 'distributed intelligence' - a powerful force for decentralisation. It is based on the notion that key decision-making information is not best generated by feeding it into a central computer - but by the formation and reformulation of networks connecting a number of previously independent systems on a 'per occasion' basis. Utilising this system of distributed intelligence, he argues, will 'for the first time, take advantage of a modern educational system that is turning out literate, original, and independent minded individuals' (Taylor, 1982).

There are at least two major ways in which decision-making may be affected by microelectronics. First, electronic media can be used to replace either written or verbal communication, or both. Second, microcomputers can be used to provide direct access to both internal and external data bases.

Replacement of Written and Verbal Communication. Taylor's argument about decentralisation is supported by a study carried out by Leduc (1979). This study reports on the results of the application of electronic communication/computing technology to the Business Policy Group of Bell Canada. This technology linked the fourteen individuals in the group to one another, as well as linking them to outside experts doing similar work. It was found that the hierarchical pattern of communication hitherto present, when the main medium of communication was the written memo, tended to be replaced by a more open 'all channel' everyone to everyone network of links. This occurred because of the perceived informality of the electronic messaging system and the ease of transmitting duplicate copies to all group members.

Other empirical work has provided results consistent with this finding. Hiltz and Turoff (1978) compared decision-making through the use of computer conferencing with conventional face-to-face negotiations. They found participation in the communication process was distributed more equally and the emergence of specific opinion leaders was suppressed under computer conferencing. Individuals were more likely to express opinions, even if they diverged from those of other members. However, by the same token, groups using computer conferencing found it much more difficult to develop a consensus and reach agreement on decisions to be taken.

However, a study by Pieper (1982) of a fifteen month field trial of a computer conferencing system in a West German research organisation did not support these results. The users were fourteen individuals organised in five subgroups working in different locations. Rather than a relatively equal distribution of communication it was found that a 'gate keeper' tended to emerge in each subgroup, who took primary responsibility for communicating with the other subgroups. Within each subgroup communication increased but was not distributed equally.

Over time communication between subgroups took on a more informal 'conversational' tone but never developed much beyond what Pieper calls a 'comfortable message system'. The system was not used to enhance the group's capacity for information processing and problem solving. He attributes this primarily to a software problem and suggests several standards that need to be met by systems design. These include 'proximity of reference' - which will allow the user to access other messages easily while building a message, possibly through use of a split screen. Another is 'reconstruction of context' - development of a method that will allow the user to easily access past messages relevant to full understanding of the present message. Clearly, the kind of electronic 'filing' system developed for electronic mail has major implications for the extent to which organisational problem solving capacity will be improved.

Hirschheim (1984) points out that using electronic media to replace verbal communication may have differing implications from use of microelectronics to replace written communication. He suggests the following potential benefits: (a) more communication; (b) more thoughtful communication; (c) greater community feeling; and (d) a written record of communications. More communications can take place between geographically separated locations because teleconferencing eliminates the time needed to travel to meetings, thus making them more convenient. Replacement of many telephone calls which do not require simultaneous interchanges by electronic mail will also free up time through elimination of 'small talk', as well as saving the time that would be required to transmit the same message to several persons.

99

More thoughtful communication could result since individuals are not required to respond immediately, as they would in a simultaneous communication. More community feeling could result from the ease of including additional persons in the communication process. Finally, a written record of communication should reduce misunderstandings as well as the need to repeat messages or to 'confirm in writing'.

On the other hand, reduction of verbal communication might have some undesirable implications. First, the use of verbal communication allows instantaneous feedback, both for message clarification and response, while electronic communication does not, thus slowing communication. Furthermore, reduction of interpersonal contact may reduce the quality of interpersonal relationships in the organisation, which are crucial for the building of trust and understanding between individuals. Most experts also feel that verbal, face-to-face communication is the most effective form of communication, and should be used whenever possible. Furthermore, much important information is obtained through 'serendipity' - that is, chance comments or remarks in the process of communication about the intended subject. Finally, the fact that messages are being recorded could restrict true communication, if individuals are over-concerned about making any statement they may regret. This would be aggravated if these messages could be accessed by other individuals in the organisation.

Indeed, the recording and storage of previously unrecorded messages presents the organisation with even better opportunities for controlling individuals, particularly if other means of communication (e.g. the telephone, travel allowances) are restricted. The ability of a superior to surreptitiously review the total contents of a subordinate's communication could effectively stifle true communication, as well as initiative and creativity. More overtly, it might now be more feasible for a supervisor to require review of outgoing communication prior to transmission.

Indeed, a major problem is the extent to which communication stored on electronic media should be accessible. On the one hand, it can be argued the computerisation of communication creates an invaluable data base never before possible. Argyris and Schon (1978) noted that in many, if not most, organisations, the organisation may 'know' much less than the sum of other knowledge possessed by individual members. Computerisation may be way of solving this problem. For example, a manager investigating a particular problem may be able to call up all correspondence in the organisation related to that subject and discover the magnitude of the problem, as well as clues as to how it may be solved.

Despite the apparent value of accessing this type of stored communication, there are serious problems. For example, certain conversations must be kept in confidence, yet without proper controls it would be difficult to guarantee this.

Superiors may well object, on valid grounds in many cases, to subordinates having access to their correspondence, while subordinates may resent access by superiors to their communications. In order to ensure that electronic media are not bypassed or, worse, that information to be communicated through electronic media is not distorted or withheld entirely, senders must be able to control its accessibility by others than the intended receiver. Of course, as in any communication the receiver still has the ability to make the message accessible to whom he pleases.

In sum, replacement of verbal communication with electronic means does have the potential to make limited improvements to the communication process and to quality of working life. However, there are a variety of possible dangers, including the reduction of effective communication, the distortion or suppression of information, increased organisational control over members and a loss of the personal contact which is crucial to developing trust and understanding. Organisations which implement such systems need to develop means to ensure the confidentiality of messages transmitted in this fashion, while still optimising benefits as a data base. Furthermore, such systems should not be used to supplant other verbal means of communication, by, say, unduly restricting the use of telephone or face-to-face meetings. Indeed, it is possible some individual managers would overuse electronic means, and steps may be needed to prevent this, in order to maintain personal contact.

However, just because the technology will exist to support the free flow of communication throughout the organisation, this does not necessarily mean that managers will use it in this way. Indeed, top managers who possess classical values and beliefs about managing - and there remain many of these - can be expected to attempt to use the technology to centralise decision-making. For many top managers a radical shift in beliefs and values will have to take place before true decentralisation will occur.

A case in point involves the application of electronic point-of-sale (EPOS) equipment in retailing. Child et al (1983) studied a British department store chain and a supermarket chain which had recently installed EPOS equipment. In both cases senior managers 'looked to the introduction of the EPOS as a means to enhance their control over store operations and staff behaviour'. In fact, the system did operate to reduce the discretion and autonomy of middle and lower management. In the supermarket departmental supervisors were no longer required to exercise discretion in the display and quantity of stocks on the shelf since these were predetermined by the system. Their discretion with regard to the pricing and reordering of stock had also become seriously constrained, a result which also occurred in the department stores. In neither case were these managers consulted in any way with regard to the design and the implementation of the new technology.

Finally, Taylor himself (1982a) foresees some problems with regard to unrestricted flow of organisational communication. Aside from the risks of 'information overload', the organisation may lose its capacity to 'absorb uncertainty', which is now done by the filtering and interpretation of information by various organisational units before it reaches key decision makers. Although some of this filtering process might be taken over by the computer, it will provide no substitute for interpretation by experts in a given function.

Direct Access to Data Bases. Ever since the advent of electronic computers, enthusiasts have made dramatic claims about their abilities to assist or even supplant managerial decision-making. Yet, more than twenty years after widespread application of the mainframe computer, few of these claims have been realised. Why should the microcomputer alter this?

Mintzberg (1973) suggests that this limited success has been due to a lack of appreciation of the true nature of managerial work. Managers need information that is timely and specific to their immediate needs. However, the type of information required changes from decision to decision and much of the information needed is not known in advance but is discovered through an iterative process.

Information provided by central computing systems generally has fallen well short of what is required. First, the information provided is based on the analyst's understanding of the manager's job, which is usually an oversimplified view. The manager himself feels peripheral to the whole process, except when he has to provide the information specified by the computing department, in the exact form demanded by the computing department. Because of the nature of centralised computing it is not well geared to producing specific information in response to specific problems. To attempt to compensate for this, systems analysts try to design information systems that produce every type of information that could possibly be required by any user. Of course, this is limited to information which can easily be collected and coded on a regularised basis. The result is the inch-thick printout appearing on each manager's desk every week. There may be some useful information buried in there, but line managers do not have the time to dig it out and manipulate it in such a way that it bears directly on a particular problem. Requests for specific types of information not now produced, but needed in an expedited fashion, receive short shrift from computer processing.

However, the microcomputer has the potential to put the data base at the disposal of the manager, rather than vice versa. 'User-friendly' systems should enable users to recall, combine, and analyse data in new kinds of ways as the notion strikes them or the need arises. Not only might they receive timely information specifically oriented to their needs, the interactive process could help managers to 'explore' the data base in previously unimagined ways. This is particularly true when external data bases can be combined with internal data bases.

For example, the government of Canada is now making available to industry a variety of machine-readable data bases. One data base includes annual survey of users of national parks for the previous ten years. A marketing manager in a recreational products firm could combine these data with his own data about sales by product type, to discover problems or new opportunties. The possibilities offered by this technique are limited only by the imagination of the manager. Under this approach, the data base is under the control of the manager, and the role of the systems analyst is to ensure that hardware and software are available and compatible to maximise these opportunities, and to help the managers to learn how to best use it.

The Hierarchy and Managers

The traditional organisation structure is likely to be affected in a number of significant ways, depending on the extent to which automation is introduced. First, there will be fewer persons needed for the routine manipulation of information as electronic mail and other types of direct interconnections develop between the actual users of the information. Since there will be fewer lower level workers to supervise, there will likely be a reduction in the number of supervisors and lower level managers required, thus reducing the number of hierarchical levels in the organisation, as well as the size (Plowright and Booth, 1982), other things being equal. In their study of British Insurance Companies, Barras and Swann (1983) found that some companies expected to reduce their hierarchies by one level - from five levels to four, in one example - as a result of microelectronic technology.

Those supervisors who do remain can expect to have their roles changed from a control or surveillance type of function to a broader role definition, as computer monitoring takes over this role. Instead, they will focus on training and helping to implement new organisational systems as procedures and technology are continually improved, as well as performing 'boundary roles' - this is, linking the unit to the greater organisational system. Linkages between the relatively few workers still needed for routine data input and those who use the information may become electronic, rather than physical. Indeed, as will be discussed later, these information workers may not even be physically located on organisational premises.

Overall, the picture this view presents is of smaller, flatter organisations, where authority is more evenly shared because of the free flow of information these devices will encourage. The surveillance and routine coordination roles will be substantially reduced or eliminated.

These predictions are based on the assumption that microelectronics will eventually reduce the need for information workers by automating their routine functions. However, to what extent will managerial functions be automated? While electronic technology can certainly help managers deal more efficiently with routine aspects of their jobs such as acquiring or disseminating information, those who expect office automation to directly replace managers may have a faulty understanding of a manager's true role. As Kasurak et al, (1982) put it:

> 'Electronic systems certainly have the ability to overcome time and space barriers, but this capability is often overrated by persons who lack an understanding of the nature of managerial work. It is true that managers "plan, organize, direct, and control". More importantly, managers negotiate, conciliate, inspire and lead. These functions are not easily automated, leaving more than one system designer puzzled at the "perverse" behaviour of managers who find their electronic system of little relevance to their work.' (Kasurak et al, 1982)

In other words, organisations are much more than just devices concerned with the processing of concrete information, as many of the enthusiasts of the 'automated office' seem to imagine. Instead, they are also systems that generate power and influence, which is then used to allocate resources and execute tasks, and they are dependent for their success on a complex web of interpersonal relationships that often takes years to develop. Mintzberg (1973) notes that managers frequently need to base key decisions on information that is unsystematic, diverse, fragmented, and not highly amenable to codification or even recording. The environment of a modern organisation is exceedingly complex and it is still an art to select and correctly interpret what is relevant to the organisation. Furthermore, because an organisation is a political mechanism, managers may not always find it in their personal interest to share key information, even though this may be in the best interest of the organisation as a whole. All of these factors militate against the prospect for significant automation of managerial functions.

There is some empirical evidence to support this latter view. Brophy (1981) reported on an attempt to install an integrated office system into a head office department of Shell Canada. The main objective was 'to demonstrate the potential for professional and managerial time saving through machine dictation, word processing and the delegation of work as well as the potential for new technologies, such as electronic

mail'.   The major emphasis was to attempt to push some of the
more routine responsibilities of higher levels down the
hierarchy, right to the lowest level which would then shift its
most routine responsibilities to automated equipment, such as
word processors.   Rather than being deskilled, these
'information workers' at the lowest levels received training in
communication skills, problem solving, decision-making and
conflict resolution.   The goal at this level was to create a
semi-autonomous group, with responsibility for their own
procedures, work allocation, and vacation scheduling.

Implementation of the system took considerably longer than
expected, and was accompanied by substantial resistance to the
depth of change required: 'Managers seemed to experience
difficulty both in delegating tasks and in redefining their
roles to make the most productive use of time freed up through
delegation.   The redefinition of roles was also found to be
time consuming and interfered with day to day business
activities' (Brophy, 1982). Cost savings during the first six
months were about half of what was anticipated.   Brophy
attributes the limited success of the programme to a failure to
sufficiently consider the social factors involved or to take a
socio-technical approach.

A socio-technical approach was used at Bell Northern
Research where a group of '19 knowledge workers were given
electronic work stations to help them with various aspects of
their jobs, including electronic mail, word processing,
information retrieval, administrative support and data
processing' (Greenberg, 1981).   Participants indicated
increased job variety, accomplishment, creativity and
satisfaction, according to quality of working life measures
administered before and after the implementation.   No changes
were found in a comparison group.

Whether these results would generalise to other types of
managerial jobs is not clear.   It should be noted that these
individuals were explicitly 'knowledge workers' (e.g.
researchers), in the most complete sense of the term, and this
type of function may be particularly receptive to the type of
information made available under 'automated' systems.   In most
organisations the most receptive users of microelectronics
appear to be functional experts (e.g. engineers, actuaries in
insurance companies, marketing specialists) who mainly use
microcomputers to extend their calculating ability.

Flexibility of Work Hours and Place

One effect of microelectronics technology will be to allow work
to be done away from the traditional office building.   A number
of potential benefits of this immediately come to mind.
Persons who are bound to the home by reason of handicaps, need
to care for family members, or other reasons may now find it
possible to gain employment.   Time and money now wasted in

commuting could be eliminated. Individuals may be able to optimise their work schedules and productivity by working as their own biological rhythms, as well as other commitments, dictate.

One example of this type of system has been adopted by a major Dutch newspaper. A study indicated that the costs of providing each reporter with workspace in the head office amounted to 150,000 guilders in capital costs and 2,000 guilders per month for upkeep. As a result the newspaper relocated the video display units already in use by the reporters to their homes and paid them an extra allowance of 2,000 guilders per month as compensation for this. Most of the released office space was then let out, except for a few rooms where periodic meetings of reporters take place. Most reporters are apparently delighted with the new system.

However, there are a number of concerns, particularly among women's groups. They point to the potential for reisolating women in the home and burdening those with responsibilities for care of family members with two jobs instead of one. This type of home work, they claim is not only devoid of the opportunities for social interaction that most jobs afford, it also takes away the visibility with superiors that is important for promotion. Finally, they fear that such systems may allow employers to treat these employees as independent contractors – thus relieving organisations of the need to provide fringe benefits. A report by Labour Canada (1982) suggests establishment of labour standards on these matters as well as on working conditions.

Another concern deals with the possibility of installation of video display terminals (VDT) into the homes of professional and managerial employees, thus placing implicit demands on them to continue their work outside of normal hours, perhaps to the detriment of their family lives (Phillips, 1982). On the other hand, if the alternative to work at home is work at the office, then the use of home computer terminals may actually increase time available for the family.

Although estimates are difficult to make, the extent of 'teleworking' as a replacement to office working in Britain appears to be extremely limited at this time. Dover (1983) could find only two firms that used teleworking in any significant way. The most extensive use has been made at International Computers Ltd. (ICL) where two hundred programmers (mostly female) scattered across Britain work from home, although not always on an on-line basis. They are supervised by project managers who also work from their homes. These individuals are considered as regular employees and are paid on a similar basis to that of other employees, although some (it is not known how many) work part-time and are paid on a pro rata basis.

The second major example is quite different in nature. Involved in a cost cutting program, Rank Xerox found that building rents and rates were costing three times the salaries paid to office staff. They also wished to streamline the upper management structure, while still having the necessary expertise available when required.

Their solution was to develop a scheme whereby a certain number of senior managers would be provided with electronic work stations in their homes. Not only would this save on office space, but these individuals would now be considered as subcontractors, rather than regular employees, thus eliminating the necessity to provide fringe benefits. Payment is to be based on output only, but in the first year Xerox provided a fixed contract to ensure income stability during the transition period, while also encouraging them to develop their own freelance work.

Although some of these individuals have appeared to adapt very well to the new system, not all are highly enthusiastic. Regardless of what it is called the scheme is a type of 'disguised redundancy', and those selected had no choice in the matter. Some of the specific problems cited by these individuals include a lack of direct contact with colleagues, learning the self-discipline to work intently in the home environment, organisation of working time and space, being taken seriously as workers, and lack of secretarial support.

Apart from these examples most of the remaining teleworkers consist of single individuals working at home on a temporary basis for a particular reason, such as during pregnancy, or an executive taking a terminal home for a few days to complete an important job. In a few cases disabled persons are working from home on a permanent basis, some as a result of a 1982 programme by the UK Department of Industry.

There are, however, many instances of employees with home terminals which may be used either outside of normal work hours or on a part-time basis within the normal working week. For these individuals it is the best of both worlds, since they not only retain their prerogatives as employees but also gain some flexibility. Not surprisingly, workers required to work at home, who lose fringe benefits and receive lower pay, often seem unenthusiastic. Whether the concept itself is at fault is not clear. However, while little empirical evaluation has been done, it is quite likely that, depending on their needs and personal circumstances, and given equal pay and benefits, there may well be a substantial number of individuals who would welcome the opportunity to telework.

Effects on Lower Level Employees

What will be the effect on the lives of lower level workers – the 'information worker' rather than the 'knowledge worker'? The previous material has already suggested that there will likely be fewer of them in the future, particularly as phase 2 of the microelectronic revolution takes place. However, it is unlikely that these effects will be as severe or as immediate as the pessimists fear. As will be seen, the word processing revolution has not had the severe effects imagined even two or three years ago, which were largely based on 'optimistic' (to use a kind expression) claims by manufacturers of the equipment.

Furthermore, phase 2 is not likely to progress as fast as either the optimists or the pessimists believe. This will be at least partly due to the inherent difficulty in automating management tasks, and not least of all by the resistance of managers concerned with not disturbing their hard-earned power and status in the organisation. Ironically, to the chagrin of women's groups, one of the major saving graces will likely be the reluctance of executives to give up the status and convenience of a personal secretary. None the less, some reduction in employment can be expected and programmes are necessary to encourage retraining for other positions within the organisation, or more likely, new occupations entirely.

The category of employee in perhaps the greatest danger of redundancy at this time is the routine data entry personnel in the data processing department, as Barras and Swann (1983) found in their study of British insurance companies. As another example, the British Southwestern Electricity Board is currently converting to a system where meter readers will be provided with portable minicomputers which are capable of printing bills on the spot. At the end of the day the data are fed directly into the main computer. This has substantially reduced the number of clerks necessary for routine data entry, as well as some of the clerical personnel formerly required in handling and posting the bills. Moreover, this phase 1 type innovation is likely to be replaced at some future time by a second phase in which meters will be connected directly to the computers, thus eliminating more clerical personnel, as well as the meter readers.

The effects on the task itself are not clear, and will likely vary from organisation to organisation. Clearly, a deskilling is not inherent in the technology, and there have been instances where introduction of microelectronics has improved the quality of jobs, as a study of bank tellers commissioned by Labour Canada (1982) found. Tellers reported increases in variety, use of skills and interest in their jobs due to implementation of microelectronic technology. Barras and Swann (1983) found that distributed processing in the British insurance industry has resulted in the computer taking over the routine tasks, leaving the more interesting jobs for people. They report how a variety of fragmented tasks, such as filing, typing, and quotations, have been merged in some companies into jobs performed by single individuals with upgraded skills. Land et al (1983) describe how distributed processing improved the quality of jobs and employee satisfaction at a branch of a British medical insurance company. On the other hand Menzies (1981, 1982) has documented cases where the quality of jobs has been adversely affected. This issue will be further discussed in the following section.

ELECTRONIC WORD PROCESSING

The use of word processors attached to either micro or main frame computers and their accompanying VDTs, have become to many synonomous with the microelectronics revolution. Use of this technology has sparked heated debate among a number of groups, and some empirical evidence is now available. Four main areas of concern have arisen. First, the employment effects. Will use of this technology lead to a net reduction in the number of clerical workers needed? If so, what is to be done about these 'surplus' workers? Second, are there physical or mental hazards related to the use of VDTs? Third, what will be the effects on job design? Will this technology create a new class of boring and meaningless jobs or will just the reverse occur? Finally, what will be the impact with regard to control and supervision? Does supervision and monitoring of an employee's work without his/her knowledge constitute a demeaning and/or unethical practice?

Employment Effects
Predictions of the employment effects of introduction of electronic word processing vary enormously depending primarily upon when they were made. Early predictions tended to be dramatic - in 1980 it was predicted that 'between four and six jobs are eliminated every time a word processor is installed in an office' (Brunet, 1980). However, empirical evidence has not borne out such drastic effects although there have been instances where reductions in employee numbers have taken place. Steffens (1983) found that over 70 per cent of those British companies which had introduced word processors reported no resulting reduction in staff, although a number of these were expecting reductions in the future. Eason and Gower (1982) examined ten case examples of word processing installations and found that introduction of word processing was followed by staff reductions in only two cases, while increases took place at four firms that were expanding.

A study by the Leeds Trade Union and Community Resource Centre (1982) for the Equal Opportunities Commission found relatively few outright job losses, although some took place through natural wastage. An unofficial estimate given by an expert in the Department of Employment in late 1983 was that job losses take place in only about half the installations, where reductions may range from marginal to up to 50 per cent in extreme cases. A review of the empirical evidence by Kendall (1983) leads him to conclude that the elimination of a quarter of a job per word processor would be an average result, although this would vary considerably. These results are in line with those in other countries, such as Canada, where the Department of Communications (1983) concluded that the introduction of word processing has reduced employment somewhat, but redundancies have been avoided through the process of natural attrition.

Why have the labour savings been so modest in comparison to what optimists have hoped and pessimists have feared? There are a variety of possible explanations. First, it appears both groups may have been influenced by over optimistic claims of manufacturers. Second, many firms may have taken their productivity gains in terms of increased quality of output rather than increased quantity. Related to this, 'hidden work' often appears - work that really should have been done previously, but could not be accommodated by the system. Third, some firms have been utilising this as an opportunity to improve services to customers - as in the case of some insurance companies which are now providing 'personalized policies'. Fourth, personnel savings are frequently distributed over several locations - saving one fifth of a person-year in five locations does not equal one person-year saving. This is particularly true in smaller businesses, which have only recently started to adopt word processors. Finally, many managers are reluctant to part with the status and convenience of a personal secretary.

While the balance of the evidence seems to indicate that the most dire predictions likely overstate the short to medium run impact on employment, all parties agree that some loss of employment among the affected workers can be expected. This trend is likely to accelerate over the longer run as phase 2 technology - which eliminates, rather than simply facilitates, many present clerical functions - comes into more widespread use. Particularly concerned are women's groups since women are the primary holders of the jobs likely to be displaced. Among others, they suggest that organisations need to create more 'bridging' positions to enable a smoother transition for workers in administrative support jobs to positions offering greater opportunities for career advancement.

Physical and Mental Health

Ever since the widespread introduction of VDTs, there has been a rash of complaints from workers and unions about the possible health hazards associated with these machines (see DeMatteo, 1981). The most serious of these complaints deals with a disproportionately high rate of miscarriages and birth defects among pregnant VDT operators (Chernier, 1982). Although some have theorised that a type of radiation leakage may be a contributing factor, extensive testing has revealed no evidence to suggest any type of radiation hazard.

One possible explanation for the disproportionately high

number of problematic pregnancies among VDT operators has been suggested by Labour Canada (1982). Citing a prominent physician, they point out that:

'while VDT Operators' complaints of eye strain, fatigue, and stress do not, in themselves, lead to birth defects, they are very likely to result in increased smoking and the increased use of tranquilizers and other drugs - factors known to have an adverse effect on the unborn child'.
(Labour Canada, 1982)

There is some evidence reported by the US National Institute for Occupational Safety and Health (1981) that VDT operators do suffer higher levels of stress than other office workers.

That VDT operators do experience physical symptoms in excess of those experienced by similar employees is quite clear. For example, in a carefully controlled study of 1,166 clerical employees at Ontario Hydro, Mallette (1983) found three symptoms that occurred more frequently among VDT operators than other clerical employees: (a) eye strain; (b) aches in neck and shoulders; and (c) blurred vision. He also found these symptoms to be related to the amount of time spent on the equipment in a given day as well as individual concern about possible radiation dangers. A review by Treurniet (1982) of prevailing literature on this issue produced virtually identical conclusions. He went on to note that the causes of these symptoms are, by and large, correctable. For example, visual fatigue was related to improper ambient lighting, poor display quality, and ophthalmological deficiencies, while muscle pain and fatigue were related to poor work station design.

A major two year study just completed in the United States (Time, 1983), similarly concluded that physical and mental health symptoms 'are probably not due to anything inherent in the VDT technology' and recommended against mandatory standards. However, Labour Canada (1982) concluded that there is a need for ergonomic standards to cover the physical environment and design of office equipment and furniture relative to VDTs. In the absence of such standards they suggest some guidelines for employers, including right of reassignment of pregnant VDT operators, a maximum limit of five hours per day on a VDT, hourly rest breaks, and annual ophthalmic testing and provision of any necessary ophthalmic devices at employer expense.

Job Design

Views on the impact of introduction of this technology on the quality of jobs themselves cover both ends of the spectrum. Some contend that:

'there are few who will deny that ...video display
terminals... and other microimage equipment intensi-
fies the pace of office work in the name of productivity, while increasing monotony and boredom in many
jobs.' (Johnson, 1983).

On the other hand, promoters of the equipment suggest that use
of the new technology can improve and enrich jobs by automating
many simple and routine tasks, thus freeing up time for the
more complex and challenging tasks that cannot be automated.
What is the empirical evidence on this issue? In general,
it appears that the initial reaction in some organisations was
to create a central word processing pool, where all VDTs and
their operators were centralised. A major rationale for this
was the desire by purchasers to amortise the high cost of this
equipment by keeping it constantly in use. Another rationale
was that personnel who specialised as VDT operators would
become more proficient, and that this would result in
minimisation of training costs. In some cases, particularly
large firms, word processing pools simply replaced the typing
pools that had existed previously. This Tayloristic approach,
by all accounts, resulted in most of the problems feared by
critics, such as narrowing of jobs, reduction of autonomy,
variety, and meaningfulness of jobs, as well as curtailing the
ability for human interaction.
One empirical study of this type of arrangement was
reported by Buchanan and Boddy (1982), who studied effects of
conversion from conventional typing to word processing at a
British consulting engineering firm. They found that the
change to a centralised pool has 'reduced task variety, meaning
and contribution, control over work scheduling and boundary
tasks, feedback of results, involvement in preparation and
auxiliary tasks and communication with authors'. None the
less, number of pages produced per typist increased
tremendously - by a factor of five at least - and typing staff
was reduced from 28 to 16 persons, despite a slight increase in
workload. However, authors of the material were not entirely
satisfied with the new system. Turnaround time had not been
reduced, and they felt they spent more time correcting drafts.
Furthermore, they were now separated from their work by the
word processing centre supervisor, possibly causing them to
feel a loss of control of the workflow.
Interestingly, it was not found that application of the
new technology in itself led to any deskilling, as many
unionists fear. Indeed, in some ways the new technology
required a higher skill level as typists needed to learn a
complex set of codes and then keep updating their knowledge of
them as programs changed. The operators themselves stated
'that they enjoyed handling the equipment but resented being
pooled and remote from the authors'.
Manchee (1980, 1983) agreed that moving from a typewriter

to a word processor in itself cannot be considered deskilling –
quite the reverse in fact – based on four years of experience
using word processors and conducting training on them. She
suggests major reasons for the myth that little skill is
required, are selfserving claims by suppliers and a lack of
actual experience with the equipment by most persons writing
about the topic.

There seems to be ample evidence that the technology
itself need not detract from the quality of working life, but
if implemented properly, may actually enhance it. One such
case is described by Mumford (1983). In order to deal with
problems resulting from the initial introduction of word
processors, secretaries at a British firm participated actively
in designing a new structure for their use. The result was an
efficient system which was also highly satisfying to the
secretaries. Mueller (1981) reports similar results at Shell
Canada where a change away from centralised word processing was
based on quality of working life principles and employee
participation.

Other things remaining equal, simple replacement of the
typewriter by the word processor in itself seems to be regarded
favourably by typists, and appears to increase their job
satisfaction. Bird (1980) examined nine case studies involving
introduction of word processing in British firms and found in
these cases that word processors were simply brought into
existing typing pools, where a distinction between copy typists
and personal secretaries had already been established. Thus,
full-time word processor operators were not downgraded
secretaries, but former copy typists, although in five of the
firms personal secretaries were allowed to use the word
processors. In a survey of the full-time operators, Bird found
that 51 per cent reported more variety in their work and 71 per
cent considered the work more satisfying, although 75 per cent
also found the pace and pressure of work had increased.

Two case studies done by the Work Research Unit (1982) of
the British Department of Employment concluded that the
introduction of word processors did not affect quality of
working life adversely, even though in one case a pool was
created where it did not previously exist. Key factors in this
result were the following. First, the typing tasks undertaken
in this organisation (the British Standards Institution) were
extremely repetitive and tedious on conventional typewriters.
Second, the pool was staffed by new recruits, rather than
downgraded personal secretaries. Relieved of their tedious
typing responsibilities, these personal secretaries have now
had their jobs enriched by increased administrative
responsibilities.

When interviewed, it was found that word processing
operators were not unhappy with their jobs. They generally
felt that production of complicated documents using the word

processor was both challenging and interesting. Also of major importance was the participative management style used in the centre as well as a team approach to working. As a postscript however, one should note that while this was considered a successful case, it did create a category of jobs narrower in scope than previously existed, although other jobs were broadened.

In their review of a number of cases where word processors were implemented, Eason and Gower (1982) found examples where skills were increased and jobs improved and cases where the reverse occurred. Although no conclusive evidence exists on what the overall balance is, one expert in the Department of Employment believed that skills were increased, and thus jobs improved in about 75 per cent of the cases he had seen.

Therefore, it seems clear that the technology itself does not dictate any particular job design. Instead, as Buchanan and Boddy (1982) found, managerial values and beliefs play a key role. In their study, management believed that the opportunities for tighter control and increased specialisation posed by the technology would result in greater efficiency.

In their research Kasurak et al (1982) make the same point about managerial choice. However, they are somewhat optimistic that the central pool may lose some of its perceived attractiveness as the real cost of this type of equipment continues to decline. Part of the original motivation for central pools, they pointed out, was based on the belief by managers that full utilisation of the equipment at all times is the only cost-effective way of implementing it. As experience with word processors has increased, users have increasingly become aware of the detrimental effects and hidden costs of pooling. Where pools do exist there seems to be a movement away from large pools toward more decentralised, smaller pools. Another force against the continued growth of pools is that for the smaller firms, only now adopting word processing, they are not practical.

Computer Monitoring of Work

A major concern of various labour groups is the extent to which the new technology permits constant, close, and surreptitious monitoring of employee performance, although this issue seems to receive more attention in North America than Britain. (Indeed, to some managers this ability to monitor performance and productivity may be one of the most attractive features of the new technology). Johnson (1983) argues that:

> 'The ability of the computer to provide a precise measurement of input is a constant source of tension between senior management and shop floor workers. Workers complain of speedups, higher production quotas, and increased stress'.
> (Johnson, 1983)

Related to this, arguments are made that these measures do not take into account the varying difficulty of the work and quality of output, thus resulting in questionable validity. Employees may also be kept in the dark about what acceptable standards are and may not be provided with feedback on whether they are meeting them.

Aside from the stress that such constant monitoring can cause, civil libertarians have argued that electronic monitoring can be considered an invasion of privacy. A Labour Canada Task Force has concluded that the concerns on this issue are so serious that the process should not be allowed under law:

> 'The Task Force regards close monitoring of work as
> an employment practice based on mistrust and lack
> of respect for human dignity. It is an infringement
> on the rights of the individual, and an undesirable
> precedent that might be extended to other environ-
> ments unless restrictions are put in place now.
> We strongly recommend that this practice be
> prohibited by law'.   (Labour Canada, 1982)

A report by the Canadian Department of Communications (1983) does not go so far as to propose an outright ban on the use of such information, but it does suggest that 'employees at all levels should be consulted and should be allowed to participate in decisions about the type of data collected and how it is used to monitor their productivity and to assess their performance'. Where possible, they suggest that use of evaluation systems that are not based on computer generated data be seriously considered.

Certain approaches could also be used to control the effects of computer monitoring. For example, employees could participate in setting reasonable standards for production and would receive feedback on their productivity whenever they desire it. As long as their overall production falls within these norms over a specified time period, short term fluctuations in output would be irrelevant. A simple procedure such as this could reduce uncertainty and stress considerably.

CONCLUSIONS

The application of microelectronics to the office has the potential to affect quality of working life in both positive and negative ways. It could result in the creation of humanised work organisations in which employees, freed of tedious and repetitive tasks, concentrate on tasks that require judgement and skill. Alternatively, it could create a type of organisation beyond the wildest dreams of Frederick Taylor – where machine controlled human automatons endlessly repeat identical tasks. Which of these scenarios will prevail? While it is clearly too early to tell for certain, there are some encouraging trends.

Clearly, the technology itself does not dictate one or another of these outcomes. Instead, managerial values and beliefs seem to be the most important determinant. After a false start toward Taylorism in the office, it appears that the forces away from Taylorism are gaining strength. Perhaps one of the strongest forces for centralisation - economics - is declining in importance as the real cost of the equipment continues to decline and the hidden costs of Taylorism become more evident. Interest groups concerned about the potential negative effects have met with some success in publicising their views, although the current recession may have distracted some attention away from quality of working life issues. Through the publication of successful alternatives to Taylorism, managers are beginning to realise that they do have a choice in how to apply the technology (e.g. Work Research Unit, 1982).

None the less, progress will likely be uneven, with some firms in some industries not electing to use the new technology in a progressive way. Changes in certain labour standards may be required in order to deal with some of the concerns discussed earlier. In addition, governments must do all they can to encourage employers to consider the broader human issues involved with the implementation of the new technology and to consult with employees at an early stage in the adoption of such technology.

Aside from the impact on the quality of work life itself, great concern has been expressed about the employment effects of the technology, particularly for lower level 'information workers'. However, while there is little doubt that some jobs have been lost, it does not seem the impact has been as rapid or as deep as many have feared, for a variety of reasons.

In the light of these somewhat disappointing (by some standards) results, enthusiasts now suggest that the real savings will occur with the introduction of phase 2 of the electronic revolution and the 'automation' of managerial jobs. However, these individuals may not be recognising that organisations are not only information processing mechanisms, but are also systems of power and interpersonal relationships. Managerial work involves far more than simply making routine decisions based on standardised information. As a result, managers and their tasks will likely prove less amenable to automation than some might expect. Furthermore, managers will turn out to have a much higher ability than lower level employees to successfully resist changes they perceive as threatening.

Thus, while microelectronics will be introduced into higher levels in the office, implementation and usage will likely be slower and more limited than believed by both the pessimists and the optimists. None the less, certain types of jobs will be reduced or eliminated and both employers and governments must develop programmes to allow the affected workers (particularly women) to retrain for other jobs. Particularly important will be the need to help 'information workers', assume productive roles as 'knowledge workers', whose ranks are expected to expand markedly in coming years. As discussed throughout this chapter, a variety of progressive management policies aimed at using the new technology to enhance and extend human abilities and skills will be necessary for the organisation and society to realise the potential benefits of this new technology.

REFERENCES

Argyris, C. and Schon, D.A. (1978) Organizational Learning: A Theory of Action Perspective, Addison Wesley, Reading, Mass.

Barras, R. and Swann, J. (1983) The Adoption and Impact of Information Technology in the U.K. Insurance Industry, The Technical Change Centre, London

Bird, E. (1980) Information Technology in the Office: The Impact on Women's Jobs, Equal Opportunities Commission, Manchester

Brunet, L. (1980) 'Word Processors: Source of Emancipation or Alienation for Office Workers?, Quality of Working Life: The Canadian Scene, 3(4), 17-19

Brophy, L.M. (1981) 'Office Automation in the Employee Relations Department Shell Canada Limited', QWL Focus, The News Journal of the Ontario Quality of Working Life Centre, 1(3), 9-12

Buchanan, D.A. and Boddy, D. (1982) 'Advanced Technology and the Quality of Working Life: The Effects of Word Processing on Video Typists', Journal of Occupational Psychology, 55, 1-11

Chernier, N.M. (1982) Reproductive Hazards at Work, Canadian Advisory Council on the Status of Women, Ottawa

Child, J., Loveridge, R., Harvey, J. and Spencer, A. (1983) 'Microelectronics and the Quality of Employment in Services', Paper presented to the British Association for the Advancement of Science

DeMatteo, B. (1981) The Hazards of VDT's, Ontario Public Services Employees Union, Toronto

Department of Communications, Canada (1983) The Human and Social Issues of Office Communications Technology, Report of the Human and Social Impact Committee on Office Automation, Department of Communication, Ottawa

Dover, M. (1983) The Impact of Teletravail on Living and Working Conditions, Technology Policy Unit, University of Aston, Birmingham

Eason, K.D. and Gower, J.C. (1982) Report on the Extent of Introduction of Electronic Machinery in The Office, University of Technology, Loughborough

Greenberg, M. (1981) 'Bell Northern Research Applies Integrated
Office Systems and the Quality of Working Life', QWL Focus, The
News Journal of The Ontario Quality of Working Life Centre,
1(3), 12-13

Hiltz, S.R. and Turoff, M. (1978) The Network Nation: Human
Communication via Computers, Addison-Wesley, Reading, Mass

Hirschheim, R.A. (1984) Office Automation, Addison-Wesley,
London

Johnson, W. (1983) 'White Collar Wasteland', Policy Options,
(4), 1, 49-52

Kasurak, P.C., Tan, C. and Wolchuk, R. (1982) 'Management and
the Human Resource Impact of the Electronic Office', Optimum,
13, 57-68

Kendall, P.M. (1983) Evaluating The Impact of Chip Technology
on Conditions and Quality of Work, Metra Consulting Group,
London

Labour Canada (1982) In the Chips: Opportunities, People,
Partnerships, Report of the Labour Canada Task Force on
Micro-Electronics and Employment, Labour Canada, Ottawa

Land, F.F., Detjejarutwat, N. and Smith, C. (1983) New
Information Technology and Social Control, Report from EIFIP to
EEC, Frankfurt

Leduc, N.F. (1979) 'La Communication Mediatisse par Ordinateur:
Une Nouvelle Definition du Dialogue Groupal', Memoire de
Maitreses-Sciences de la Communication, Department de
Communication, Universite de Montreal

Leeds Trade Union and Community Resource Centre (1982) New
Technology and Women's Employment: Case Studies from East
Yorkshire, Equal Opportunities Commission, Manchester

Mallette, R. (1983) A Survey of the Attitudes and Perceptions
of Video Display Operators at Ontario Hydro, Human Resources
Research Report prepared by the Personnel Applied Research
Branch, Ontario Hydro, Toronto

Manchee, J. (1980) Drowning in the Pool: Word Processing and
the Organization, Institute of Canadian Studies, Carleton
University, Ottawa

Manchee, J. (1983) Skill, Word Processing, and the Working
Class, Unpublished manuscript

Menzies, H. (1981) Women and the Chip, Institute for Research on Public Policy, Montreal

Menzies, H. (1982) Computers on the Job: Surviving Canada's Microcomputer Revolution, Lorimer, Toronto

Mintzberg, H. (1973) The Nature of Managerial Work, Harper and Row, New York

Mueller, M. (1981) 'Overview of the Automation and Reorganization of the Word Processing Centre at Shell Canada Limited's Head Office', QWL Focus, The News Journal of the Ontario Quality of Working Life Centre, 1(3), 7-9

Mumford, E. (1983) Designing Secretaries: The Participative Design of a Word Processing System, Manchester Business School, Manchester

National Institute for Occupational Safety and Health, United States, (1981) Proceedings of a Workshop on Methodology for Assessing Reproductive Hazards in the Workplace, US Department of Health, Education and Welfare, Cincinnati, Ohio

Nexos, U. (1982) as cited in Eason and Gower (1982) op.cit.

Phillips, D. (1982) 'The Human and Social Impact of Office Communications Technology', Presented at the 4th International IDATE Conference (Institut pour le Developpement et l'Anenagement de Telecommunications et de l'Economie), Social Experiments in Telematique, Montpellier, France

Pieper, M. (1982) 'Computer Conferencing and Human Interaction', Proceedings of the Sixth International Conference on Computer Communication, London, 653-657

Plowright, T. and Booth, P.J. (1982) A Study on the Social Impacts of Office Automation, Report prepared for the Department of Communications, Canada, Department of Communications, Ottawa

Steffens, J. (1983) The Electronic Office: Progress and Problems, Policy Studies Institute, London

Tapscott, D. (1982) 'DP Professionals Face Major Challenge in Automated Office', Computer Data, 7(2), 22-32

Taylor, J.R. (1982a) 'Computer Aided Message Systems: An Organizational Perspective' in Neffah, N. (ed.) Office Information Systems, INRIA/North-Holland Publishing Company, Amsterdam

Taylor, J.R. (1982b) New Communication Technologies and the Emergence of Distributed Organizations: Looking Beyond 1984, Unpublished manuscript, Department des Communications, Universite de Montreal, Montreal, Quebec

Taylor, J.R. (1982c) 'Office Communications: Reshaping our Society', Computer Communications, 5, 174-180

Time (1983) 'Screen Test: Discounting VDT Hazard', July 25, 35

Treurniet, W.C. (1982) Review of Health and Safety Aspects of Video Display Terminals, Ottawa, Department of Communications, Canada

Work Research Unit (1982) Meeting the Challenge of Change: Case Studies, Department of Employment, London

Chapter 7

NEW TECHNOLOGY AND FUTURE
WORK PATTERNS

Paul Blyton

In the wide-ranging reader, The Microelectronics Revolution,
Forester (1980) divides writers on the employment consequences
of new technology into optimists and pessimists. Optimists,
such as Robinson (1980) and Davies (1980) tend to couch their
arguments in terms of labour displacement (rather than loss)
and in the lessons of history.   The experience of past
technological breakthroughs (the invention of steam power, the
internal combustion engine and the electric motor, for example)
is offered as evidence of the way in which such developments
can lead to major economic growth, wealth creation and the
overall   expansion   of   employment.   Widespread   labour
displacement - for example, the massive exodus from the land in
Britain at the beginning of the nineteenth century due in part
to more labour efficient farming methods - is characterised as
a short term problem in the pursuit of a greater long term
benefit (economic growth).   In terms of the new technologies,
the optimists picture labour displaced by robots, word
processors and the like, as encountering an expanding labour
market resulting not only from the production of technological
hard- and soft-ware, but also from new employment fields
created by the wealth generated by the application of new
technology.   And in case anyone is left unconvinced by this
argument, the optimists point to the likely consequences of not
applying the various innovations.   The outcome of such an
action is portrayed as a growing inability to compete with
other industries and countries which have adopted the available
technology, and a consequent loss of employment substantially
greater than that lost as a direct result of introducing new
technology into home industries.   This last argument has been
of particular importance in influencing the responses of
employee organisations to the introduction of new technology.
     In recent years, however, pessimistic interpretations of
the effect of new technology on employment have become more
prominent.   The main focus of this argument concerns the
displacement effect of new technology being potentially far
greater than has generally been acknowledged, resulting in

severe long term unemployment unless particular courses of action are taken, notably in relation to the way working time is organised. One of the most significant contributions to this argument has been made recently by the Nobel Prize winner, Wassily Leontief, who argues that the present technological developments are qualitatively different from any predecessors, therefore past experience cannot serve as a reliable guide to the impact of the current generation of technological advance.

'With the advent of solid state electronics, machines that have been displacing human muscle from the production of goods are being succeeded by machines that take over the functions of the human nervous system not only in production but in the service industries as well... The relation between man and machine is being radically transformed.' (Leontief, 1982, p.152)

Further, the potential employment consequences are seen by many to be exacerbated by the economic climate in which they are being introduced - one characterised by a zero or low growth in domestic and world trade, high unemployment and growing competition from newly-industrialising (and low labour cost) countries. Moreover, the long term transformation of a number of traditional manufacturing industries - a transformation which has been associated with 'de-industrialization' (Blackaby, 1978) - means that these are no longer likely to act as an employment 'sponge' as they have at the end of previous economic recessions.

Clearly, like those viewing the employment consequences of new technology as manageable within present institutional arrangements, the proponents of a bleaker view are hindered not only by a dearth of detailed empirical evidence on the effects of introducing new technology, but also by their inability to predict changes in government policy which could markedly alter the economic setting in which the diffusion of innovations takes place. Hence, various assumptions are required not only in relation to the rate and breadth of application but also concerning future economic conditions and the extent to which market demand will be conducive to rapid diffusion. Among other ways, the limitations inherent in such an assumption-based argument manifest themselves in the wide variation in predicted employment effects of the new technology. For example, whilst Curnow (1981) has estimated an overall job loss of between 7 and 20 per cent by the mid 1990s, Stonier has argued the probability that 'by early in the next century it will require no more than ten percent of the labour force to provide us with all our material needs' (Stonier, 1980, p.305).

Nevertheless, despite the shortcomings of available evidence, the strength of the 'pessimistic' argument appears to be growing, partly as the potential breadth of application of new technology becomes clearer, together with the extent of the indirect as well as the direct employment consequences and the comparatively low levels of employment which have already been created in advanced industrial societies by new technology industries. On this last point, it is becoming clear that the question is not just one of job displacement on a national level, but rather employment being shifted around the world in search of lower labour costs.

Moreover, it is generally recognised that certain employment groups are likely to experience technological unemployment to a much greater extent than others. Those in low-skilled and repetitive jobs – both blue- and white-collar - appear most threatened by technology in the short term. According to Blatt (1979) the result will be to make an increasing proportion of the population unemployable, a process which he terms the 'village idiot' effect. (In pre-industrial times, Blatt argues, the village idiot could still perform a useful role, for example as a shepherd. Only with the mechanisation of farming does this individual become unemployable since he is both unable to learn the necessary skills and unable to embrace the new practices without endangering the lives of himself and others):

> 'Technological progress imposes an upward change in the minimum level of ability to carry on useful productive work' (Blatt, 1979, p.8).

This author goes on to argue that many of those with relatively low levels of intelligence will be unable to absorb the training required to take an active part in computer-assisted employment, and so like the village idiot will become increasingly unemployable. A gap is thus envisaged opening up between the minimum level of skill required to operate the new technology and the maximum level of skill which some groups currently in employment will be able to offer. Nor is Blatt the only writer identifying the lower skill levels as the group most likely to bear the initial brunt of the displacement effects of new technology. Barron and Curnow (1979), for example, identify workers performing assembly tasks, carrying out repair and maintenance work and various grades of clerical workers (particularly the lower levels) as being the types of labour most threatened by the substitution of microelectronic technology.

These predictions are made all the more significant when we consider the current pattern of unemployment which shows that it is already the lowest skill levels who are disproportionately represented among the unemployed. In their study of unemployment Moylan and Davies (1980), for example, found that 40 per cent of the sample had last worked in semi-skilled or unskilled manual jobs, whereas those categories comprised only 19 per cent of the general population. This overrepresentation of lower grades was also reflected in former earnings; the previous earnings of half of the unemployed fell into the bottom fifth of the earnings distribution (Moylan and Davies, 1980, p.831). Nor is this pattern of unemployment unique to the post-1979 recession. Analysing data from the 1972 General Household Survey, Nickell (1980) found that whilst the overall unemployment rate was 4.5 per cent, among semi-skilled manual workers the rate was 6.7 per cent and among unskilled manuals it was 14.2 per cent. Hence, in relation to lower grades of manual workers, the predicted effects of new technology, if borne out, will exacerbate the situation of workers already seriously disadvantaged in terms of their propensity for becoming unemployed. Further, the fact that the burden of unemployment is already becoming heavier is indicated by the continued increase in long term unemployment. At the beginning of 1981, for example, 18.8 per cent of the unemployed population in Britain had been workless for a year or longer. By April 1983, this proportion had risen to 36.1 per cent (figures from the Employment Gazette, July 1983).

The unique aspect of the predictions about the new techno-logy's impact on job opportunities is the anticipated demise of large numbers of clerical jobs, initially the lower skilled ones. On the whole white-collar unemployment is a recent phen-omenon, and follows a long period of expansion in the white-collar sector resulting from the expansion of service indus-tries and government administration, and the demands of large-scale enterprise for expanded clerical and managerial func-tions. Non-manual unemployment remains substantially below that experienced by manual workers. However, this differential could reduce with the full development of current and future microelectronic equipment in the office as well as on the shop-floor. Also, as Werneke (1983), Joseph (1983) and others have argued, these changes will impact particularly upon female employment since their concentration in lower non-manual grades could make women especially vulnerable to replacement by less labour intensive technology. Overall, there appears to be a widespread belief that without significant changes in the way work is organised, unemployment could become as severe in the lower levels of white-collar employment as in the blue-collar sector.

OFF-SETTING TECHNOLOGICAL UNEMPLOYMENT BY REDUCING WORKING HOURS

To counteract the potential threat to employment posed by new technology, little support has emerged for the non-adoption of innovations. There has been a general concurrence among trade unions and elsewhere with the view that technological innovation is essential to maintaining a competitive position, and that the employment consequences of retaining a technological status quo could be even worse than full adoption of new techniques. Jenkins and Sherman (1979) are one example of this way of thinking:

'Remain as we are, reject the new technologies and we face unemployment of up to 5.5 million by the end of the century. Embrace the new technologies, accept the challenge and we end up with unemployment of about 5 million' (p. 113).

Trade union objectives have in general involved the acceptance of new technology, whilst seeking involvement in decisions about its introduction and the achievement of 'no redundancy' agreements. Longer term proposals for adapting to new technology have centred around the call for shorter working time, to mitigate the translation of a large drop in demand for labour into widespread unemployment. Leontief (1982) is one of many arguing the necessity and feasibility of this step as a key adaptive response to the long term challenge of:

'how to enable a modern industrial society to derive the benefits of continued technological progess without experiencing involuntary technological unemployment and resulting social disruption'. (Leontief, 1982, p.155).

By way of supporting evidence, Leontief cites a large scale Austrian study which modelled the effects of technological adoption and changes in the length of the working week, on employment and unemployment. Some of the results of this study are summarised below in Table 7.1. These results suggest that whilst the full application of technology and maintenance of a 40 hour working week would lead to highest levels of GDP, this strategy would also create highest levels of unemployment. A reduction in the working week is projected to bring unemployment down to the levels enjoyed by Austria in the 1970s and early 1980s (unemployment has risen only slightly in Austria, and in May 1983 stood at 3.9 per cent; figures from Employment Gazette, July 1983).
Other writers have similarly argued for a reduced work week to combat technological unemployment. Blatt (1979), for example, discusses cutting working time in half; Jenkins and Sherman (1979) advocate a 4 day, 32 hour week (falling to a 3 day, 24 hour week by the year 2000), as well as longer holidays, more flexible retirement provision and greater access to sabbatical leave. The general point being argued by these and other writers is that from a societal point of view, the extra productivity resulting from the application of new technology should be used to facilitate reductions in working hours, rather than, say, substantial wage increases for those in employment. The general objective is the avoidance of a 'two nation' position comprising, on the one hand, a progressively smaller, highly skilled and highly paid employed group, and on the other hand a growing body of unemployed becoming increasingly unempoyable as technology makes further advances.

Table 7.1:   The Projected Impact of Technology on the Austrian
            Economy by 1990

	1976	1990			
		Unchanged Work Week		Shortened Work Week	
		No Mechan-isation	Full Mech-anisation	No Mechan-isation	Full Mech-anisation
GDP (1976=100)	100	160	161	151	156
Per Capita Wages (1976=100)	100	149	157	130	136
Average working week (hours)	41.1	39.6	39.9	35.2	35.3
Unemploy-ment (%)	1.7	6.4	11.2	0.8	2.2
Employment (1000 persons)	3,222	3,221	3,056	3,413	3,366

Source: Adapted by the Author from Leontief (1982)

Yet the reduction of working time has already been
receiving growing amounts of attention as a possible response to
the current high levels of unemployment.   Indeed, by examining
the changes in working time that have already occurred in
different countries in recent times, and more specifically the
obstacles which have frustrated major developments in this area,
it will be possible to more fully evaluate the proposal to
combat potentially large scale technological unemployment via
changes in working time patterns.

RECENT CHANGES IN WORKING TIME: A BRIEF REVIEW

At various times of high unemployment, support has been voiced
for shortening the length of the working day or week, and
distributing the available work among more people (for an
example of support for work-sharing as far back as 1824, see
Webb and Webb, 1902, p. 341).   The current wave of interest in
work-sharing grew in the latter part of the 1970s, during a
period when levels of unemployment in many Western industrial
societies began to move considerably beyond the norms
established in the late 1950s and 1960s.   Within the trade union

movement this support for reduced working hours was focused by a now well-known Resolution by the European Trade Union Confederation, in May 1979, which stated that the ETUC would seek to achieve a 10 per cent reduction in working time without loss of pay, by one or a mixture of the following changes:

1. reducing the working week to 35 hours;
2. extending annual holidays to 6 weeks;
3. giving workers the right to a full pension at 60 years;
4. raising the school leaving age to 16 years and extending the right to time off for vocational training and further education. (ETUI, 1979)

At the same time the European Community has been considering the reduction and reorganisation of working time, though progress has been slow and to date largely limited to information gathering and the drafting of guidelines for Member States (European Industrial Relations Review, 1983).

Just as at international level the issue of reduced working time has generated more debate than action, so too at national level, progress towards significantly different work patterns has to date been very modest, though considerable variation in activity is evident between different countries. Most changes which have occurred are connected to reductions in the working week (and year) and greater provision for earlier retirement. Before outlining some of the reasons why changes have not been greater it is worthwhile looking briefly at the developments which have occurred in these areas.

Working hours vary significantly between different countries and between different industries within single countries. In the late 1970s, for example, according to Vater (1980) the average hours worked in West Germany was 1,812 hours per annum, whilst in Britain and the USA the average was approximately 5 per cent higher (1,892 hours and 1,907 hours) and in Japan almost 9% higher at 2,083 hours (Kotaro (1980) points out that this disparity in the Japanese average work time per annum is due not so much to a longer working week as to the practice of shorter holidays and the tendency for employees not to take all their holiday entitlement). Similarly at the industry level, disparities are evident with some industries (e.g. mining and printing) tending to operate with lower average hours than others (e.g. agriculture and catering). However, whilst these national and international differences have persisted, a small reduction in hours has occurred in many (though not all) countries in recent years. In Britain, for example, where the basic working week at the beginning of the 1970s was generally 40 hours, it has recently been estimated that about 6.5m manual workers (about two-thirds of the total) are now covered by agreements which reduce basic hours below 40 (TUC, 1983). Following the precedent of the 1979 engineering agreement, many of the agreements reached subsequently have involved a one hour cut to 39 hours. It is worth noting, however, that despite these reductions in the basic hours of manual workers, they remain substantially higher than those worked by non-manual employees; in mid-1982 the average basic hours for non-manual men was around 37 hours (TUC, 1983).

Elsewhere in Europe reductions in weekly hours are also evident. In France, for example, the standard working week was reduced in 1982 from 40 to 39 hours; to encourage further reductions, the French government offers employers a grant of 1000 Francs per employee per hour reduction below 39 hours (Incomes Data Services, 1983a). The French aim of using reductions in working hours to lower the level of unemployment is made more explicit in recent agreements in Belgium and the Netherlands. In Belgium, despite initial opposition from employers' organisations, a government decree for employers and unions to reach agreements on reduced working time appears to have met with some success. The requirement for employing organisations to reduce working time by 5 per cent and increase employment by 3 per cent* has been occasioned by the high level of unemployment in Belgium (given as 18 per cent in the Employment Gazette, July 1983). According to a recent report (Incomes Data Services, 1983b) agreements on reduced hours covering more than one million employees have been reached and the Belgian government estimated that between 52,000 and 66,000 jobs had been preserved or created as a result of cuts in working time. In the Netherlands the system of pay indexation (which links pay increases automatically to price rises) has been suspended with the intention that the cash withheld from wages be used to finance a reduction in hours in order to save or create jobs (the Employment Gazette, July 1983, gives the Netherlands unemployment level as 16.1 per cent). By April 1983, agreements covering one and a quarter million employees had been reached on how reduced working time would be introduced (Incomes Data Services, 1983c).

This work-sharing initiative in Belgium and the Netherlands is also evident in a number of early retirement programmes introduced nationally in recent years. Whilst individual companies have sought to use early retirement as a way of reducing overall manpower levels, national early retirement schemes have sought more to reduce the labour supply and alleviate the level of unemployment and redundancy among younger age-groups. In Britain and Belgium, this aim has been explicit since the national schemes contain a 'replacement

---

*The required increase in employment is 2 per cent in companies employing less than 50 people. Reductions in working time are not required if companies put forward alternative plans which increase employment. Those not complying with the decree incur a fine, equivalent to the cost of the required increase in employment, which is paid into an Employment Fund and used to fund job creating projects.

condition' requiring employers to replace the retiree with someone from the unemployment register (in Belgium the replacement must be under 30 years of age). Other early retirement schemes operate in Scandinavia, France, West Germany, the Netherlands and Luxembourg (Blyton, 1982), and in Sweden the opportunity for earlier retirement was extended in 1976 by the introduction of partial retirement whereby employees between 60 and 65 years can apply to transfer from full-time to part-time work, and receive a partial pension which compensates for 50 per cent of their loss in earnings (for a recent assessment of this scheme, see Blyton, 1984).

Apart from changes to weekly hours and early retirement provision, other smaller reductions in working time have occurred through increases in holiday entitlement. In Britain in 1981, for example, 88 per cent of full-time adult males in employment were entitled to four weeks or more paid holiday per annum, a marked increase on the position in the late 1970s. Further, though there is not space to cover the subject in detail here, aggregate reductions in hours worked have also occurred due to the decline in full-time employment and marked growth in part-time working, particularly among women and in the service sector. In Britain, where the level of part-time working is high, the number of employees working full-time declined by 800,000 between 1971 and 1980, whilst the number of part-time workers increased by over one million (Clark, 1982). Recently, interest in part-time working has been growing, partly as a result of the greater attention being paid to the concept of job-sharing, whereby two people undertake to fill one full-time job (Olmstead, 1979).

Hence, the pattern of working hours is not static but is shifting slowly downwards as a result of collective agreements on hours and holidays, the greater provision of early retirement and the spread of part-time working. Yet, given the scale of unemployment in most advanced industrial societies, and compounding factors such as the potential labour substitution effect of new technology, it is apparent that both the scale and the rate of these changes in working time are inadequate, if they are to contribute significantly to a lowering of unemployment in coming years. However, to contemplate a change in gear, resulting in an accelerated and substantial reduction in the time people spend at work, requires an appreciation of the obstacles hindering the progress of such a development.

OBSTACLES TO MAJOR REDUCTIONS IN WORKING TIME

In fact, viewed from a standpoint of economic recession, with its accompanying low level of demand, over-capacity, ebbing trade union power and the ascendancy of relatively right-wing administrations in the UK, USA and elsewhere, the barriers facing a large-scale reorganisation of working time appear daunting. At the same time, to summarise the arguments of several aforementioned writers, the severe costs (social, psychological, economic and political) resulting from long term unemployment are likely to be sufficient to eventually overcome these barriers, though whether this is sooner or later will depend on a variety of factors.

A major obstacle facing any proposal to substantially reduce working time is the employers' criticism that the outcome would be a substantial increase in labour costs which, it is argued, would so damage the competitiveness of those industries reducing hours, that the result would be <u>fewer</u> rather than more employment opportunities (CBI, 1980). Underlying this argument is not only the assumption that simultaneous national and international reductions in hours could not be effected, but also a perceived unwillingness among the labour force to accept a proportional reduction in income (an unwillingness voiced by trade unions in the ETUC resolution outlined above). In Britain, the state has similarly emphasised the increase in costs likely to accompany a shorter working week; in 1978 it was estimated that a 35 hour work week, whilst potentially reducing unemployment by as much as 480,000, could increase labour costs by up to 8.5 per cent (Department of Employment, 1978b).

This question of costs has not yet been fully explored. For example, relatively little is known about different groups of employees' potential willingness to trade off a proportion of earnings for a cut in hours (Best, 1978). Moreover, in many countries the nature of the trade union movement has meant that counter arguments, in terms of the costs of unemployment, have not been put as forcefully as they might. Partly this reflects a receding of trade union power resulting from job insecurity, high unemployment and reductions in trade union membership. In addition, however, union movements have continued to give greater priority to the interests of their employed membership, rather than the unemployed. Reductions in working time have been achieved; however, the main objective of the reductions has evidently been to improve the condition of employment of those in work, rather than to create the basis for translating the reduced hours into additional employment.

Further, it has been argued (Institute of Manpower Studies, 1981) that until the issues of working time and work-sharing become more salient at local level, any general resolutions by trade unions or other groups at national and international level will have little impact. This is no doubt true, and nowhere is it more clearly represented than in relation to the continued high level of overtime working in Britain; local resistance to reducing overtime has so far nullified any general union or employers' federation statements about the need to reduce overtime working. Yet, whilst in no way denying the importance of the local level in any effort to reduce hours, it could also be argued that in those countries where trade unions lack established institutional involvement in national policy-making bodies, progress towards a substantially modified working time structure is likely to be significantly impeded. Hence, to bring about the necessary changes, trade union influence is required at both national level (to influence manpower policies towards creating a framework conducive to the reduction of working time), and at local level (to influence the implementation of such changes). The lack of established tripartite machinery (involving unions, employers, and government) in several countries, coupled with the current shift in power away from both the trade union movement and pro-union political parties (notably the Labour Party in Britain) could represent a considerable obstacle to the mobilising of pressure to modify working time patterns in the near future.

So far, governments in Britain have shown less interest in developing work-sharing initiatives than some of their European counterparts. Certain measures introduced in the 1970s have been retained (concerning early retirement and short time working), and a temporary scheme to encourage job-splitting has recently been introduced. However, whilst each of these contains a work-sharing element, their coverage is restricted, and indeed are tending to become more rather than less restricted as time goes on (for example, in 1982 the period of subsidy for short-time working was reduced from nine months to six; likewise having progressively extended eligibility for early retirement under the Job Release Scheme, this is shortly to be restricted again to 64 year old men and 59 year old women). On the grounds of increased costs the state in Britain has been generally unenthusiastic towards either a substantial reduction in working hours or a general reduction in the age of retirement (Department of Employment, 1978a; 1978b). The recent Select Committee report on age of retirement likewise forebore to make recommendations which would allow a fundamental change in working time over life. A notional common pension age of 63 years by the 1990s was recommended; larger reductions in pension age, together with any national provision for phased retirement (along the lines of the Swedish partial pension scheme) were rejected, again primarily on the grounds of cost (House of Commons Social Services Committee, 1982). Overall this pattern of government reaction appears to reflect an unwillingness to consider the shortage of employment as a long term and multi-causal problem, requiring more than traditional Keynesian or monetarist patterns of response.

A further obstacle to the initiation of action on a sufficiently large scale to alleviate not only current unemployment but also the potential unemployment resulting from the full adoption of new technology, is the pattern of unemployment itself. As noted above, the employed and the unemployed tend to be drawn from different groups, thus the experience of unemployment is far more widespread in some social groups than in others (the concentration of the experience of unemployment is indicated in a finding by Moylan and Davies (1980), where more than three-quarters of the sample of unemployed had experienced at least one other spell of unemployment in the previous five years, and a quarter had experienced three or more periods of unemployment). Following the argument by Gregory (1982), if 13 per cent unemployment (the official rate of unemployment in Britain at the time of writing in August 1983) meant that each worker was unemployed for 13 per cent of the year (or at least that unemployment was experienced by a far wider cross-section of the working population than actually occurs) the perception of unemployment and the motivation to seek ways to reduce it - including the reorganisation of working time - would be substantially different to that currently prevailing at national and local levels. Moreover, the effect of this concentration of unemployment within lower skill levels is exacerbated by the lack of direct political pressure exerted by the unemployed (for a variety of reasons which there is not space to examine here; see Schlozman and Verba, 1979).

Nor are these the only obstacles facing a fundamental reorganisation of working time. Others include the difficulty of effecting <u>major</u> changes during periods of recession; the ability of employers in recession to make <u>minor</u> reductions in working hours without stimulating a positive employment effect (White, 1982); the problem of seeking to reduce overtime when a substantial proportion is worked by those on low basic wage rates; the need to protect the rights of workers from, for example, compulsory early retirement; and the problem that a strong work ethic poses for creating a greater willingness to work fewer hours. Together these factors appear to represent a context largely unsupportive towards major changes in working time in the near future. However, the pace of change has been greater in some countries than others and this differential allows us to consider possible factors which could stimulate a substantial modification in working time practices. Whilst several potentially important factors can be identified, the role played by the state in bringing about changes appears to have been particularly salient in those countries where working time changes have been greatest.

THE ROLE OF THE STATE

A review of initiatives already taken underlines the role of the state in initiating change or adding impetus to changes already under way. This is evident, for example, in the reduction of working hours in France, Belgium and the Netherlands; in the restriction of overtime in countries such as the Netherlands (Whybrew, 1968); and in broadening the eligibility for early retirement (e.g. France and West Germany) and partial retirement (e.g. in Sweden). These examples reflect the state playing a directive role (e.g. in France and Belgium), and also a facilitative role which involves, for example, passing legislation (such as the Swedish Partial Pensions Act) to remove obstacles to the agreement of specific working time changes. Other examples of the state facilitating change would be the subsidising not only of hours reductions (as currently in France) but also the quasi-fixed costs of employment (e.g. costs of hiring and training) in order to reduce the difference in costs of employing, say, one full-time worker or two part-time.

The state, however, has no magic qualities and in countries such as Britain which have been characterised by a low level of state intervention in the workplace, a directive role would be likely to meet with considerable opposition. On the other hand, if a rapid development of new technology results in much greater numbers being displaced than new jobs created, the burden of very high levels of unemployment is likely eventually to stimulate increased involvement of the most non-interventionist of governments in the labour market and in the organisation of working hours. Following the argument outlined above, it is in those countries where established tripartite machinery exists at national levels that developments towards shorter hours are likely to be greatest. The recent experience of Belgium and the Netherlands, for example, suggests that progress is most likely where a package of agreements (or at least understandings) can be reached not only about hours, but also about wages and other conditions of employment.

Hence, whilst highlighting the possible role of the state in directing and/or facilitating change, the approach of employers and trade unions to this issue will similarly have a critical bearing on future developments at both national and local levels. On the union side the question appears to be, in part, a general one about the handling of the unemployment issue and the priority which should be given to working time changes, compared to other trade union objectives. Among employers, one requirement appears to be an evaluation of their traditionally fairly rigid approach to working time. For example, in the past only limited opportunities have been available for individuals to exercise a degree of choice over their pattern of work hours, or the degree to which income can be traded-off for extra leisure. Yet the criticism that greater diversity of work patterns would create undue problems for administration and work allocation, has not been borne out by, for example, the development of 'flexi-time' in Britain and elsewhere, or the development of phased retirement in Sweden. If adaptations are possible, further research is justified on the types of trade-off between work, income and leisure which those in employment would be in favour of making.

Indeed, for the issue of working time changes as a response to new technology developments to be advanced, greater investigation is needed of the possible implications for different groups of workers. Some studies already exist, for example, on the psychological effects of early retirement (McGoldrick and Cooper, 1980) and desired trade-offs between income and leisure (Best, 1978). Though valuable, these studies nevertheless are insufficient to fully evaluate the different work options. Moreover, in terms of the impact on employers of, for example, higher levels of part-time working, restrictions on overtime or the operating of diverse working time patterns, the dearth of enquiry is even more pronounced.

CONCLUSION

In terms of the potential impact of new technology on employment we have dealt here with only one aspect of the optimistic/pessimistic scenario - the quantitative impact on jobs and the possible adaptive response of changes in working hours. This is not to undervalue the possible qualitative impact, that is the implications of new technology for the nature of people's jobs, their levels of discretion, job satisfaction, health, etc. Indeed this latter aspect is clearly important and is attracting increased attention, particularly from occupational psychologists. However, in societies where citizenship, income, status and self-regard continue to be so strongly linked to paid employment, it is the potential widespread loss of jobs which for many remains the more pressing issue. As we have seen, in contrast to the optimistic view which predicts sufficient job creation to counteract technological job displacement, a growing pessimistic analysis has pointed to a scale of labour displacement far exceeding that compensated for by a growth in new industries and related revival in demand. Under this latter view, the labour market would come to be characterised increasingly (that is, more than it is already) by, on the one hand, groups of relatively secure, high income and career progressive workers, and on the other, a growing proportion of the working population unemployed or increasingly insecure, lacking both the appropriate skills and access to the education and training necessary to acquire those skills.

A widely canvassed proposal to mitigate the potential impact of technological unemployment involves the reorganisation of working time patterns - reducing hours and dividing more equitably the total volume of work available. This proposal is already current in relation to the present unemployment problem, though from the foregoing analysis it is evident that whilst certain changes have been introduced, substantial obstacles confront a more fundamental reorganisation of working time. Not least of these is the level of priority currently being given to fuller evaluation and action in this area by governments, employers and trade unions. It remains to be seen whether the further advance of new technology and the potential threat that it poses for the overall level of employment available, will be sufficient to create the necessary will to establish a more equitable balance of employment in the future.

REFERENCES

Barron, I. and Curnow, R. (1979) The Future with Microelectronics, Open University Press, Milton Keynes

Best, F. (1978) 'Preferences on Worklife Scheduling and
Work-Leisure Tradeoffs', Monthly Labor Review, 101, 31-37

Blackaby, F. (ed.) (1978) De-industrialisation, Heinemann,
London

Blatt, J.M. (1979) 'Technological Unemployment', Australian
Computer Bulletin, February, 7-10

Blyton, P. (1982) 'Early Retirement: An EEC Perspective', Three
Banks Review, 136, 32-44

Blyton, P. (1984) 'Partial Retirement: Some Insights from the
Swedish Partial Pension Scheme', Ageing and Society, in press

Clark, G. (1982) 'Recent Developments in Working Patterns',
Employment Gazette, 90 (7), 284-88.

CBI (1980), Jobs - Facing the Future, Confederation of British
Industry, London

Curnow, R. (1981) 'The Effect on Employment' in B.C. Twiss
(ed.), The Managerial Implications of Microelectronics, Macmillan, London, pp.61-79

Davies, D.S. (1980), 'The Computer Revolution, Industry and
People', in T. Forester (ed.) The Microelectronics Revolution,
Blackwell, Oxford, pp. 334-44

Department of Employment (1978a) 'Measures to Alleviate
Unemployment in the Medium Term: Early Retirement', Gazette,
86(3), 283-5

Department of Employment (1978b) 'Measures to Alleviate
Unemployment in the Medium Term: Work-Sharing', Gazette, 86,
(4), 400-402

European Industrial Relations Review (1983) 'Working Time in
the EEC: European Commission Memorandum on the Reduction and
Reorganization of Working Time', EIRR, 109, 28-31

ETUI (1979) Reduction of Working Time in Western Europe,
European Trade Union Institute, Brussels

Forester, T. (1980) (ed.) The Microelectronics Revolution,
Blackwell, Oxford

Gregory, R.G. (1982) Work and Welfare In the Years Ahead, Discussion Paper No. 47, Centre for Economic Policy Research, Australian National University, Canberra

House of Commons Social Services Committee (1982) Age of Retirement, HMSO, London

Incomes Data Services (1983a) International Report No. 185, p.4

Incomes Data Services (1983b) International Report, No. 193, 1-2

Incomes Data Services (1983c) International Report, No. 194, 1-2

Institute of Manpower Studies (1981) Work-Sharing Potential: An Examination of Selected Firms, IMS, Sussex

Jenkins, C. and Sherman, B. (1979) The Collapse of Work, Eyre Methuen, London

Joseph, G. (1983) Women at Work, Philip Allan, Oxford

Kotaro, T. (1980) 'The Effect of Reductions in Working Hours on Productivity' in S. Nishikawa (ed.) The Labour Market in Japan, University of Tokyo Press, Tokyo, pp.67-83

Leontief, W.W. (1982) 'The Distribution of Work and Income', Scientific American, 247(3), 152-164

McGoldrick, A. and Cooper, C.L. (1980) 'Voluntary Early Retirement - Taking the Decision', Employment Gazette, 88 (8), 859-864

Moylan, S. and Davies, B. (1980) 'The Disadvantages of the Unemployed' Employment Gazette, 88 (8), 830-832

Nickell, S.J. (1980) 'A Picture of Male Unemployment in Britain', Economic Journal, 90, 776-794

Olmstead, B. (1979) 'Job-Sharing: An Emerging Work-Style' International Labour Review, 118, 283-97

Robinson, A.L. (1980) 'Electronics and Employment: Displacement Effects', in T. Forester (ed.), The Microelectronics Revolution, Blackwell, Oxford, pp.318-33

Schlozman, K.L. and Verba, S. (1979) Injury to Insult: Unemployment, Class and Political Response, Harvard, Cambridge, Mass.

Stonier, T. (1980) 'The Impact of Microprocessors on Employment' in T. Forester (ed.), The Microelectronics Revolution, Blackwell, Oxford, pp. 303-7

TUC (1983) Campaign for Reduced Working Time, Progress Report No. 9, Trades Union Congress, London

Vater, K. (1980) The Conflict Over Working Hours, Inter Nationes, Bonn

Webb, S. and Webb, B. (1902) Industrial Democracy, Longman, London

Werneke, D. (1983) Microelectronics and Office Jobs, International Labour Office, Geneva

White, M. (1982) Shorter Working Time Through National Industry Agreements, Department of Employment, Research Paper No. 38, London

Whybrew, E.G. (1968) Overtime Working in Britain, Royal Commission on Trade Unions and Employers Associations, Research Paper No. 9, HMSO, London

PART III

MANAGEMENT IMPLICATIONS
IN INDUSTRIAL RELATIONS

Chapter 8

NEW TECHNOLOGY AND INDUSTRIAL RELATIONS: THEORETICAL AND
EMPIRICAL ISSUES

Michael Poole*

INTRODUCTION

It is almost impossible to understate the effects which the so-
called 'microelectronics' revolution is likely to have on
industrial relations in the years ahead.   In several
industries, its implications have already been manifested in
radical changes in the content of work, as well as in the
structure of decision-making and in labour practices generally.
Moreover, the advanced 'Silicon Valley' style companies may
well be prototypical of the types of management labour
practices which will emerge across a range of enterprises in
the future.   It is thus undoubtedly opportune for some of the
implications of the new technologies, for plant-level labour
relations, to be set out in a coherent and empirically informed
manner.
     In this paper, then, it is our aim to chart some of the
effects of microelectronics and other advanced technologies on
industrial relations.   The account begins by a theoretical
analysis of the role of technology in this sphere, with special
reference to on-going debates on the labour process and on the
use of technology as a form of administrative control.   A
prototypical case of the employment philosophies and labour
practices of a company in the 'Silicon Valley' (Santa Clara
Valley, California, USA) is then examined.   This forms the
prelude for a more detailed appraisal of the likely modes of
'human resource' management, trade union structure and
strategy, the role of women and minority ethnic groups and the
links between work and domestic roles and relationships
accompanying the rise of new information technologies.   In our
conclusions, the implications for control and autonomy,
conflict and the accommodation of interests, the levels and
styles of bargaining, and the possibility of collective
bargaining being replaced by other regulatory mechanisms in the
productive and distributive spheres are assessed.

* The author wishes to thank Professor Eliezer Rosenstein
  for his help in obtaining the data from the 'Silicon
  Valley' company, which are reported in this chapter.

THEORETICAL CONSIDERATIONS

Scholarly interest in the implications of technology for the evolution of modern societies and for the patterns of control, authority and administration in contemporary and future social orders, has a wide and impressive ancestry in the annals of the social sciences. Naturally, technology includes materials and knowledge as well as operations (Kmetz, 1978; Gerwin, 1979; Fry, 1982). Moreover, a typical classification would encompass mechanised manual, mechanised, integrated mechanised, automated, and integrated automated production (ILO, 1966). Again, while it is the last mentioned mode of technology with which we are particularly concerned here, it is necessary to say something at the outset about the implications of technological advance for industrial relations generally.

At its broadest level, the view that technology is related to an essential 'logic of industrialism', which produces a substantial measure of convergence between societies with different cultures, ideologies and politico-economic structures, is particularly associated with the work of Clark Kerr and his colleagues (1962). It should be emphasised, however, that in his most recent work, Kerr (1983a) has modified a number of the arguments contained in the original treatise. In The Future of Industrial Societies, Kerr thus notes several areas of comparability, increasing similarity and continuing substantial dissimilarity between 'capitalist' and 'socialist' societies. Areas of comparability include the utilisation of technology, utilisation of large-scale manufacturing enterprises and increased occupational and geographical mobility. Meanwhile, in his view, there is increasing similarity in such areas as the percentage of the population in agriculture, the percentage of adult women in the labour force and the percentage of the labour force in service and white-collar occupations. However, there are persistent, marked dissimilarities in ownership of property, the distribution of ultimate political power, the goals of the economic and political systems and in religious beliefs, national and ethnic identities, and so on. Nevertheless, the derivative proposition that the closer any activity is to the 'inner technological core' of a given society at a particular stage of development, the more likely it is for comparability or convergence to be manifest, remains essentially intact.

At a macro-social level, a concern over the impact of technology is, of course, particularly associated with Weber's (1968) view that value rationality has been increasingly destroyed by the narrow concerns of purposive rationality during the course of the twentieth century. Again, writers such as Friedmann (1962) and Ellul (1965) have also noted the pervasive characteristics of 'technical civilizations' with the latter noting an ever-expanding and 'irreversible' role of technique, in which there is a 'quest for continually improved means to carelessly examined ends', and a commensurate loss of quality in human life. More radically, too, Marcuse (1964) once noted the suppression of individual liberties and the close inter-twining of political power, technical organisation and mechan-ised processes as a primary cause of this state of affairs.

In the more focused industrial sociological and industrial relations literature, there have been two main departures which merit special attention. The first involves the classical con-tributions of the so-called 'technical implications' school and, the latter, the more radical accounts of the 'labour pro-cess'.

The Technical Implications School

To begin with, then, in classical industrial sociological lit-erature, a series of contributions involved relating the extent to which the technical organisation of work could have far-reaching implications for patterns of human organisation in the enterprise (Blauner, 1964; Woodward, 1965; Touraine, 1965). Many of the essential propositions were rather rudimentary, but the basic conception was that of a technical scale, which im-plied a gradual movement from craft forms of production, through various intermediary machine-tending and mass produc-tion types, to fully automated or process enterprises. More-over, in this view, there were likely to be profound con-sequences of this change for industrial relations. For Blauner (1964), in particular, in continuous process or fully-automated modes of technology the worker's sense of control over the immediate work process was restored and there was far more scope for self-fulfillment in such milieux, than in machine-tending and assembly-line technologies. The nature of work encouraged a scientific, technical orientation and the changing character of technology resulted in opportunities for learning and personal development for a considerable section of the blue-collar labour force. And, as a result, it was not un-reasonable to suppose that industrial relations would be far more harmonious than in the intermediary types of technological environment.

Such a view, however, has been challenged in more recent radical accounts of the labour process by industrial sociolog-ists and scholars of labour economics. This is not the context to enter in any great depth into the considerable literature on the so-called 'Braverman thesis', but certain essential points of the main arguments and developments should be presented. The thesis of Braverman (1974) has thus stimulated an extremely rich debate within industrial sociology (Nichols, 1977; Friedman, 1977; Brighton Labour Process Group, 1977; MacKenzie, 1977; Cutler, 1978; Elger, 1979; Littler and Salaman, 1982; Wood, 1982; Storey, 1983). Briefly, in Braverman's view, as a consequence of being geared to profit and not human needs, 'capitalism' not only engendered the progressive transformation in the nature of work in the twen-

tieth century (re-structuring of work organisations along
scientific management lines and later the application of
science to production), but also occasioned, in this process,
fundamental problems of control within the enterprise. These
were resolved by the 'degradation' of work, a continuing process of deskilling, which resulted in the removal of knowledge,
responsibility and discretion from working people in the actual
process of production, and their transfer to managerial and
supervisory employees. Braverman argued, too, that the same
process had occurred in the Soviet Union, because here the
state rather than individual employer had assumed the role of
capitalist agent (1974, pp.22-3).

Such a thesis has been criticised on a number of counts.
These include its determinism, its narrow conception of the
conflict between capital and labour as the source of managerial
control, its over-concern with consciously intended managerial
activity, its neglect of the varying types of managerial control, its weak theoretical foundations and its failure to
develop the realm of politics, ideology and consciousness
(Hill, 1981; Storey, 1983). These all suggest, too, the
possibility of substantial variations between societies in the
extent to which the 'degradation' of work in the twentieth century has eventuated.

The Labour Process: USA and Japan

However, many of the essential arguments of Braverman have been
echoed in the work of labour economists on the nature of labour
markets. Prior to the influential contribution of Doeringer
and Piore (1971), the original distinction between 'structure-
less' and 'structured' labour markets was closely associated
with the so-called 'California school' (see e.g. Kerr, (1983b)
for a review). Subsequently these categories have been refined
in the more complex notions of differentiation and labour market segmentation, associated with independent and subordinate
primary and secondary jobs respectively.

To illustrate the value of this type of analysis two key
examples have been chosen: the development of labour within
the United States and the Japanese pattern of segmentation. In
the first case we rely heavily on the recent work of Gordon
et al (1982) for whom the 'historical transformation of
American labour' reveals three main periods accompanying the
long-swings in the economy and technological change within the
enterprise. Initially, a period of proletarianisation between
the 1820s and 1830s and the late 19th century witnessed the
development of a wage system in an organisational milieu of
unstandardised work practices. This situation enabled many
workers to control their own labour processes and several
diverse internal systems of labour control to emerge (Gordon,
et al 1982, pp.13-14). The period of 'homogenisation of
labour' from the late 19th century to the 1920s and 1930s
closely matched the long-swings in the American economy and

was characterised by mechanisation, greater use of foremen to supervise workers, decreasing reliance on skilled labour, and the 'drive system'. Moreover, in the larger corporations increasing attention was paid to the personnel function and generally to greater employer control over the labour process and labour markets (Gordon et al 1982, pp.14-15).

The segmentation of American labour was largely a product of the Second World War and the post-war period, and arose during the rapid accumulation of capital in the most recent of the long-swings in the economy. A series of 'social and governmental' arrangements encouraged employer recognition of trade unions, grievance procedures and security rules for layoffs and promotions. Employers, in their turn, gained discretion over the organisation of work provided that they granted regular increases in wages. Above all, there was a separation of labour along two dimensions. The first involved the distinction between primary and secondary jobs that arose as a consequence of large corporations adopting structured internal systems of labour management. The second was reflected in new systems for generating and deploying skills, with craft methods being replaced by independent primary jobs (in which considerable employee autonomy was still evident), and subordinate primary jobs (in which discretion was largely circumscribed).

The saliency of segmented labour markets in understanding the differential life chances of members of the working population is also well demonstrated by the Japanese experience. Familiarly, in this milieu, there is a dual economic structure, a term which 'contrasts the large-scale firms which pay relatively high wages and have good working conditions to the mass of small and medium-sized enterprises, often family-owned, which subsidize the major enterprises' (Cole, 1971, p.37). By contrast with 'traditional' enterprises, the 'modern' firms are thus larger and employ more capital per worker. They are also more likely to have a bureaucratic corporate structure, a trade union and a formalised wage structure, to contract out work and to have research departments. In addition, they are liable to have higher labour productivity, higher wages and lower labour turnover (Dore, 1973, p.302). Above all, the 'modern' sector is characterised by permanent employment, a seniority-based wage and promotion system ('nenko') and welfare corporatism.

As Jacoby (1979) has pointed out, there are three main explanations for this pattern. The first focuses on the unique cultural heritage, and the second on specific human capital requirements of modern technologies. By contrast, the third involves a multivariate historical approach in which firm size and complexity, changes in skilled labour organisation, and an employers' strategy to forestall unionisation, are particularly relevant.

To begin with, then, the emergence and continued importance of permanent employment and the 'nenko' systems have been
frequently envisaged as a logical extension of unique cultural
traits and, more specifically, of the modified Confucian world
view which prevailed in pre-industrial Japan, and which
encouraged benevolent paternalism. Moreover, the absence of a
revolutionary change in employment practices between feudal and
contemporary periods is also frequently cited in this respect
(see e.g. Abegglen, 1958; Levine, 1958). However, this
argument is not entirely supported by the historical record
which indicates considerable labour mobility in the first two
decades of the twentieth century, and hence the absence of an
effective permanent employment system up until the end of the
First World War. Hence, a further proposition which has gained
considerable currency involves tracing the growth of the
permanent employment system to firm size and technological
complexity, which made workers' skills increasingly enterprise
specific (Doeringer and Piore, 1971; Sumiya, 1977). But again
such a view is difficult to substantiate on historical grounds
since, as Jacoby (1979, p.189) has noted, 'it is not at all
certain that machinery or technology was becoming more
enterprise-specific at the time of the formation of internal
labour markets in Japan'.
    In a multi-causal explanation of the origins of the dual
labour market in Japan, then, although culture and growing size
of enterprise and technological complexity are regarded as important variables, emphasis is also placed on the concern of
employers to limit the powers of a form of independent skilled
labour organisation. This was accomplished with the emergence
of capital-intensive oligopolistic forms of enterprise by the
use of firm-specific training, and universalistic personnel
practices. This analysis, too, as we have noted, closely parallels the arguments propounded by Braverman (1974) in the case
of the USA.
    Moreover, whatever the correct explanation, there is no
doubt that dual-labour market theorists (alongside analysts of
the labour process) have placed considerable importance on the
role of technology in shaping labour relations practices. It
is now necessary to examine a number of empirical issues which
bear upon these debates of considerable theoretical moment.

EMPIRICAL THEMES (1) A CASE STUDY

So far, then, we have seen that the theoretical literature on
the role of technology in shaping different aspects of industrial relations is extensive, and has been the focal point for
substantial controversy and keenly fought intellectual debates.
However, attempts to use empirical data to test some of the
most interesting derivative arguments and hypotheses have been
remarkably limited. Of course, we cannot attempt here other
than a brief indication of likely tendencies, but it is worth

(a) highlighting a number of salient issues by means of a case study; and (b) drawing more generally on empirically-informed literature to evaluate some of the more far-reaching consequences of technological change.

The case study is used to address the following points. Do advanced prototypical companies still maintain a commitment to profitability and consumer interests as a result of operating in a market economy, or do other considerations (e.g. long-term growth, managerialism, and so on) weigh increasingly heavily in corporate philosophies? To what extent are employees in advanced enterprises regarded as 'human resources' of considerable importance to the survival and development of enterprises and, consistent with the 'segmented labour' hypothesis, encouraged to remain in the company by a variety of advanced personnel techniques? Are opportunities for personal growth and development of individuals encouraged and to what extent are 'quality of work-life' programmes initiated and fostered? To what extent is responsible autonomy encouraged? More specifically (and crucially in so far as radical accounts of the labour process are concerned) to what extent is control 'stripped away' from individual employees and vested either in central management or in bureaucratic structures of administration? Again, do the policies of management in these respects reflect either R-strategies (moving quickly to exploit resources and encouraging considerable enterprise autonomy and decision-making flexibility) or less flexible K-strategies (designed to compete successfully in densely settled environments) (Brittain and Freeman, 1980). These distinctions, too, it should be mentioned, parallel but are by no means identical with the early Burns and Stalker (1961) work on organic versus mechanistic structures of management decision-making. And, perhaps most crucial of all, in so far as industrial relations are concerned, to what extent do managements in advanced companies prefer to operate on the basis of a 'human resourcing' employee-centred style of decision-making, in which there is no room whatsoever for the intervention of wider representative channels (and notably, of course, for trade unions)?

A Case Study: The Silicon Co

The company which forms the basis of our case study was founded in 1969, to produce general purpose computers that could withstand the severe, rugged environments encountered in military applications. Currently, Silicon Co's products are aboard most ships in the US Navy, most planes in the US Air Force and a variety of Army vehicles. The philosophy of the company is that its most important asset is its employees and a primary objective is to 'challenge employees so that they can achieve maximum job satisfaction'. It endorses equal employment opportunities and affirmative action. It encourages employees with problems to use in-house grievance channels (via supervisors and the personnel department). And it embodies a wide range of 'Japanese-style' integration policies including profit sharing, subsidised cafeteria, discount cards, assistance for employee financial needs for colleges, universities 'and other institutions of learning', petty cash vouchers, employee assistance programmes (covering drinking problems, narcotics problems, marriage counselling, financial counselling, legal aid, depression/anxiety/suicide, day care centres), and a host of other related practices.

On a more general level, as the following data indicate, the company appears also to endorse the policies below, which are illustrated with quotations from the company.

1. A major commitment to profitability, which is seen as basic to (rather than as an alternative to) long term company interest or managerial control: 'A primary reason for the existence of most businesses in our economic society is to make a profit. Making a profit is necessary to finance the business intelligently. On a continuous basis we need additional funds for doing research and development, expanding facilities, upgrading equipment, maintaining inventories, and strengthening sales and service channels. Silicon Co profits, with the exception of those distributed in our employee profit-sharing plans, have always been totally reinvested in the business. Further, making a profit is necessary to have the flexibility to make the correct long term decisions for the company. A consistent profit advance provides a secure basis for thoughtful examination of future possibilities. Undue profit pressure forces an environment in which decisions may be made with poor planning and a short-term view'.

2. A long term commitment to growth based on a high level of profitability and the personal growth and development of each individual employee: 'A company can compete successfully with others only if it grows. Further, the ultimate reward for our stockholders' investment is profitable growth. At Silicon Co we recognise two other major reasons for steady, planned growth. First, there is a strategic reason. Silicon Co competes against the giants of the computer and telecommunications industries. Success in this competition is marked by gaining market share from companies that are less responsive and creative. We must grow to supply these large markets in which we choose to operate. Secondly, there is a basic human reason for corporate growth. The environment that we continue to create at Silicon Co is one of expanding opportunity and challenge for our people. The opportunity for the growth of each individual is dependent upon the healthy growth of Silicon Co Corporation. Conversely, the growth of Silicon Co Corporation is dependent upon the growth of each individual'.

3. A high level of concern for consumer or customer interests: 'Silicon Co has a single basic reason for being in existence: to provide the finest quality products and customer support. We have been and will continue to be distinguished by

our excellent products and our efficient customer support. The goods that go out our back door - our products, our hardware - are conceived and manufactured to be of the highest possible quality. Silicon Co customers are led to expect the finest. Silicon Co people are committed to delivering the finest. However, our products are only a portion of the total quality Silicon Co offers. We are also committed to providing the best customer support in the industry. This includes: meeting customer needs quickly, interacting with customers professionally, focussing on uptime, and offering a complete range of services. In this manner, we strive to earn the loyalty of our customers'.

4. A commitment to advanced 'human resourcing' techniques and 'quality of work-life' programmes: 'The first three goals of Silicon Co are shared by many companies throughout the world. The fourth, "To Create a Great Place to Work" is rare. We know of no other organization that makes this one of its basic goals. We do this quite simply because we want to attract and motivate the best and brightest people we can. In order to attract and motivate the best and brightest people Silicon Co promotes a humane and challenging work environment, a very competitive compensation and benefits plan, and physical surroundings befitting the qualities of Silicon Co people.

The humanity and challenge of the Silicon Co work environment is predicated on a dual responsibility. Silicon Co Corporation acts to provide equal opportunity to grow and be promoted; fair treatment for each individual; respect for personal privacy; encouragement to succeed; opportunity for creativity; evaluation based on job performance in the context of Silicon Co philosophy. Silicon Co people are expected to respond by being individually accountable; being helpful toward others to enhance teamwork; performing to the best of his/her abilities; and understanding and implementing the Silicon Co philosophy'.

5. Commitment to an organic rather than mechanistic structure of decision-making and, arguably, rather more to R than to K strategies:

(a) Attributes of success for all Silicon Co. People:

    '. Avoid bureaucracy; keep practices simple, but make sure they are communicated, understood, and effective.

    . Freely communicate ideas and suggestions.

    . Show initiative to assure you understand the performance expectations of your job.

    . Avoid "finger pointing". When you see a stalemate, encourage discussion to get the problem solved.

    . Discourage rumors by communicating facts upwards, downwards, and sideways throughout the company.

    . Use written communications when it makes sense

to do so. Recognise the value of face-to-face
communication.
. Focus on substance;   it is always more important
than form.
. Take a large view of your job; do whatever it
takes to make your tasks succeed whether or not
it is part of your "job".
. Focus on the important issues; let the
inconsequential slip.
. Build teamwork inside and outside your work
group; it avoids the need for bureaucracy.
. Fix problems as we grow; don't stop growing
to fix problems. Don't fix things that aren't
broken; try to anticipate things that may
become broken.
. Set personally challenging and difficult goals
that support departmental and Corporate
objectives.'
(b) Additional Attributes of Success for Silicon Co Managers:
' . Level with people. Communicate your expectations –
encourage honest response.
. Get decisions made as close to the action as
possible; don't second-guess them unless you
have good reasons which you communicate. Let
people plan and control as much of their own
work as possible.
. Assume that people understand job performance
expectations; then encourage their individual
initiative to expand.
. Promote from within whenever feasible; seriously
consider Silicon Co people if they want promotion.
. Identify and create an environment that motivates
all Silicon Co people.
. Maintain equal opportunity and affirmative action
practices that meet the spirit as well as the
letter of the law. Assist individuals to compete
and succeed and reward them on the basis of merit.
. Recognise individual accomplishment in and out of
your immediate work sphere. Praise in public;
criticize in private. Don't point to third
parties to rationalize your failures.
. Help Silicon Co people build their self-image;
treat them as individuals.
. Assure that people are paid fairly considering
the labour market, internal equity, and individual
worth to the Corporation; then give merit
increases only.
. Communicate praise to individuals in the group;
buffer them from group criticism; make sure they
are aware of any real short-comings.
. Give salary and performance reviews on time.

. Use written PPGs to document practices, policies
and guidelines for routine tasks critical to
the smooth functioning of the organisation.   If
PPGs don't reflect reality, rewrite them.
. Follow important projects and take continual correc-
tive action, if necessary, to keep them on track.
. Manage by walking around. Recognise potential
problem areas before they become major.
. Encourage each individual to develop his/her
skills for career advancement.'

6. A pronounced adherence to a 'unitary' rather than
'pluralist' conception of the organisation: 'One of the
reasons we are a successful organization is because we are an
employee-oriented as well as customer-oriented company. All of
us at Silicon Co strongly believe that:

1. Work should be a challenging, stimulating
and enjoyable experience.
2. Everyone contributing to our success should
be able to grow, lead and be financially
rewarded.
3. The workplace should be pleasant, convenient,
attractive and safe.
4. We should have an environment where every
employee can enhance their self-image.

Because we have these philosophies, have followed them in the
past, and intend to follow them in the future, we do not need
third parties (unions) to change these ideas. We believe that
a union would be of no advantage to you. On the contrary we
believe unions are likely to cause artificial tensions and work
interruptions that could cause all of us to defocus from our
objectives of making Silicon Co a great place for work while we
are satisfying our customer's needs'.

EMPIRICAL THEMES (2) SOME GENERAL IMPLICATIONS OF THE NEW TECH-
NOLOGY

To what extent such philosophies have been fully implemented is
difficult to determine with precision.   But there are good
grounds for supposing that an employee-centred but anti-union
philosophy is likely to feature increasingly prominently in
managerial strategies for labour relations in the years ahead,
and that this applies particularly in advanced, 'prototypical',
'Silicon Valley'-style companies. A rather different set of
issues are involved in the question of what happens within
existing organisations as a result of the application of information technologies.   In this section, then, some broader
questions involved in the implications of new technologies for
current patterns of industrial relations are considered.
There is a broad-ranging literature in which the effects

of microelectronics on industrial relations have been charted (see e.g. Forester, 1980; Martin, 1981; Warner, 1982; Hunt and Hunt, 1983; Wilkinson, 1983; Sorge et al 1983) and it is only possible to address some of the most salient issues here in the following form:

1. The effects of microelectronics are likely to be fundamental in terms of the structure of employment, the nature of jobs and quality of working life and on socio-economic institutions and practices generally.

2. In so far as the changes in employment are concerned, in manufacturing there is likely to be increased employment in design and development, and sales and maintenance, with fewer opportunities in the production of final goods and parts. More generally, too, there will be a shift from non-information to information occupations (e.g. managers, scientists and computer analysts) (OECD, 1981).

3. Nevertheless, the overall employment effects of such a change have not been agreed upon amongst leading commentators. At one extreme, Jenkins and Sherman have argued that:

'remain as we are, reject the new technologies and we face unemployment of up to 5.5 million by the end of the century. Embrace the new technology, accept the challenge and we end up with unemployment of about 5 million'. (Jenkins and Sherman, 1979, p.113)

Yet, in other accounts, it has been observed that high technology industries create more employment opportunities than low technology industries, while the supporting infrastructure of education, training and re-training which is required results in an expansion of jobs in the 'knowledge field' (OECD, 1981).

4. Eventually the computer-integrated automated factory and the automated office will be realised although this may not be evident in Britain in ten years time. But while a certain amount of decentralisation of control is occasioned by the new technology, the predominant impact of microprocessor electronic digital technology is to reduce discretion in work functions and to increase centralisation. As the OECD report points out: although the interest of the work may be enhanced, so also is stress and possibly alienation from work. Hence, even though the new technologies will contribute to greater abundance, they will not create equity in themselves (OECD, 1981, p.269).

5. Indeed, in so far as the quality of working life is concerned, jobs will become increasingly demanding mentally, but less demanding physically. Again, there are strong prospects that employment will increase for professional and skilled workers, but that other types of occupation will be deskilled, made more routine and even, as we have observed, eliminated entirely. This may create an increasing polarisation in work between the qualified and unqualified and the educated and less-educated as opposed to the skilled and unskilled in a con-

ventional sense.

6. The effects of these changes in the trade unions are
also very interesting, since clearly the trend towards white-
collar, professional and managerial unionism at the expense of
trade unionism amongst traditional manual workers can only be
further exacerbated. The official view of the Trade Union Advisory Committee to the OECD is that trade union participation
should be encouraged in the formative stages of decision-making
in this context at enterprise, industry, national and international levels; that the growth of the electronic sectors
should be 'planned, balanced and accountable'; that corresponding policies of qualitative and quantitative growth (especially in the service sector) should be pursued; that increased
leisure and reduced working time should be logical accompani-
ments of this movement; and that rapid adjustments in the
labour market (especially in training and retraining) should be
a major objective. (OECD, 1981, p.272). Similarly, as part of
the day-to-day consultative process, it has been suggested that
employees should elect special representatives ('data shop
stewards') to represent them in the processes of
decision-making.

7. With respect to the employment opportunities for women
(and, by extension, for minority ethnic groups), although in
some types of production occasioned by the new technology the
dominant group will be female, at the same time, it has been
observed that some of the jobs most at risk from the microelectronic revolution are now largely performed by women.
Hence, drawing on Australian data, Smith has noted that over 50
per cent of the female workforce is 'employed in occupations
that are in risk of significant labour displacement' as opposed
to only 25 per cent of the male workforce. Hence it may well
be the case that 'women will disproportionately bear the burden
of job displacement imposed by the widespread adoption of the
new technology'. (Smith, 1981, p.241).

8. It is vitally important, however, not to view the
effects of technology in a deterministic fashion, but rather to
acknowledge the centrality of 'human agency' and social choice
in the patterns which develop (cf. Loveridge and Mok, 1979).
Of relevance, too, are a series of subjective satisfactions and
discontents that are 'anchored in changes in family composi-
tion, consumption pressures, job patterns, income flows, and
debt loads as they interact and vary over the life cycle'
(Wilensky, 1981, p.261). In other words the individual's
reaction to technological change may well depend on a series of
wider circumstances linked with life-cycle stresses. These are
particularly acute at transition stages (e.g. at the birth of
the first child, particularly if this is associated with the
wife leaving gainful employment).

CONCLUSIONS

But what, it may be reasonably asked, are the implications of the foregoing analysis for such central industrial relations themes as: (a) control and autonomy in a work environment; (b) conflict and the accommodation of interests; (c) the levels and styles of bargaining; and (d) the possibility of collective bargaining being replaced by other regulatory mechanisms in the productive and distributive spheres?

To begin with, then, in so far as control and autonomy are concerned, it seems unlikely that any one long trend can be easily identified. Rather, it would appear that divergent groups are likely to be affected very differently by the advent of new technologies. Many routine jobs will almost certainly be deskilled further and some eliminated entirely. But in the independent primary sector of the labour market, considerable autonomy and on-the-job control is likely to be exercised by individual employees. Moreover, as our case-study from a 'Silicon Valley' company revealed, this group is likely to be the beneficiary of a major 'human resourcing' drive by management to persuade such employees to contribute fully to, and to remain in, any given employing enterprise.

Turning to conflict and the accommodation of interests, a great deal here would appear to depend on wider labour market conditions, rates of inflation, and so on (cf. Crouch and Pizzorno, 1977a; 1977b), and to seek some 'technologically-determinist' explanation for developments in this area is unlikely to be fruitful. However, insofar as technological change is linked with fundamental changes in the patterns of control then this could be a source of some very intensive struggles for 'job rights' (cf. Edwards, 1981; Martin, 1981), and this is especially so when a series of longstanding craft practices are being substantially undermined.

Managerial 'human resourcing' strategies are also entirely consistent with a trend towards corporate or plant level bargaining at the expense of negotiations at a national or regional level. Hence, in so far as managements of 'prototypical' companies are prepared to deal with labour organisations at all, the trends which have been witnessed towards plant-level and company bargaining in the post-war years (cf. Brown, 1981) can only be intensified by his process. Moreover, given the weakening of trade unions by adverse labour market conditions, it is only really a change in state or governmental policy (to encourage centralised bargaining) that could be expected to offset the pronounced preference of managements for developing 'in-house' procedures for bargaining and for the settlement of disputes.

It is worth speculating finally on whether we are likely to witness a movement away from the institutions of collective bargaining to either managerial paternalism (or, in some circumstances, authoritarianism) or, more especially, to a participative structure of decision-making. Indeed, in countries such as the USA in which trade union density is now well below 20 per cent of the employed population, it must be emphasised that collective bargaining is no longer the principal means for reaching agreements either in the production or distributive spheres. Moreover, the primary deficiency of collective bargaining has always been that the distribution of power and the willingness to pursue 'brinkmanship' tactics becomes decisive in the rewards which accrue to different sections of the workforce, and between the workforce and employers and managerial personnel (cf. Poole et al, 1984). This ensures that the positive forces for creativity become vitiated in the continuing struggle for control, which oscillates from one group to another, but has no final resting place. It is at the heart of the economic and industrial problems of a country like Britain and, while on a temporary basis, management paternalism or authoritarianism may be increasingly manifest, this state of affairs is likely to continue until new types of work relationships are fashioned, based on the full-hearted consent of the workforce via the systematic sharing of gain, knowledge and power, on the basis of some agreed principles of social justice. More practically, too, this must find its expression in a comprehensive programme of industrial democracy based on employees and working people, with union officers and shop stewards (in countries with high union densities, at least) becoming the essential supports rather than focal points of any emergent framework. But whether or not such a goal will be achieved, or whether (particularly in Britain) a worsening of industrial relations accompanying technical change becomes the dominant theme of the next ten years, will depend a great deal on a series of strategic choices by governments, employers and managers, trade unionists and working people. After all, the future of industrial relations is not a series of fixed events following an inevitable path governed by an 'iron law' of technical determinism, but rather consists of a variety of types of human adaptation to predictable and unpredictable changes in the environment and reflects, in substantial measure, the values of strategically-placed decision makers among the principal groups concerned.

REFERENCES

Abegglen, J.C. (1958) The Japanese Factory, Free Press, Glencoe, Illinois

Blauner, R. (1964) Alienation and Freedom, University of Chicago Press, Chicago

Braverman, H. (1974) Labor and Monopoly Capital, Monthly Review Press, New York

Brighton Labour Process Group (1977) 'The Capitalist Labour Process', Capital and Class, 1, 3-42

Brittain J.W. and Freeman, J.H. (1981) Organization Proliferation and Density Dependent Selection, Reprint No. 441, Institute of Industrial Relations, University of California, Berkeley

Brown, W. (ed.) (1981) The Changing Contours of British Industrial Relations, Blackwell, Oxford

Cole, R.E. (1971) Japanese Blue Collar, University of California Press, Berkeley

Crouch, C. and Pizzorno, A. (eds.) (1978a) (1978b) The Resurgence of Class Conflict in Western Europe Since 1968, Vols. 1 and 2, MacMillan, London

Cutler, A. (1978) 'The Romance of Labour', Economy and Society, 7, 74-95

Doeringer, P. and Piore, M. (1971) Internal Labor Markets and Manpower Analysis, Heath, Lexington

Dore, R.P. (1973) British Factory-Japanese Factory, Allen and Unwin, London

Edwards, P.K. (1981) Strikes in the United States, Blackwell, Oxford

Ellul, J. (1965) The Technological Society, Cape, London

Forester, T. (ed.) (1980) The Microelectronics Revolution, MIT Press, Cambridge, Mass.

Friedman, A.L. (1977) Industry and Labour, MacMillan, London

Friedmann, G. (1962) The Anatomy of Work, Free Press, New York

Fry, L.W. (1982) 'Technology-Structure Research: Three Critical Issues', Academy of Management Journal, 25, 532-52

Gerwin, D. (1979) 'The Comparative Analysis of Structure and Technology: A Critical Appraisal', Academy of Management Review, 4, 41-51

Gordon, R., Edwards, R. and Reich, M. (1982) Labour Market Segmentation in American Capitalism, Cambridge University Press, Cambridge

Hill, S. (1981) Competition and Control at Work, Heinemann, London

Hunt, H.A. and Hunt, T.L. (1983) Human Resource Implications of Robotics, Upjohn Institute for Employment Research, Kalamazoo, W.E.

International Labour Office (1966) Technological Change and Manpower in a Centrally Planned Economy, Labour and Automation Bulletin No. 3, Geneva

Jacoby, S.M. (1979) 'The Origins of Internal Labor Markets in Japan', Industrial Relations, 18, 184-96

Jenkins, C. and Sherman, B. (1979) The Collapse of Work, Eyre Methuen, London

Kerr, C. (1983a) The Future of Industrial Societies, Harvard University Press, Cambridge, Mass.

Kerr, C. (1983b) 'The Intellectual Role of Neorealists in Labor Economics', Industrial Relations, 22, 298-318

Kerr, C., Dunlop, J.T., Harbison, F.H. and Myers, C.A. (1962) Industrialism and Industrial Man, Heinemann, London

Levine, S.B. (1958) Industrial Relations in Post War Japan, University of Illinois Press, Urbana, Illinois

Littler, C. and Salaman, G. (1982) 'Braverman and Beyond', Sociology, 16, 251-69

Loveridge, R. and Mok, A.L. (1979) Theories of Labour Market Segmentation, Martinus Nighoff, The Hague

MacKenzie, G. (1977) 'The Political Economy of the American Working Class', British Journal of Sociology, 28, 244-52

Marcuse, H. (1964) One Dimensional Man, Sphere Books, London

Martin, R. (1981) New Technology and Industrial Relations in

Fleet Street, Clarendon Press, Oxford

Nichols, T. (1977) 'Labor and Monopoly Capital', Sociological Review, 25, 192-4

OECD (1981) Micro-electronics, Productivity and Employment, Organization for Economic Cooperation and Development, Paris

Poole, M.J.F., Brown, W., Sisson, K. Rubery, J., Tarling, R. and Wilkinson, F. (1984) The Future of Industrial Relations, Routledge and Kegan Paul, London

Smith, J.S. (1981) 'Implications of Developments in Micro-Electronics Technology on Women in the Paid Workforce', in OECD, Micro-Electronics, Productivity and Employment, OECD, Paris

Sorge, A., Hartmann, G., Warner, M. and Nichols, I.J. (1983) Micro-electronics and Manpower in Manufacturing, Gower, Aldershot

Storey, J. (1983) Managerial Prerogative and the Question of Control, Routledge and Kegan Paul, London

Sumiya, M. (1977) 'Japanese Industrial Relations Revisited', Japanese Economic Studies, 5, 3-65

Touraine, A. (ed.) (1965) Workers' Attitudes to Technical Change, OECD, Paris

Warner, M. (1982) 'New Technology, Work Organizations and Industrial Democracy', Paper to I.D.E. Group Meeting, Free University of Amsterdam

Weber, M. (1968) Economy and Society, Bedminster Press, New York

Wilensky, H. (1981) 'Family Life Cycle, Work and the Quality of Life', Reprint No. 442, Institute of Industrial Relations, University of California, Berkeley

Wilkinson, B. (1983) The Shopfloor Politics of New Technology, Heinemann, London

Wilkinson, F. (1981), The Dynamics of Labour Market Segmentation, Academic Press, London

Woods, S. (ed) (1982) The Degradation of Work, Hutchinson, London

Woodward, J. (1965) Industrial Organization: Theory and Practice, Oxford University Press, London

Chapter 9

THE IMPACT OF NEW TECHNOLOGY ON
PARTICIPATIVE INSTITUTIONS AND
EMPLOYEE INVOLVEMENT

Malcolm Warner

INTRODUCTION

An early attempt to examine the impact of computers on democracy was published at a time of student and industrial turbulence at the end of the 1960s. In that paper, Bodington (1968,
pp.104-113) argued that:

> 'The key question about computers is how are they to be
> turned to the advantage of the community or, to put the
> same point in a more political and more realistic way -
> "How are socialists to use computers?" By this I do not
> mean what role will be assigned to computers in blue
> prints for some planned Utopia of the future. I mean what
> should socialists be doing about computers beginning from
> here now.' (1968, p.107)

It is clear that such problems do not loom large in most
management text-books! And yet, that short paper raised a number of major issues of control over 'the information revolution' which need further examination.
Bodington (1968) went on to discuss the ways in which
'routine control of productive operations' could be taken over
by the computer, namely, automation, and how models could be
created for 'almost any of the "systems" out of which our
complex society' is constituted. He goes on to argue that
democratic control of productive activities could be simulated
to show how alternative plans could be made and discussed
between the chief executive and his elected works council.
The author thought he was being a little 'Utopian' - and he was
- for little has yet emerged, in practice, from this scenario.
Taking into account recent trends this paper will specifically
examine the potential impact of the advanced technology, which
is now very much with us, on existing participative
institutions and practices. It takes as its point of departure
such existing bodies as works councils or equivalent
representative organs and looks at how microelectronics will

affect them, and the implications for employee involvement.
This procedure develops issues raised by an earlier paper
(Warner, 1982) which examined the impact of new technology on
industrial democracy.

We argued there that the more the new technology spreads,
the more firms will resemble existing service sector organisations. This will mean that with greater computerisation and
automation, there will be greater numbers of employees with
higher education, skill and technical-training levels.   We
also asked whether there are greater chances for
decentralisation of decision-making, and/or greater involvement
of employees in this process. We tentatively concluded that
the effects of technology on industrial democracy are
relatively indeterminate, given that new technology may permit
a range of organisational and manpower solutions.

THE IMPACT OF NEW TECHNOLOGY ON WORK ORGANISATIONS

The impact of computers on organisational decision-making must
be still seen as problematic. Some writers have, of course,
taken a deterministic point of view, and argued that technology
inevitably pushes organisations in an unambiguous direction.
One version of this view is that the computer merely reinforces
conventional decision-making structures by making them more
centralised.   Another less deterministic view might argue that
the new technology is neutral in its effects. Finally, some
might argue it basically decentralises and devolves authority,
which is a view I would basically subscribe to.

> 'Current computer technology has enormous potentials for
> the integration of systems and subsystems. This is prob-
> ably one of the factors that make us label it "new techno-
> logy" and speak of a new industrial revolution. It is to
> be anticipated that the computer will impose its logic on
> the organisation.
>
> The computer is a very formalized tool. When the computer
> is used in various functions and processes, it requires
> considerable (pre)programming: "what", "when", "who",
> etc., have to be decided in advance... It can therefore
> be expected that the degree of preprogramming will
> increase with more extensive use of computer-based infor-
> mation systems.' (Hennestad, 1983)

This development would, according to this line of argument, affect the autonomy and discretion of the worker and his
unit. Jobs in which skill and reflection were previously
needed and decisions had to be made, would become preplanned,
or programmed. Planning activities would be separated from
operating tasks and thus from the work role. They would then
be carried out by specialists from planning and programming

departments.   If this trend continued, skills would be programmed and become part of the technology (Braverman, 1974).
From something that gave the worker his identity, 'skill is
transformed into reified knowledge that, as part of technology,
manipulates the worker.' (Hennestad, 1983, p.56).

On the other hand, findings derived from a cross-national
study carried out by the present writer (with colleagues at
Henley, and Berlin) on microelectronics and manpower in manufacturing, have pointed in the opposite direction (see Sorge et
al, 1983).   The study, which looked at the effects of Computer
Numerically Controlled (CNC) machine-tools on organisational,
and related manpower variables, such as personnel, training and
industrial relations, found that deskilling was not necessarily
determined by the change in the technology and that the
introduction of CNC did not necessarily lead to the negative
consequences described by Hennestad (1983).   While we did not
look at employee participation and industrial democracy per se,
we found relatively indeterminate organisational consequences.
For example, the presence of institutionalised norms in West
Germany did not, in the cases studied, lead to the works
council (where indeed there was one) necessarily becoming
involved in decisions to introduce new technology;   nor did the
absence of such norms in the UK necessarily exclude worker
influence.   Even the trade unions did not take a position
positively or negatively, although they usually regard
technological progress 'as a good thing'.

The impact on industrial democracy is not easily ascer-
tained, as pointed out elsewhere.   There are different consequences which result from more decentralisation, or conversely
greater centralisation.   It depends on where the representative
bodies in the firm are situated.   If more decisions are pushed
upwards, the role of worker directors becomes more important;
if they are pushed downwards, the role of the works council,
for example, may become more significant.

The previous research cited strengthens the view that new
technology may de facto decentralise both decision-making and
skill profiles, even if it does lead to a reduced work-force.
The degree to which this occurs may vary with the rate of technological innovation.   Incremental changes in technology may
not have immediately noticeable effects, but more widespread
innovations may lead to readily discernible changes.   The
effect of microprocessors in the workplace is already extensive, and it is clear that the faster the rate of technological
change, the greater the need for organisationally adaptive
mechanisms will be.   If new technology is introduced into
firms which do not adopt new structures, then the costs of
implementation may be high and the benefits diminished.   Organisations which have participative mechanisms may have fewer
problems of initial acceptance of new technological developments than those which do not, or which have fewer.   The faster
the rate of technological change, the greater the need for

consensus–generating mechanisms within organisations, not only within the managerial strata but between the 'top', and 'bottom', of the decision–making structure. There needs to be not only sharing of information, but also ways of co-determination of technology strategy as well as the tactics of implementation.

DISTINGUISHING BETWEEN ENDS AND MEANS

We can possibly distinguish between participation in decision-making concerning: first, the introduction of the new technology as such, and second, the implementation of non-technological changes but where the new technology is a means to bring about such a change. In practice, it may be difficult to distinguish between ends and means. Further, the new technology may help in how firms go about introducing new systems. At the moment, the problematic decision issues facing workers' representatives relate to the introduction of new information technology. Once EDP becomes the norm, it may at the same time become the means of greater participative decision-making. Rather than arguing that technology puts constraints on worker autonomy, it may be the case that it potentially enhances it. Direct personnel supervision may be diminished, and access to information enlarged in the course of carrying out the set of daily tasks.

Hennestad concedes that decentralisation is a possibility, which is 'primarily of management policy' (1983, p. 64). If the total amount of information in the company increases, distribution may not be even; yet it can also be said that access to it may be more widely diffused by the new technology. The ways by which workers' councils and representatives on supervisory boards will cope with such information is an open question.

THE EFFECT OF PARTICIPATIVE INSTITUTIONS

If more new technology thus offers greater possibilities of greater decentralisation, how will our existing participative institutions be affected? If we examine this problem at the works council level (or its equivalent), we find that such a body may have need of on-line access to company operational data via ▸DUs, when they are conducting their deliberations, as well as prior access to data from minis, micros, or main-frame set-ups for print-outs of say, personnel information relating to the problem in hand.

Members of works councils, in the course of their daily duties on-the-job, may also require greater access to data compared with what has previously been the case. The same will also be true of worker directors. They may also need privileged access to restricted files; hence needing special 'passwords' giving access to data-sources blocked to the bulk of employees. This points to the need for special training for workers' representatives vis-a-vis information systems, if they do not already have this in the course of their daily work. The more this is preponderant in the workforce, the less the need for special training. In many industries, an increasing percentage of the employees will occupy technical, white-collar or managerial roles and hence may be better motivated and indeed educationally equipped to participate in decision-making via the new technology.

A further level of participation concerns the so-called 'data-stewards', whose role on the shopfloor is to monitor the introduction of new technology. The need for training here will be greater, and will depend on the general training philosophy operative. If deskilling is positively discouraged, and craftsmens' skills developed to use the new technology, the general level of ability and preparation will be greater for potential participation.

A novel characteristic of new technology will be its ability to create participative systems in so far as all levels in the organisation will be able to interact with others in networks and thus instant feedback may be facilitated (at least theoretically). There is clear potential for better two-way communication, consultation and even co-determination both directly and indirectly. The individual will be able to be involved directly, or his representative's access to the system will be facilitated. This scenario is, of course, only a potential, and is as yet only hypothetical: it will not happen overnight, but the possibilities are there!

If a system is created, various participative subunits could be on-line with each other. Theoretically, the worker directors on the supervisory board could have direct access to their 'constituency' whilst representing the latter, or they could be on-line to works councillors and shop-stewards. Parity of access to such two-way systems should be the goal of workers' representatives, vis-a-vis the data privileges of management. Whether such parity will be easily achieved is another matter, and one suspects it will only come about, if at all, after hard bargaining in organisations which might concede it.

Such access could cross plant or even company boundaries, in the last analysis even crossing national frontiers. Even if corporate consent were not forthcoming, public lines of data transmission could be used.

In so far as VDUs are relatively silent, communication between participative sub-units in the middle of meetings would be unobtrusive and could be on-going. However, the advantages to the workers' representatives could be counterbalanced by those available to management, as speedier communication between each side's spokespersons between plants, companies and other groupings could lead to information flows consolidating the bargaining potential of the respective sides. Computers

have already been used by both sides in labour-management negotiation in the United States.

The reduction in the cost of data processing systems would
probably be to the relative advantage of the side with less
command over resources, and hence be a power-equilibrating
mechanism. Bodington has pointed out that:

> 'Democratic social application of computers such as that
> suggested above implies that massive information will be
> freely available. This points immediately to an important
> political issue. The stock-in-trade of privilege and
> class power is restricted information..... Rapid analysis
> of massive information can, under certain circumstances,
> be a powerful instrument of control and domination by
> small select groups ruling over others, but the same
> technological facilities can provide instruments of
> democratisation and effective continuous participation in
> decision-making. Which way things go is the political
> issue that has to be fought and this is the issue here and
> now.' (Bodington, 1968)

A fear of many concerned observers is that the information
revolution will create major imbalances of access to
information, both in organisations and society. If this were
the case, it might lead to greater oligarchic control over
information in major institutions, both private and public.
If, on the other hand, information became less difficult to
'hoard' because of system openness in networks, then the social
implications are clear. It may be difficult to control and
restrict information in multi-access networks, based on linked
micro computers.

New communication technology could therefore be intrinsi-
cally more 'democratic', as it would potentially enhance the
greatest influence of the greatest numbers, to paraphrase
Bentham. The slogan might then be 'Computing Power to the
People!'. In a way, this parallels an earlier technological
development, namely the printing press which, by reducing
communication costs, increased the potential for democratic
practices. Greater democracy could result from the new
technology via greater access to information within
organisations, both for employees and their representatives, as
well as for management. An ultimate goal, of course, would be
as much disclosure of all corporate information to such
representatives as feasible, subject to constraints of
organisational confidentiality and commercial secrecy.
Nonetheless, access to personnel information, now increasingly
computerised, would be a good place to start.

Elections for worker directors and works councillors could
also take place electronically in the workplace, as indeed
could (hypothetically) contests for union office. This practice could supplement other forms of voting, could be secret

(with the use of a suitable security code), and potentially increase rates of participation and 'turnout'. Endorsements on a frequent basis could be inexpensively carried out. Given the fact that the capital costs of EDP systems are a given, that is, provided by the enterprise for commercial purposes already, the costs of elections could be considerably reduced, both for the consultative system as well as for the union, if it chose to be involved.

New technology could also assist the process of democratisation by enabling worker directors and works councillors to operate 'instant' referenda on key issues which they are asked to co-determine. This could become the analogue of what has already been proposed for citizens in households, in the broader political sphere and which now seems technically feasible via interactive cable systems.

Whether this would be desirable or not, is another question, but 'instant' referenda are now at least technically feasible. The diffusion of new technology to households could have other important consequences for industrial democracy, given the wider use of home computers. Theoretically, information flows of the kind described earlier could be available off-the-job, particularly to those who could not have access due to part-time working, or multiple shifts. Requests for information could be input from the home to the workplace vis-a-vis representatives' activities, and output by the latter back to the home computer screen.

In addition to their role in the workplace, and say their co-determination body, the representative may have access to EDP systems outside and parallel to the company data sources. The trade union will need to have its own electronic information system, for example, both on a centralised or decentralised basis. The United Automobile Workers, in the United States, have for many years kept a central data bank of information for collective bargaining purposes on all the major companies they deal with, which has also been made available to other metal workers' unions internationally, but this has been exceptional. The role of EDP in trade union organisation is a little-researched area, but no doubt is of potential importance. It is not the focus of this paper, but there is little doubt that unions will have to provide extended services vis-a-vis the new technology, both in the form of information they collect and make available to their officials, as well as rank and file, and facilities for training for workers' representation and 'data-stewards', let alone formulating technology policies on behalf of their members.

Trade unions in Britain are, however, sadly lacking in both skills and resources, at present, to service their members. Although computers are fairly widely used for keeping records of membership and union dues, the research departments of unions have very limited staff and expertise to keep abreast of new developments in the EDP field. Bodington foresaw the problem:

> 'Trade unions, production councils or whatever bodies are
> appropriate might do well to consider discussing with
> managements at once how they are currently using and how
> they plan to use computer techniques. Without doubt any
> computer installation will be much improved if the man on
> the job helps plan the project. His views and experience
> will point to possibilities that otherwise would be missed
> and he will best see that it takes proper account of
> conditions of work.' (Bodington, 1968)

To some degree, joint management-labour consultation on
implementing technological change has emerged in a number of
organisational change projects and especially where quality of
working life experiments have been attempted, for example in
Norwegian firms.

In Britain, shopfloor reactions have been mixed, and at
best pragmatic:

> 'On the whole, workers in Britain have been relatively
> successful in resisting the harmful effects of new
> technologies: job loss, the loss of traditional skills,
> the speed-up of work with increased physical and mental
> stress, the loss of immediate job control. Perhaps this
> is because the British working class had a much stronger
> dose of technological change very early on, during the
> industrial revolution.'
> (CSE, 1980)

Given the recent high levels of unemployment, it is surprising that there has not been greater resistance to technological change; perhaps the slack labour market has made it difficult for both individual workers and for their trade union
representatives to have much to negotiate about! Even so,
trade unions have already started to bargain for better conditions regarding the introduction of new technology. In some
cases, they have concluded what are known as Technology Agreements:

> 'trade unions appear to have made less bargaining headway
> on the issues of job design than on the question of equip-
> ment design. The former is an area over which systematic
> knowledge is much less precise. However, since this area
> is one in which worker experience is paramount, it could
> be argued that the trade unions would be in the best posi-
> tion to evaluate different options in work organisation,
> without deferring to "the experts".' (Williams and
> Moseley, 1982)

We would be wrong to suggest that trade unions have had no
impact on these areas of decision-making. They are often best-

168

placed to know the options which are relevant because they have first hand contact with shopfloor conditions over very long periods. Shop stewards particularly have often worked with the production systems involved, and have a pragmatic rather than textbook perspective on potential problems. In these matters the long tradition of trade union/worker resistance to the 'scientific management' of production may exert its influence informally over implementation of the new systems of 'the information society' (Williams and Moseley, 1982)

Rather than bargaining about the details instead of the strategy of technological change, trade unions may move to the strategic level in future, as the threat of greater unemployment increases. In any case, the existing health and safety legislation will to some degree take care of the potential hazards (Williams and Moseley, 1982). But as long as there is a dual channel of representation, with a strong trade union structure paralleling other forms of workers' representation such as works committees or councils, the separate process of bargaining over technological innovation will continue. Where, however, the statutory works council and union representation are more closely interwoven, then there might be less need for formal Technology Agreements as such.

CONCLUDING REMARKS

As time goes on, it is tempting to argue that more decisions in which workers have an influence will involve new technology, both as means and/or ends. However, it must also be said that in due course innovations in technology, in some areas of work at least, may cease to be 'problematic', as they become the norm. Thus, the subjective perception of the 'problem' may change. In less traditional industries, a less defensive attitude is already the case. In economies where less traditional attitudes have prevailed, innovation has been less controversial.

In the short run, whether co-determination on issues involving technological innovation will be more difficult in the countries of the European Community, now that the recession is upon us, is difficult to predict. Moreover, new technology is a 'great leveller' and often adversely affects white-collar as well as blue-collar employees. Greater unionisation of office workers over the last decade has also led to their institutionalised representation more closely resembling that of their shopfloor counterparts.

I would argue that rather than the new technology being the 'Trojan horse of Taylorism' (Cooley, 1977), it could potentially be one of Industrial Democracy, and that through it, participation enters by the back-door. Beyond this, organisation design can ensure that greater participation is built into new structures, as well as modifying old ones. Clearly, these potentialities only represent an agenda for the future, and their implementation will depend on, as yet latent, social and organisational developments.

REFERENCES

Bodington, S. (1968) 'Socialism, Democracy and the Computer' in K. Coates (ed.), Can the Workers Run Industry, Sphere Books, London, pp. 104-118

Braverman, H. (1974) Labour and Monopoly Capital: The Degradation of Work in the Twentieth Century, Monthly Review Press, New York

Cooley, M. (1977) 'Impact of CAD on the Designer and Design Function', Computer-Aided Design, 9, 238 ff.

CSE Microelectronics Group (1980) Microelectronics: Capitalist Technology and the Class, CSE Books, London

Hennestad B. (1983) 'Computer Technology, Work Organisation and Industrial Democracy', International Studies of Management and Organisation, 12, 54-72

Sorge, A., Hartman, G., Warner, M., and Nicholas, I.J. (1983) Microelectronics and Manpower in Manufacturing: Applications of Computer Numerical Control in Great Britain and West Germany, Gower Press, Aldershot

Warner, M. (1982) 'New Technology, Work Organizations and Industrial Democracy', Paper to I.D.E. Group Meeting, Free University of Amsterdam, March, to be published in Warner, M. Organizations and Experiments, Wiley, Chichester, (in press)

Williams, R. and Moseley, R. (1982) 'The Trade Union Response to Information Technology' in Bjorn-Andersen, N., Earl, M., Holst, O. and Mumford, E. (eds.), Information Society: For Richer, For Poorer, North-Holland, Oxford, pp. 231-46

Chapter 10

THE MANAGEMENT/UNION RELATIONSHIP IN
THE INTRODUCTION OF NEW TECHNOLOGY

Annette Davies

INTRODUCTION

This chapter focuses on two empirical questions which are
concerned with the management/union relationship during
technological change.   The data on which the paper is based
were collected between March and August 1982 from samples of
managers and trade unionists within the UK brewing industry, as
well as from similar groups representing a range of different
industries.

When one reviews the literature which surrounds the technological debate, the role of choice and discretion in determining the outcome of technological change is highlighted, by
many, as being one influential factor.   Given the pluralist
nature of industry, such choice and discretion may potentially
be influenced by different interest groups who have partially
conflicting objectives.   The concern of the present paper,
therefore, involves an analysis of the relative influence of
management and union sub-groups, and the relationships formed
between them, in the introduction of microtechnological
equipment.

Over the past thirty years, the trade union movement has
attempted to establish technological change as an issue for
collective bargaining, and therefore the first empirical question concerns trade union success in achieving this objective
in relation to microtechnology, and indeed the extent the trade
unions influenced the direction and outcome of such technological change.   A number of specific trade union demands in
relation to the introduction of microtechnology have been outlined in the policy statements and model arrangements of many
trade union organisations, and the question is to what extent
these are being achieved at 'grass roots' level.   Secondly, in
looking more closely at the type of management/union relationship achieved in this potentially conflictual context, is there
evidence of a consensual <u>integrative</u> approach between management and unions, and what are the underlying conditions and
behaviours for such a relationship to occur?   As defined by

Walton and McKersie (1965), the <u>integrative</u> approach refers to a system of activities instrumental to the attainment of objectives which are not in fundamental conflict with the other party. <u>Distributive</u> bargaining was also studied, and, in contrast, refers to the process of resolving pure conflicts of interest between the parties. This integrative relationship was investigated in contrast to one of more <u>distributive</u> bargaining.

TRADE UNION INFLUENCE ON CHOICE

The first conclusion to be drawn in relation to this issue, is that a number of the substantive trade union demands invest-igated were consistently not being achieved. These included: a reduction of working hours; increases in holidays; earlier retirement and work-sharing – all schemes which, it has been argued, could prevent job loss during the introduction of microtechnology. It seems that management is not choosing, being persuaded, or even is not able, to adopt such schemes, and although the most often quoted union objective in the cases of technological change studied was to preserve as many jobs as possible, there is very little evidence of the trade unions being able to achieve this, and thus avoid redundancies. Surveys of new technology agreements have already highlighted the lack of these provisions in such documents (Williams and Mosely, 1981) and therefore the present study provides further support for these findings in situations where agreements have not necessarily been signed. Seventy four per cent of the total sample of managers and trade unionists indicated that little improvement in terms and conditions of employment had resulted from the installation of the new equipment. There were only five areas where fifty per cent or more of the sample indicated that improvements had been made; these areas were: job evaluation, job enrichment, new skills and retraining, health and safety and improved job satisfaction.

While the above outcomes are only 'perceptions' of what occurred, it is significant that the only major difference bet-ween the four groups sampled was the relatively high percentage of full-time union officials who indicated an increase in pay resulting from microtechnological change (64 per cent of full-time officials, as opposed to 44 per cent of brewery trade unionists, 34 per cent of brewery managers and 33 per cent of general managers). However, the full-time officials interviewed stated that increases in pay had only been achieved at the expense of most other things. A number of cases were outlined where, in return for slight pay increases, companies had been given <u>carte blanche</u>. There were also indications that employees were not getting increased pay for retraining, with management and unions often disagreeing about whether the technological change had led to a significant work change to warrant extra payment. Many managers believed that job satisfaction had been increased as a result of changing technology, and saw that as a sufficient reward in itself. This attitude was usually coupled with a reluctance to 'pay' for technological change, and it was usual for managers to try and dissociate changes in terms and conditions of employment from the introduction of any new equipment.

The above findings are consistent with information which was collected from managers in the brewing industry regarding the reasons for the introduction of microtechnology. These reasons for innovations were shown to follow closely manufacturers' promises of increases in control, improved cost-efficiency and labour reductions, and it was generally the case that production was increased by between 25 and 75 per cent in these companies. A survey of the advertising literature of brewing equipment manufacturers showed that, in most, emphasis is being placed on eliminating dependence on the human factor in operations thereby 'reducing the risk of error, and variation in the process constants'. The managers interviewed fully realised the potential for increased control with the new technology, as one interviewee commented, 'there is no longer a reliance on individual expertise' and 'discipline is easier when the computer dictates the orders'. Such statements are far removed from the design principles outlined by Davis (1971) and Mumford (1977), which embodied the notion that workers should control the technology and not vice versa.

Evidence was also found of the isolation of tasks and the breakdown of social relationships in work situations where microtechnology had been introduced on a large scale. In many companies, managers reported that workers complained of loneliness, and it was felt that the isolation of jobs had reduced feelings of team spirit among employees. Therefore, whereas a surprising 61 per cent of managers in the brewing industry indicated that job 'enrichment' had occurred during the technological change, the increased responsibility and initiative demanded of employees, which was the basis of such enrichment, would seem also to have had a number of negative consequences in the form of increased managerial control and reductions in the numbers employed (cf. Kelly, 1980). While there were a few occasions when managers stated that manual aspects had been purposely maintained or built into the new processes 'to prevent boredom and improve job satisfaction', it must be concluded that such considerations were not viewed as main priorities in the adoption and implementation of new technology. Very few managers indicated that improvements in working conditions, or matters concerning health and safety, were important reasons for changing technology.

THE LIMITED NATURE OF UNION INVOLVEMENT

The failure of the trade union movement in influencing

managerial discretion, and in achieving many of their demands, must be partly attributed to their limited involvement in many aspects of the change process. Of eight decision-making areas which were investigated, five may be outlined where the unions were not being involved in any meaningful way. These related to the decision to invest, the cost-benefit analysis, the type and extent of technology to be implemented, job redesign and the selection and training of employees.

Greater union involvement, either in a joint decision-making or distributive bargaining capacity occurred in relation to such issues as: redundancy; pay and grading; and health and safety. Such findings are what would be traditionally expected, and therefore there is no evidence of an extension of collective bargaining over change – a procedural demand included in many trade union policy statements.

In all the companies visited, decisions concerning new technology were always finalised by management committees, before they were put to employees and their unions. Even in one case where the union indicated that they were satisfied with their involvement in the project, it was found that discussions between the two sides had not begun until approximately four years after the initial management decision to invest. In fact, the most common complaint among the trade unionists interviewed was that they were not being involved at an early enough stage to exert much influence over the process.

Such findings support a growing literature which outlines the relative lack of trade union influence in strategic decision-making. Wilson et al (1982) found that although decisions concerning new equipment or plant were the second largest area of union involvement in strategic decision-making, the degree of influence in these decisions was still found to be minimal. For example, in a decision to open a new plant in an engineering firm, it was departments such as manufacturing, finance and purchasing that had a good deal of power, as did the managing director; and externally the supplier of the new equipment and a competitor spurred on the decision process and set its pace. The union, on the other hand, was found to be one of the least influential interest groups.

Therefore, as was concluded from the surveys of new technology agreements (Williams and Mosely, 1981), the present paper can provide little evidence of the TUC objective of 'change by agreement' being achieved. There was no instance of technological change being negotiated, although some 'effects' of the change were subject to collective bargaining. Three important factors highlighted in the present research may explain this lack of union involvement.

MANAGERIAL ATTITUDES AND STRATEGIES

It was clear from the research that management did not view

technological change as a 'negotiable issue'. Many managers
interviewed resented the bargaining stance which they felt was
prevalent in the union approach towards technological change.
They believed that there were certain 'givens' in the
situation, such as labour reduction, which made it impossible
for trade unionists to participate, or to be seen to
participate. There was a fear (which was usually found to be
unwarranted) of union reaction to such changes, and therefore
information was passed to the other side only with extreme
caution. It is significant that much of the information
collected from management had not yet been discussed with the
union side, and the fact that many managers refused access to
union representatives, at their plant, is perhaps indicative of
their strategy to exclude the unions from this potentially
controversial area. Many of the managers interviewed outlined
a number of reasons for their apparent success in deterring
union involvement, and ensuring the implementation of the new
technology in their 'desired way'.

The relative ease of gaining acceptance to change at a
time of economic recession was fully appreciated by management,
and the position of the trade union is obviously very much
weakened. A number of instances were outlined where employees
were threatened with the closure of their plant, if the union
could not reach an agreement, and fear was easily generated
amongst employees by highlighting the competition they faced in
the industry from those companies with much more sophisticated
technologies. Not surprisingly therefore, many trade unionists
stated that it was difficult to get support for any industrial
action, as employees became increasingly concerned about keeping their jobs at a time of high unemployment. Significantly,
only 33 per cent of the management sample indicated that there
had been a threat or occurrence of an industrial dispute during
technological change, and in twenty five companies visited,
only six instances of industrial conflict were found. These
were caused mainly by grievances over substantive issues such
as pay, reduction in hours or increased status, rather than
procedural issues such as the exclusion of trade union representatives from early stages of decision-making.

Many managers also pointed to the usefulness of what was
termed a 'softly, softly' approach to technological change, in
reducing the drama of the situation and thereby deterring the
necessity of union involvement. In one company, the manager
stated that the plan followed was to deal firstly with those
areas which were the least contentious - that is, those with
limited manpower implications. After these so-called
'innocent' changes had been implemented, more controversial
changes would then be made, with the position of employees to
resist obviously weakened. The implications of piecemeal
changes carried out in a gradual way may be difficult to appreciate in the short-run and they do not initially appear dramatic enough for the trade union organisation to attempt, or to

succeed, in gaining benefits for their members. In one company information was given concerning a five year plan of separate micro-applications, and this provided an insight into the cumulative effect such changes could produce. The aim of the plan was a 25 per cent reduction in manpower, and a movement towards the 'operator technician'.

A final factor, which may explain the success of managerial strategies, related to the strength and expertise of the management team. The questionnaire responses showed that the majority of managers were confident: about the clarity of their team's objectives (89%); about their preparations for decision-making (89%); the adequacy of their knowledge about the new equipment (78%); and, their technical ability to play a meaningful role in the situation (54%). A number of examples were also found of companies actively involved in the establishment of managerial expertise in this area. This either revolved around one person who had been specifically employed to look at various applications, or there would be a project team with the requisite skills to make such decisions. In the brewing industry, it was found that professional bodies such as the Brewers Guild organised courses to explain the new technology to management and help them to cope with it. Also, this industry consists of a very close and tight network of management teams, and frequent exchange visits are organised by the different breweries so that each may learn from the experiences of others. Management expertise is an often-quoted objection to arguments for increased shopfloor involvement in decision-making, and as pointed out by Marchington and Loveridge (1979):

> 'the idea of non-useful and generally destructive contributions from the shop-stewards would appear to exert a particularly pervasive influence over British management thought'.

Many managers felt that the trade unions lacked knowledge and expertise in this area, and would be unable to provide much feedback in the conceptual stages of the introduction of new technologies. While it could be argued that such statements may be used by management merely as rationalisations for a desired course of action (Marchington and Armstrong, 1981), there is evidence that weaknesses in trade union organisation and strategy, in the present situation, are also partly accountable for their failure to achieve greater involvement in decision-making regarding new technology.

Trade Union Weakness
Managerial perceptions of trade union influence and strategies were indicative of the weakness in the union position. In six of the companies visited, management was surprised at the absence of any trade union reaction, and their lack of concern

about future plans and applications. For example, one manager commented that the trade union did not seem to realise the implications of production being increased by about 65 to 70 per cent with no extra jobs being created. Also, in the majority of companies visited, there had been no initiative from the trade unions for any formal agreements on new technology.

The majority of managers felt that the union strategy had lacked expertise and preparation and that their reaction could at the most be described only as 'suspicious' or 'defensive', when it occurred at all. This was illustrated in one brewery by an incident during the annual negotiations, when the electricians' union had enquired about what the company was doing about new technology. Not surprisingly, management's reply was 'nothing special', which to management's astonishment brought an end to the discussion. In only one company was it stated that certain applications had not been made because of the possibility of adverse relations with the trade unions.

The ignorance of many trade unionists concerning future plans for technological change, resulted at times in an unwarranted complacency on their part. An example of this was found in the brewing study where in one company the trade union official dismissed the issue of technological change as being 'of no great consequence' and 'something which happened all the time', while his management counterpart spoke of plans to eventually 'automate everyone out of the process'.

Trade Union Organisation

The brewing study also highlighted an aspect of trade union organisation which militated against union involvement at an early stage in decision-making. A complete lack of coordination was found between the union representatives in the various operating companies of the same brewing group, which provided management with a major advantage in carrying out technological change in this industry. Although management, in many of these operating companies, stated that over the last five years they had become profit centres within their group and could initiate changes as long as they were cost-effective, it would seem that the decision to make a technological investment on one site – resulting in the closure of others because of excess capacity – would have to be a central one. Although this was found to be a prevalent trend in the brewing industry, and probably in many others, there was no union organisation at this central level, to even claim involvement in decision-making. The predicament of many trade unions is perhaps summed up by one interviewee, who felt that 'his union had woken up five years too late, finding themselves in a hurricane of new technology with no planning for it'.

Finally, from the above discussion, it may be observed that there are a number of problems which render the task of tracing the manpower implications of technological change very difficult, and which may also therefore inhibit trade union involvement. Firstly, it is not difficult for management to completely dissociate technological change and manpower savings, and the present economic climate has made the task even easier. Secondly, any redundancy which occurs may be blamed on poor market performance after or before microtechnological change has occurred.

In a recent study by the Labour Research Department (1982) it was also found that in two-thirds of the cases where jobs were lost during microtechnological change, these jobs were not lost when the equipment was being introduced, but some time later. Thirdly, the more common gradual and piecemeal application of microtechnology has enabled companies to reduce their labour force in a less dramatic fashion through natural wastage. Finally, the case study of the brewing industry illustrated that the manpower impact of technological change may not necessarily be felt only on the site where the changes are taking place, and may even have more serious implications in other companies within the group. In at least four cases, technological investments in one brewery have resulted in the closure of a number of smaller breweries within the respective organisations.

In view of these findings, it has to be concluded that any trade union influence on managerial discretion during microtechnological change must, indeed, have been slight. In the vast majority of cases, trade unions have effectively been excluded from the important areas of decision-making, and therefore when they finally are involved, the scope left for discussion - and their ability to change management decisions - was obviously limited. However, when the unions were involved, especially in distributive bargaining there was a strong association with an increased degree of perceived improvement in terms and conditions resulting from the change, for both management and union respondents. Integrative bargaining, on the other hand, only showed significance in this way in the union data, but even there it did not seem to have resulted in the creative and innovative solutions to manpower problems one may have hypothesised from the literature. It is to these relationships, and discussion of their influence that we now turn.

A CONSENSUAL, INTEGRATIVE BARGAINING APPROACH BETWEEN MANAGEMENT AND UNIONS

It is well-documented that the achievement of an integrative or cooperative bargaining approach is not without difficulty in a conflict-based industrial relations system. The most ardent opponents of such cooperation have outlined the dangers for the union organisation in becoming too closely identified with management (Clegg, 1960), while there are also many fears amongst management of losing their prerogatives in decision-making.

However, in contrast, it is also argued that the achievement of more integrative agreements is advantageous to both sides, being tantamount to achieving 'the greatest good for the greatest number'. However, certain issues may be more amenable to such integrative relationships than others, and it was assumed in the present study that negotiations concerning technological change, in covering such a wide variety of issues, will have this potential for the development of cooperative management/ union relationships. However, in relation to this assumption, it is significant that 20 per cent of the total sample indicated that there had been no such cooperation in the management/ union relationship. In fact, the majority of both managers and trade unionists (60 per cent of managers and 54 per cent of trade unionists) indicated that less than 25 per cent bargaining with the other side had been integrative.

Many of the managers interviewed had felt that it was impossible for the both sides to participate in this way. As one manager stated, 'even if the unions do recognise the need for the new technology, they will not be a party to a reduction in manpower and will fight hard to get the best terms'. The main reasons outlined by management both in the questionnaire and in the interviews, for the introduction of microtechnology was the reduction or avoidance of labour costs, and such 'rationality' was not open to debate or discussion with the trade unions. In contrast, most of the trade unionists interviewed welcomed a more participative relationship with management during the introduction of microtechnology. The view commonly held was that the new equipment and techniques would be introduced even without their involvement, and therefore only by increasing their degree of participation in the procedure could they hope to influence it. However, a few did outline the potential problems of such participation, and indicated that at times - for example, in a redundancy situation - they would not be able to cooperate with management. In keeping with these findings, the questionnaire data revealed a strong positive correlation between union satisfaction with the technological change and the occurrence of integrative bargaining between the two sides, while no such correlation was found in the management data. It may therefore be concluded that whereas increased participation and integrative bargaining was the preferred negotiating relationship of the union team, this was certainly not the case for the majority of managers surveyed.

Further support for this conclusion is available from an analysis of the conditions and behaviours which were found to underlie the occurrence of integrative bargaining between the two sides. In the management data, not one of the variables describing the strength and expertise of the management team was significantly correlated with the degree of integrative bargaining in the relationship. Interestingly, the only significant relationship found, with any of the above variables, was between a well-prepared decision approach by the management team and a mainly consultative relationship with the other side. The team strength and expertise of the union side was, however, highly correlated with the occurrence of integrative bargaining, and the fact that such strength and expertise was found to be very limited in the present context, may provide an important reason why such a low degree of integrative bargaining occurred. Many variables relating to communication between the two sides were found to be important for the occurrence of integrative bargaining in both samples, but variables relating to a cooperative relationship between the two sides were only significant in the union data. Unionists also perceived a greater degree of integrative bargaining when there were 'formal negotiations', and when issues concerning new technology were isolated from other issues - two conditions management have attempted to avoid.

All the unionists interviewed outlined factors which described the underlying conditions and behaviours of the negotiating process, as being those most important for integrative bargaining to work in this situation. These factors were: strength and expertise of the union side; trust and honesty between the teams, and management commitment to participative structures. The interview data, therefore, provided some support for identifying causality, or at least antecedent conditions.

It may be concluded from the above findings that the trade union data provide some further support for the factors associated with integrative bargaining, which were highlighted by Walton and McKersie (1965) and tested by Peterson and Tracy (1976). This is true for most of the subvariables relating to a cooperative working relationship and the frequency and openness of communications. Also, variables relating to team expertise, which were found to be important for integrative bargaining in Peterson and Tracy's work, were also significant in the trade union data. However, amongst management respondents, support for Walton and McKersie's model was only found for the variables relating to contact and communication between the sides. Generally, management lacked the motivational orientation for integrative bargaining during technological change. Therefore, it may be argued that if such a relationship occurred, it was not because both sides wanted it, an assumption of Walton and McKersie, but because the union side had enough expertise or procedural advantage to demand it.

The union respondents in the survey seemed firmly convinced of the effectiveness of a joint management/union approach to the problems of change, and the attainment of improved terms and conditions as a result of their increased involvement in this way. In fact, an analysis of the questionnaire responses showed that an increased amount of integrative bargaining in the management/union relationship was highly correlated with less redundancy and deskilling, improvements in bonus payments, productivity bargaining and retraining; and the interview information provides some justification for tentatively concluding that there is a causal link between them.

However, similar correlations were not found in the management data. It is certainly the case that very little integrative bargaining was perceived at all, and therefore one perhaps could not expect to see an effect. But the difference between the responses of management and union negotiators in relation to integrative bargaining raises the question of the 'reality' of the influence perceived by the unions. The lack of union involvement in the important areas of decision-making was very clearly observed, and therefore it is quite probable that the influence of the integrative bargaining, which was reported to have occurred, was largely 'subjective' with no basis in 'objective reality'. There is much evidence in the literature of the ease with which people can be made to feel that they have participated (Wall and Lischeron, 1977) and the influential effect that 'subjective participation' may have on one's perceptions of events.

In addition, it is interesting and perhaps alarming that the unionists who 'felt' they had participated in an integrative way with management showed a marked difference in their attitudes towards new technology, compared to those who perceived less involvement. It was observed that these unionists fully embraced the introduction of microtechnology, outlining the advantages that would result, rather than any of the drawbacks. One emphasised the financial side of his union, which looked closely at the cost-effectiveness of various computer technologies, and it was stated that the union would always support the most efficient technology, even though it might result in a loss of jobs.

There were also strong feelings amongst many of these unionists that the adoption of work-sharing schemes to preserve jobs was not cost-effective. These findings indicate that the unionists who felt involved in an integrative relationship with management, adhered strongly to what could be described as the 'managerial rationality' of the situation, and as such did not pose a threat to management's 'way of thinking'.

Similar findings have also been outlined in a recent study by Wilson et al (1982), where it was concluded that unions involved in strategic decision-making only get their own way when this is congruent with 'management's way'. These findings raise some problems concerning integrative bargaining, especially when the union movement is weak, and management is able to manipulate the information which the unions receive. In one company, the aim was to get people 'into the right frame of mind', so that information presented to employees could be loaded in such a way that the right questions were asked. Indeed, evidence of the influence of specialists in controlling decision-making in this way is well-documented in the literature by authors such as Pettigrew (1973) and Winkler (1974).

Therefore, the present study showed that the union respondents indicated far greater involvement in the process of technological change than was attributed to them by the managers surveyed. For example, not one manager in the sample indicated that the unions had been involved in a joint decision-making or bargaining capacity with respect to the initial investment decision or the cost-benefit analysis, and only 6 per cent indicated that such an involvement had occurred in decisions regarding the type and extent of technology. However, in the trade union responses 22 per cent indicated involvement in joint decision-making or bargaining in the investment decision, 36 per cent in a cost-benefit analysis and 49 per cent in decisions concerning the type and extent of technology. Doubts have already been raised in this discussion concerning the reality of such involvement, and its 'manipulation' by management when it occurs. Certainly, the trade unionists interviewed indicated no involvement in any investment decision or cost-benefit analysis, and one unionist who believed that he had 'fully participated', had not become involved in discussions with management until two years after the initial decision to invest.

CONCLUDING REMARKS

While it was argued at the outset that 'choices' do exist both in the design and implementation of new technology, there is much evidence in the present study to show that the new microelectronic equipment is being designed and implemented in a 'determined' way.

In the brewing industry principles of managerial control were prominent in the designs of new equipment, and cost-efficiency and labour reduction emerged as the main reasons for implementation. It is true that some decision-makers did wander from this 'determined way', and the introduction of job enrichment schemes and some attempts to make work more satisfying with microtechnology were found. However, more innovative manpower adjustment policies such as reduction in hours, job-sharing and increased holidays, are consistently not being adopted. Managers to a large extent have attempted and succeeded in dissociating improvement in terms and conditions of employment from the introduction of new equipment, and have prevented technological change from becoming a negotiable issue. Nevertheless, to conclude that there has been an 'unfettered triumph of capital over labour' would not be justified as there was evidence of conflict, dispute and struggle, as well as participation, all of which has had some impact on the outcome of technological change. What is questioned in the present paper, however, is the <u>degree</u>

of union influence and the size of its impact.

The design and choice of technology are still unquestionably managerial prerogatives, and no instance was found where discussions with the trade unions had started before management had made these decisions. By that time the scope for union influence had been severely narrowed, and the main achievement during the process of implementation has been slight pay increases, usually at the expense of everything else. The imbalance of power between management and union negotiators was very evident in many of the cases studied and confidence in their own team's strength and expertise was very much higher among the managers surveyed. While the impact of the recession cannot be dismissed as a causal factor in the trade union weaknesses identified, the present paper raises a number of important questions concerning the effectiveness of trade union policy and structure in dealing with the phenomenon of microtechnological change.

REFERENCES

Clegg, H.A. (1979), A New Approach to Industrial Democracy, Blackwell, Oxford

Davis, L.E. (1971) 'The Coming Crisis for Production Management: Technology and Organisation', International Journal of Production Research, 9, 65-82

Kelly, J. (1980) 'The Costs of Job Redesign: A Preliminary Analysis', Industrial Relations Journal, 11(3), 22-34

Labour Research Department (1982) 'Survey of New Technology', Bargaining Report, 22,

Marchington, M. and Armstrong, R. (1981) 'Employee Participation: Problems for the Shop Steward', Industrial Relations Journal, 12(1), 46-61

Marchington, M. and Loveridge, R. (1979) 'Non-Participation: The Management View?', Journal of Management Studies, 16(2), 171-84

Mumford, E. (1977) 'The Design of Work: New Approaches and New Needs' in Rijnsdorp, J.E. (ed.) Case Studies in Automation Related to the Humanisation of Work. Proceedings of the IFAC Workshop, Pergamon Press, Netherlands

Peterson, R.B. and Tracy, L.N. (1976) 'A Behavioural Model of Problem-Solving in Labour Negotiations', British Journal of Industrial Relations, 14, 159-173

Pettigrew, A. (1973) The Politics of Organisational Decision-Making, Tavistock, London

Wall, T.A. and Lischeron, J.A. (1977) Worker Participation, McGraw-Hill, London

Walton,R. and McKersie, R. (1965) A Behavioral Theory of Labour Negotiations, McGraw-Hill, New York

Williams, R. and Moseley, R. (1981) Technology Agreements: Consensus, Control and Technical Change in The Workplace. Paper presented to EEC/FAST Conference

Wilson, D.C., Butler, R.J., Cray, D., Hickson, D.J. and Mallory, G.R. (1982) 'Union Participation in Strategic Decision-Making', British Journal of Industrial Relations, 20, 322-341

Winkler, J.T. (1974) The Ghost at the Bargaining Table: Directors and Industrial Relations, British Journal of Industrial Relations, 12, 191-212

PART IV

MANAGEMENT ISSUES – INFORMATION,
CONTROL AND STRUCTURE

Chapter 11

EMERGING TRENDS IN MANAGING NEW INFORMATION
TECHNOLOGIES

Michael Earl

INTRODUCTION

The management of information technology (IT) is a relatively
new function and area of research. However, we do have a
growing body of knowledge based on the experience of, and
research into, the management of Data Processing (DP) and
computer-based information systems. Therefore, armed with such
knowledge, we can observe, interpret and comment on the
emerging issues and trends in the management of IT at large -
seeking out useful similarities and highlighting significant
differences. Such is the purpose of this paper. It will be
supported by data derived from a simple, but wide-ranging,
questionnaire survey being applied to managers of IT, and their
user colleagues, from some of the largest organisations in
Europe[1].

The paper is in five parts. First, the nature of the
management of information resources is briefly described.
Then some technological trends are identified, followed by
presentation of some of the management concerns evident in the
survey data. Then a broader analysis of contemporary experience is provided, followed by some conclusions on a management
agenda.

MANAGING INFORMATION TECHNOLOGY

By managing IT, I mean the formal management in large organisations of information resources and information technologies,
which at its most elementary involves the tasks of planning,
organising and controlling. Table 11.1 suggests some of the
recurring questions that the management of DP has entailed. It
is by no means an exhaustive list and only deals with issues at
the organisational level, and not with the system, project or
individual level. In Table 11.2 are suggested some of the more
contemporary questions being raised in large organisations
about the management of both the 'old' and 'new' information
technologies, that is of DP, Data Communication, and the

application of microelectronics in automating data-dependent tasks in factory and office operations.

Table 11.1:   Recurring DP Management Questions

Task Category	Question
PLANNING	What systems should we develop next? What is the next hardware step? Which of our competing application needs has priority?
ORGANISATION	Should DP be centralised or not? How do we resolve user-specialist conflicts? How can we involve senior management?
CONTROL	What resources should be committed to DP? Are resources being deployed efficiently and effectively?

Table 11.2:   Some New IT Management Questions

Task Category	Question
PLANNING	What is our data communications policy? What information systems do our current business strategies demand? What strategic opportunities are presented by IT?
ORGANISATION	Who should manage office automation? How will IT affect our organisation structure? Has the DP manager's job changed?
CONTROL	Are we in control of DP and IT any more? How do we control small computing? Is control of IT so important now?

The case for formal management of IT is easily made. At least seven arguments exist:

1. IT is a high expenditure activity. The Fortune top 1000 companies spend, on average, $150m per annum on DP alone, whilst my own survey data suggest that the annual DP budgets of large government and business organisations in Europe lie in the region of £50m to £100m. More significantly still, DP budgets, according to my data, are growing at about 30 per cent per annum compound, and it seems that hardware costs form less than 30 per cent of total DP expenditure.

2. Information processing is central to many business and government operations. For example, in banking, insurance, retailing, and airlines, the day to day business is computer-dependent. Often, the operations directors are DP executives. Several government operations likewise are, or soon will be, computer-driven, for instance in the Department of Health and Social Security and the Inland Revenue. In these sectors, IT has become the means of delivering services (Read, 1983) but the management questions are often no different from the past, except that they require technological know-how.

3. New information technologies are offering new business and management opportunities. Indeed, those organisations that have employed IT as a strategic weapon and have recognised the vital dependence of many business strategies on information processing are often those who now are leaders in their sectors. The converse is that those who do not recognise the strategic implications of IT or who make poor business and technological decisions are threatened.

4. IT is hitting all functions and levels of management. Thus, it could affect in differing degrees not only the ways and means of operations but the structure of organisations and the styles of management - relationships which are truly a management responsibility.

5. In one management area in particular, IT is obviously significant. In management information systems (MIS), IT offers new opportunities for data retrieval, storage, dissemination, manipulation and analysis - opportunities which managements should not only seize but maybe should direct and control.

6. Besides managers, other stakeholders are concerned with, and seeking to influence, the adoption and use of IT. Organised labour, consumers, governments and supplier or customer organisations are significant and legitimate actors in IT. For example, the business which does not appreciate or consider the implications of government regulation (such as data protection), deregulation (such as in telecommunciations) and intervention (such as in industrial policy initiatives) in the IT sector is likely to miss opportunities or be caught out.

7. Lack of management involvement and support has been a major cause of information processing failures hitherto, particularly in terms of failure to meet anticipated objectives (McCosh et al, 1981). Often initiatives and projects have been

technologically driven and increasingly this may lead us not only into major management problems but wider economic, political and social issues which perhaps only the technologists can understand.

It is to the technological trends, in terms of their management implications, that we now turn.

TECHNOLOGICAL TRENDS

Four interrelated trends in IT, important in their management implications, seem worthy of emphasis. They both change the nature of many of the planning, organisation and control questions that have faced information managers hitherto and raise new issues which managements are beginning to recognise. These trends may be described as follows: (a) IT comprises multiple technologies; (b) IT is dispersing; (c) the rate of IT change is accelerating; and (d) IT is becoming pervasive.

Multiple IT

There are now many generic and specific information technologies, whether classified by delivery or use. Besides DP, based on both mainframe and small computers, there is Data Communication and factory and office automation. By application, there are at least the IT activities listed in Table 11.3. Each is likely to be different in its hardware and software characteristics, its supply, its application and its management. From the managerial viewpoint, at least three consequences arise:

1. Each IT may stimulate its own application portfolio, each of which in turn will vary in stage of evolution. For example, the office automation application portfolio is still emerging and is immature whilst the DP application portfolio is well understood, even though it is not fully implemented. Likewise, the office automation portfolio, although important to those seeking productivity gains, is unlikely to have such strategic significance as the development of a telecommunications infrastructure. Thus, each IT will have planning, organisation and control implications, but their relative importance and balance will differ.

2. There are likely to be several IT functions, and thus managements, in any one organisation. Industry data suggest that less than 50 per cent of information processing activities today are under the regime of conventional DP managers and it has been predicted that spending on information technologies will multiply by 600 per cent or 800 per cent in the decade from 1980, only 200 per cent of this growth being explained by DP[2]. Already there exist in some organisations, separately, DP departments, communications divisions, office automation departments, manufacturing system groups etc., whilst in others there is uncertainty, ambiguity or open conflict over who ultimately controls which ITs. The immediate manifestation and management question is organisational, but

the planning and control implications are obvious.
    3.   There arises an 'architecture' problem.   Several of these technologies are converging, especially DP and Data Communications, many of them are interdependent, and major IT suppliers are themselves diversifying into all the major technologies, for example IBM, AT&T and Xerox (McKenney and McFarlan, 1982). Thus, coordination of IT is required at a policy and a technical planning level. At the same time, reinforced by the second trend of dispersing IT, some of these technologies can be, and should be, stand-alone and/or local, for reasons of both efficiency and effectiveness. Thus, IT planners have many technical challenges and dilemmas ahead, but general management also has a responsibility for ensuring that the IT infrastructure, or architecture, relates to the business and management strategies.

Table 11.3:   Information Technology Adoption and Usage
                   (44 large organisations 1982/83)

Technology	Current Usage	Planned Usage
Mainframe	High	High
Minicomputers	High	High
Microcomputers	High	High
Data Communication Networks	High	High
Word Processing	High	High
Distributed Computing	Medium	High
Facsimile Transfer	Medium	High
Viewdata	Low	Medium
Electronic Mail	Low	Medium
Teleconferencing	Low	Low
CAD/CAM*	Low	Low
Robotics*	Low	Low

        High   =   70% or more of sample organisations
        Medium =   40% to 69% of sample organisations
        Low   =   less than 40% of sample organisations

* If the sample is confined to manufacturing firms, the current usage of CAD/CAM and Robotics is medium.

Dispersing IT
Related to the first trend is the dispersion of IT, which raises important organisational questions, since the trend of many of these technologies is towards distributed, local, end-user, and personal information processing - for example, in office automation, robotics and personal computing. Others in this

volume have addressed the impact of IT on organisation in general, and so I will concentrate on the implications for the organisation of IT management. I might add, however, that experience has shown that, except in heavily information processing operations, the organisation of information processing and its management need not influence the structure of the host organisation (Whisler, 1970). There are other intervening and mediating variables.

From the IT management viewpoint, the economies of scale and the specialisation of skills arguments once favoured centralisation of DP. In time, the need for specialist-user interaction and the diverse requirements of different divisions led to decentralisation of systems development. As hardware costs reduced and distributed processing became available, decentralised DP operations - at least in part - became feasible. Planning and control of DP, however, usually remained centralised for reasons of direction and coordination. The centralisation-decentralisation argument, as ever, was an exercise in seeking a balance between effectiveness and efficiency and in managing ambiguity. Now, with dispersing technologies, the balance has to be redrawn, the ambiguities are more complex and the IT managers have to reassess their demand and redeploy their resources. Indeed, there are now likely to be several DP (or office automation, etc.) departments in any large organisation as well as the multiple functions identified above. Pressure of demand, variety of technological know-how, scarcity of development personnel and growth of end-user interest, ability and capacity, will all lead to decentralisation and dispersion of hardware, data and development, and thus to diffusion of planning, organisation, and control of IT. DP managers have the scars of resisting devolutionary pressures in the past; they will be foolish to resist in the future - indeed, centralisation of information processing is a lost cause. However, the need for some central coordination - especially for strategic planning of IT and for plotting the hardware, software and data infrastructures - will become more vital.

Second, at every level of IT organisation, specialists will be required to provide support services and facilitating skills to the increasing number of end-users. It happened with distributed computing as, after the first flush of autonomous euphoria, remote users found they needed the technical help of specialists (Down and Taylor, 1976) and it appears to be happening with the development of information technology centres or provision of personal computers - approximately every six users need a specialist 'chauffeur'.

This scenario is just dawning. My survey data reveal that in 90 per cent of large organisations the emphasis is still on centralised computer operations and that in 79% of organisations applications development is centralised. However, 77% of the firms report that users can now have their own computing, and a recent Urwick (1983) survey shows that 61% of organisa-

tions plan an increase in decentralised computing expenditure –
whilst doubtless other ITs are already dispersing.

Accelerating IT

It is a cliche to talk of accelerating rates of technological
change. Yet the recent growth in the development, adoption and
implementation of IT has been explosive. Microelectronics has
stimulated the development of these technologies, but, of
course, the price/performance ratio of computing in general has
improved dramatically. Table 11.3 portrays the current state
of IT use in the survey organisations. Considering that
several of these technologies were not easily available in
Europe three or four years ago, the data are arresting. However, I suspect that the data are describing large, successful
and innovative firms. Nevertheless, these early adopter organisations may pull the entities with whom they trade – via market pressures – into the IT era.

For example, my own institution – with its unusual market
pressures in an ancient university setting – has felt this
technological pull. Increasingly we are expected to use
microcomputers in teaching, our more commercial competitors are
exploiting word processing in their sales support activities so
that we have to match them, two of our corporate clients have
requested that we use viewdata terminals on courses to
faciliate IT awareness, one organisation has suggested we join
a commercial electronic mail network to overcome postal
problems and another is suggesting data communication access to
our library. Like many organisations, presumably, we feel that
in some of these cases we have no choice. In this context, the
management control procedures, such as cost benefit analysis
and capital investment appraisal, which were once applied to DP
acquisition decisions, now seem strangely inappropriate. The
control criteria and control variables have changed.

As we make these IT investment decisions, we are but a
microcosm of larger IT users faced with the uncertainties and
complexities of rapid technological change. Should we wait for
better price/performance ratios, for improved software, for
greater upwards compatibility, for proven reliability...? The
large organisation, in similar vein, considers whether to be a
leading-edge IT user or not. Most of our sample firms have
made a policy decision not to be, being somewhat risk-averse.
Should we seek compatibility between different ITs, with IT use
at large in the University...? Larger organisations in similar vein are implementing acquisition approval procedures and
vendor policies to ensure some degree of control. Will our
teaching methods change, do our building plans need to be IT
oriented, are our assumptions about library requirements
correct...? Like business at large, our business plans already
need to be IT-related, but the IT future, as much as our business requirements, is uncertain.

Finally, if different ITs bring different management problems, the rate of technological change may well generate managerial and organisational dyspepsia. One multinational, multidivisional firm in our sample already admits to being in chaos in terms of managing IT, since events have overtaken managerial direction.

Pervasive IT

The above three characteristics suggest that IT is hitting, or is about to have an impact on, many more functions and actors than in the past. The personal computer boom is illustrative. There are already 1.5m personal computers owned in the UK, the highest per capita ownership in the world. This, alongside other dispersed technologies and easy to acquire and use software, for example the widespread adoption of 'visicalc' and spread-sheet analysis, is stimulating a rapid growth in end-user computing. There are at least two managerial issues gestating.

First, the expectations of user communities are being raised. They are likely to be more impatient than ever for IT support. They not only expect delivery of local, personal and user-friendly information processing capabilities, but also the necessary infrastructures and interfaces which they may soon recognise are essential for more sophisticated applications. Given that conventional DP departments may have a visible backlog of two to three years development and a hidden backlog five times greater (Alloway and Quillard, 1983), the potential for frustration and conflict is high. In time, end-user development of applications may help resolve these conflicts and reduce backlogs, but there is an educational transition period to go through meanwhile.

Indeed, IT education promises the second managerial challenge. In the UK, virtually all secondary schools now have a computing facility, whilst 25 per cent of primary schools have computers also – due to the government's IT investment programme. In the USA, the major computer firms are donating computers to universities and already some university courses demand that students possess their own (approved) computer. The industry motives are obvious. As an IBM spokesman put it:

> 'there can be no factories of the future unless there
> are universities of the future educating people now'
> (Mendelson, 1983).

The result could be the creation of a cohort of thrusting agents of IT change, or a generation gap of IT interest and knowledge between young and older executives, or a subtle process of technological transfer as the older brethren are technologically rejuvenated by the young. Evidence, of sorts, exists for all three scenarios. For example, many new software and hardware ventures are resourced by young graduates. Yet, one of my undergraduates recently remarked that there was already an IT generation gap between his 21 year old age group and 14 year old schoolchildren they knew. Likewise, a schoolteacher informs me that 13 year old schoolchildren conceive of, and design, computer-based engineering applications never thought of by their seniors. Meanwhile, a recent survey (MORI, 1982) suggests that parents become interested in IT through the activities of their children. (The same has been observed of executives through the word processing exploits of their secretaries.) Such trends suggest some quite new managerial issues ahead: planning challenges, such as the management of creativity and innovation; organisational challenges, such as management and organisation development to cope with IT education gaps; and control challenges, such as the (pervasive) distribution of information processing ability and thus of power.

The management implications suggested of these four tech-nological trends, however, are somewhat speculative. What are the issues that concern today's IT managers and users?

MANAGEMENT TRENDS

Much of the professional literature and common discourse amongst DP personnel suggests that management of IT is essentially a technological issue. However, for some years it has been evident that senior executives responsible for information processing recognise that technological know-how and technological questions are only one aspect, and by no means the most important aspect, of information management. To the contrary, the traditional tasks of any management function have surfaced as key variables in the successful management of IT. To test this assertion, albeit crudely, 28 senior executives responsible for information processing were asked in my sample survey to rank the traditional tasks of management (further simplifying the admittedly simplistic PODSCORB* model of management tasks) against technological issues. The results, based on Likert scale responses, are presented in Table 11.4.

Planning questions emerge as the dominant issue. To the widely recognised pressures to plan in the conventional DP environment - setting direction, linking DP developments to business goals, resource forecasting, allocating scarce resour-ces, involving top management and managing the size and compl-exity of DP projects - are probably added the recognition that new technologies provide strategic opportunities that must be planned for; that data, hardware and software architectures will be required to facilitate the convergence of the new ITs and their applications; that more aspects of the business are
*PODSCORB is an acronym to describe the work of a manager, i.e. Planning, Organising, Directing, Staffing, Coordinating, Reporting and Budgeting.

affected, and that the problems of priority-setting and allocating scarce resources, especially liveware, will be manipulated.

Not far behind in management priorities are organisational issues. This may seem a surprising response from technologically-oriented managers, but on discussion with them it would seem to reflect two related issues, suggested in the previous section. The first is how to organise for the operation, development and management of multiple, dispersing, accelerating and pervasive ITs. The second, rather immediate status and power issue, is what are the implications for DP and information managers in particular?

The lower priority attached to control questions may reflect the fact that management control of information processing techniques and systems seem to be widely in place. How effective they are is another matter - as is how appropriate they are for the new ITs. However, our survey, for example, reveals that most large organisations run their DP departments as cost centres, that DP services are charged out on a transfer price basis, that IS projects are subject to cost benefit analysis and post-implementation audits, and that project management techniques are in general use. These are today's norms of management control of DP resources.

Finally, technology scored the lowest ranking. This does not indicate, presumably, that the management implications of the new ITs are unimportant, for other data from the survey suggest otherwise, but that technological issues per se are relatively unimportant to senior executives concerned with management of information processing - or are so at the moment.

Perhaps more revealing still are the concerns expressed by respondents in a problem-oriented manner rather than by the classifications imposed in Table 11.4. Twenty-five managers of DP functions - which in the organisations surveyed generally have responsibility for most ITs - were asked to rank, again on a Likert scale, the most important issues facing them now, and over the next five years. They had to select from a list of 17 DP management concerns widely discussed in professional and academic literature. The responses are summarised in Table 11.5.

The current priority given to planning suggested in Table 11.4 is confirmed by the concerns with strategy formulation

Table 11.4: Priorities in Managing Information Technologies

Priority	Issues
High	Planning
↑	Organisation
↓	Control
Low	Technology

and long range planning revealed in Table 11.5 – particularly
in the future. IT strategy formulation is certainly a significant topic in the professional and academic literatures and,

Table 11.5: Specific Concerns of Information Technology
Managers

Current Concerns	Future Concerns
1. Information Systems Strategy	1. Information Systems Strategy
2. User Awareness and Education	2. Information Systems Long Range Planning
3. Inadequate Staff Resources	3. Coping with New ITs
4. Information Systems Long Range Planning	4. User Awareness and Education
5. Coping with New ITs	5. User Involvement

as argued earlier, seems to be a recognition both that a
strategic approach is necessary in information processing,
because of the growing impact on business operations and
management activity, and that IT provides strategic
opportunities and threats, which are ignored at management's
peril. User awareness, education and involvement are recorded
as major concerns both now and in the future. User awareness
and involvement repeatedly figure in the conclusions of
research into key variables for successful information systems
development and information management (Gibson and Nolan, 1974;
Lucas, 1975; McCosh et al, 1981). The current concern with
inadequate staff resources reinforces other survey data
(Urwick, 1983) and coping with new ITs is interpreted (from the
word 'coping' and from follow-up discussions) to mean the
management questions that new ITs will pose.
   It is not unusual in the information processing field for
users, and their managers, and DP personnel, and their managers, to have quite different views of each other and of organisational needs and priorities (Hedberg and Mumford, 1975;
Alloway and Quillard, 1983). Table 11.6 reports the priorities
of twelve user managers who ranked, on a Likert scale, 17 user
concerns commonly recognised in the literature. Despite the
small sample, the scoring was remarkably consistent and
reflected two principal dissatisfactions. First, relationships
with the DP professionals are problematic, from the user
perspective, and we might construe that this reflects, and may
explain, the other four key concerns – namely, the recurring
problems of acquiring the systems and applications that users
demand; agreeing on what the systems should provide; and
actually getting projects or facilities developed, implemented

and maintained. To some extent, these also are problems of planning – which the DP managers recorded, but here expressed in user and application terms.

For the future, two other issues are revealed: the exploitation of new ITs and behavioural matters which are seen

Table 11.6: Specific Concerns of Information Technology Users

Current Concerns	Future Concerns
1. Relationship with IT/ DP Department	1. Exploiting New Information Technologies
2. Defining IS/IT Needs	2. Ensuring Applications Meet Needs
3. Agreeing IS/IT Priorities	3. Getting Projects Started
4. Getting Projects Started	4. Behavioural Impact of IS/IT
5. Getting Projects Finished	5. Managing Change

in terms both of impact on organisations and the management of change. Of course, users' current concerns are in part due to behavioural factors, but in the future it seems that users anticipate quite specific and explicit behavioural issues. It is interesting that, whilst research suggests that behavioural factors have been widely overlooked in the past, it is in the future – perhaps because of the perceived dramatic impact of the new ITs – that they may receive greater user management attention. It is also interesting that the DP executives did not register such concerns – confirming perhaps the managerial stereotypes.

To summarise the data so far, both DP managers and user managers recognise that the traditional problem areas of information services planning – user–DP relationships and meeting user needs – will continue to prevail, but they see new technologies throwing up new questions which, perhaps as far as users are concerned, will be especially behavioural.

MANAGEMENT ISSUES

Five of the issues identified in Tables 11.5 and 11.6 now will be examined in detail – strategies, user awareness, planning, coping with new ITs and behavioural factors. They are not only the principal concerns identified in the survey, but areas on which evidence is already emerging.

Strategies

The general case for formulating IT strategies has already been
made; the arguments may be classified as business, management
and technological. From the business viewpoint, many examples
now exist of organisations who have benefitted from strategic
deployment of IT. For instance:

> American Airlines placed terminals into travel agents for
> seat reservation enquiries. The system displays the sche-
> dules and vacancies of any subscribing airline, but is
> programmed to display American Airline offerings first,
> with obvious payload benefits. Then, any reservation
> placed with another airline is first credited to Ameri-
> can's account for subsequent re-allocation, with obvious
> cash float benefit. And, by use of a customer card,
> American has now built up a customer database for sales
> analysis. Commercial Union used computer terminals for a
> similar operation, to break into the American insurance
> broking business by offering terminal enquiry facilities,
> quoting CU policy offerings, and local brokerage account-
> ing systems. Interestingly, like other similar technology
> users, they had to commission special hardware and soft-
> ware and are now in the computing business too.

> John Deere invested in flexible manufacturing systems to
> cope with the twin threats of the recession and new compe-
> tition from small specialist manufacturers. The benefits
> have shown through in productivity, market responsiveness
> and working capital costs. Likewise, Fiat has invested in
> robotics and FMS to counter competition – interestingly,
> their production control system has attracted as much
> interest as their automation.

> Merrill Lynch used its computers to occupy a niche left
> exposed by other financial institutions. It developed
> its Cash Management Account and gained market share.
> Incidentally, it chose a small Midwest bank to provide its
> computer processing. Likewise, Reuters, traditionally a
> news and information gathering agency, has invested in
> worldwide data communication to collect, store and disse-
> minate financial information to the financial sector,
> thereby developing a new product-market, and multiplying
> profits in the process – and when many other news agencies
> are in financial distress.

These examples – using IT as a competitive weapon, as a
productivity tool for survival, as a means for delivering new
services – demonstrate the opportunities available. They also
demonstrate several further points:
  1. As ever, one competitor's opportunity is another's
threat. The laggard airlines, automotive manufacturers etc.

may perish - except that, as ever, competitor retaliation is likely, which Merrill Lynch is already discovering as other financial institutions seek to catch up, and as American Airlines are discovering since the US Congress, the Justice Department and the Civil Aeronautics Board are all investigating charges that the airlines which develop and sell these systems to agents gain competitive advantage. Indeed, regulators may soon also consider the question of technological barriers to entry.

2. IT can take you into new business. Do all businesses - indeed do Commercial Union or Bank One of Ohio (the Merrill Lynch subcontractor) - want to be in the technology business and have they the long term capability? Is this a necessary price of competitive advantage, is it an uncontrollable and unforeseen diversification or is it the first step of joint and cooperative ventures?

3. The thinking that is required to exploit IT is as much marketing, production, financial thinking as technological know-how. Organisations which seek to exploit IT need to bring about a creative fusion of functional know-how and ideation.

4. As IT, especially data communication, extends the boundaries of an organisation and its trade, who is recognising and taking the new business and political decisions involved? If the Reuters network provides duplex interaction between currency dealers, need they use the banks and brokers, and what will be the financial sector's responses? Even more dramatically, as the banks establish national point-of-sale networks, who is to be allowed into the network, and under what conditions, and with what power? Already pilot schemes accommodate banks, other financial institutions and retailers - who pays, who benefits, who controls - and what are the further implications when the consumer is networked? As Read (1983) asks, what are the politics of the technology?

5. Functional strategies may depend on IT. The ability to deliver a product-market strategy, a manufacturing strategy, a financial strategy, and so on, may rest on the implementation of IT, or at least have implications for information processing functions. Any functional or corporate strategy is today incomplete without its IT component.

Thus, these case examples demonstrate that, besides the strategic opportunities afforded by IT, general strategic questions are raised - about mission, about organising for innovation, about competitive strategy, about regulation and power, and about the linkage between IT and other strategies.

The set of management strategy arguments is perhaps less obvious. In short, it is the concern for the impact on management - particularly on structure and style (Tricker, 1982) - of IT. As the distribution, use and boundaries of IT expand, the impact on organisation structure or management style could be significant. Second, IT may offer the opportunity to change and to develop alternative management styles and structures.

Networking is one obvious technological means for change, bringing new opportunities for inter and intraorganisational functioning. The need for a management strategy, therefore, is not only positive, that is, using IT to facilitate desired change, but also defensive, that is, ensuring that IT decisions made on technical or economic criteria do not bring about unforeseen organisational change. For example, development of an end-user enquiry system, with access to central data, stimulated devolutionary pressures in an insurance firm, and use of decision support systems can foster middle management autonomy and challenge (Alter, 1976). On the other hand, some experiments on executive networking, presumably are being done with organisational benefits in mind.

The technology strategy argument is more obvious. Long term infrastructures have to be laid down, data architectures have to be conceptualised, compatibility has to be planned. Technological investment is expensive and cannot be disposable, so an ordered implementation schedule is desirable. For example, the DHSS has formulated a computing strategy for social security operations. Efficient and reliable social security operations are dependent on IT support. The strategy has a time-frame of 15 years. In formulating it, the factors considered included: future demands for social security operations; management information and policy analysis; data structures; security exposure; data privacy; national and regional administrative structure; interfaces with the Inland Revenue and other government operations; evolution of payment systems; technology futures; vendor policy; available resources; implementation schedules; working conditions; legal constraints; trade union agreements, and so on. All these factors indicate both why an IT strategic plan is necessary and what is involved.

McLean and Soden reported in 1976 that more executives talk about information systems strategic planning than do it. Seventy-two per cent of our survey organisations, however, are attempting it, but, as discussed later, it is not an easy task. Furthermore, the importance and intensity of IT strategy formulation may vary with the dependence of current and future operations on IT (McFarlan et al, 1983).

User Awareness

DP managers viewed user awareness and education as a priority concern now and in the future. User awareness, although clear conceptually, is difficult to measure and research evidence is accordingly thin. However, it is clear that user involvement in information systems development is a necessary condition for success (Swanson, 1974; Lucas, 1975; Keen and Scott-Morton, 1978), and user awareness, especially IT experience of the user community, is held to be a determinant of the stages through which managements learn to manage DP (Gibson and Nolan, 1974; Nolan, 1979). Furthermore, Drury (1983) recently has shown that DP management problems become less serious in organisations with increasing user awareness.

However, DP managers assigned higher priority to user awareness and education now, than in the future. Whether this reflects optimism over progress, or the progressive impact of new ITs, or the future dominance of other concerns is not clear. Drury (1983) was unable to conclude whether adoption of technology begat user awareness or vice versa. Perhaps the DP managers believe in the former association. Certainly the technology trends outlined earlier are taking IT to the user and, with national IT promotions such as IT82, educational and awareness benefits are evident. It was also argued earlier that these trends would impose on IT managers a necessity, if not responsibility, for providing educational and facilitative services. It is also interesting that the survey data revealed that it is now the norm for users to be represented on IT project teams, for users sometimes to lead projects, and for general managers to be involved in steering committees. Thus, perhaps user awareness and education is advancing.

Curiously, or perhaps in confirmation of this observation, user managers, however, did not rate user awareness and education as a priority. This may indicate that user managers feel they are sufficiently IT aware or educated, or that the issue is of low priority in managing IT, or that 'they don't know what they don't know'. It is probable, though, that the respondent user managers are a biased sample, since they were attending IT management courses and thus at least they themselves may already have been 'converted'. My own experience suggests that IT managers tend to complain of low immediate requirements but do not understand either the technological implications or the technological opportunities beyond, and that general managers find it difficult to link their business concerns, on which they are very articulate, to technological developments. Thus, besides personal education and awareness, what are required are organisational structures and processes to bring these groups together in a development coalition.

Planning

We have seen that on top of the traditional case for long range planning of IT applications there is now a case for strategic planning. Table 11.7 shows that 72 per cent of our survey organisations attempt long range and/or strategic planning of IT. It has been reported elsewhere that some organisations believe in IT planning, some are succeeding at it, and some have failed and despair of it (Pyburn, 1983). Table 11.8 reveals the benefits expected and realised of IT planning by the survey organisations. Respondents were asked to rank, on a Likert scale, the benefits from a list of seventeen suggested in the IT planning literature. It is interesting that both the anticipated and realised results are a mix of product and

Table 11.7:   Trends in IT Planning

Characteristic	% of 42 Organisations
Formulating IT Long Range Plans	72%
Formulating IT Strategic Plans	72%
Possess Business Long Range Plans	81%
Possess Corporate Strategic Plans	66%
Linking IT and Business Long Range Plans	41%
Linking IT and Corporate Strategic Plans	35%

Table 11.8:   Benefits of IT Planning

Expected Benefits	Realised Benefits
1. Improved Top Management Support	1. Improved Top Management Support
2. Improved User Involvement	2. Improved Resource Forecasting
3. Improved Resource Forecasting	3. Improved Business Planning
4. Improved Business Planning	4. Improved User Communication
5. Understanding the Organisation/Business	5. Understanding the Organisation/Business

process benefits. Whereas the product of better technology and
business plans were sought and achieved, top management support
- which was the dominant expected and realised benefit - user
involvement and communication, and better DP/IT understanding
of the business, were significant process gains. These process
goals are, of course, frequently cited as critical success
factors in IT management, both by research-based and more
normative literatures. Pyburn (1983) recently emphasised the
importance of communication processes and of seeking a shared
consensus between the parties in MIS strategic planning, and
McLean (1983) has suggested that process benefits were the
early outcomes of such exercises. Indeed, in that DP/IT understanding of the business/organisation, top management support
and user involvement and communication seem to be positive
gains from IT planning, it may provide one valuable means of

achieving the management coalition advocated in the previous
section. As in other functions, learning to plan may also be a
case of planning to learn, as Michael (1973) has suggested.

Nevertheless, the products of IT planning are not a minor
concern; furthermore, process benefits may be more effectively
achieved when there is an obvious product benefit being sought.
One problem in producing a satisfactory 'product' may be the
absence of long range or strategic business plans, from which
to derive IT plans, a lacuna which the IT planners may have to
remedy themselves by induction (King, 1978). Table 11.7 shows
that this lacuna is not a dominant problem, but the linking of
IT plans to business plans appears to remain problematic.
McLean and Soden (1976) identified several approaches to this
task, whilst Pyburn (1983) has classified three contingent
methodologies. It is clear that IT strategic and long range
planning methods are still under experimentation, that several
alternatives exist and that any one organisation's approach
should fit its organisational structure, management style,
strategic dependence on IT, previous experience in managing and
planning IT activities, business planning procedures,
environmental uncertainty, etc. This is suggested by Table
11.8 which reveals the more important problems experienced by
29 survey organisations, the respondents having ranked, on a
Likert scale, problems from a list of eighteen. IT planning
clearly is still immature and there are several methodological
problems to be resolved.

Coping with New ITs

Whereas the new IT era presents significant architectural challenges to IT planners, not only having to predict the divergent
and convergent development of multiple technologies, but also
the potential uses and demands of host organisations, 'coping'
with IT implies something further. It implies an expectation
that IT managers will be faced with a new set of managerial
issues when, perhaps, they feel they have barely begun to con-
quer the managerial challenges of conventional DP. Indeed, the
information manager is about to be exposed to a double sandbag.
He is expected by the user community and top management to continue the improvement in managing traditional forms of information processing, in particular, resolving the current planning
and organisational issues identified in Table 11.6, extending
the DP applications portfolio, and tackling the requirements
backlog. Concurrently, top management will be expecting major
gains from the new ITs and the user community will be expecting a rapid provision of end-user, local, personal facilities.
Faced with such expectations, some healthy and some naive, and
armed with over 20 years of hard-won DP experience, it is no
wonder that many DP managers are the new conservatives of management. They sense danger in the adventurous years ahead.

Yet, is it not likely that lessons learned from the past
will be applied to the future? This is a somewhat controver-

sial question.   Nolan (1979) has developed a widely-accepted
hypothesis that organisations and their managements learnt how
to manage DP in stages, each stage delineated by a crisis to
which new managerial responses were made.   This learning curve
of four, or perhaps six, stages is thought to be technologically driven, with each stage lasting several years and
representing in the later stages increasing sophistication
(although not necessarily rigour) of management and automation
of information processing functions.   Each stage represents a
balance of tight and loose, control-oriented, and innovation-
oriented management.   Subsequent empirical testing (Lucas and
Sutton, 1977;   Drury, 1983) has been inconclusive, but the
hypothesis is by no means disproven, and certainly is accepted
by many managers.   At the same time, the idea of evolutionary,
or stage by stage, adoption of technology and management of
change, in general, is not without support (Schein, 1961;
Greiner, 1972).   The key question is whether a process of
technology transfer will occur, such that learning from
managing DP will be applied to adoption of office automation,
data communication, etc.   Early research evidence suggests not
- stages of learning are being identified in office
automation, for example (Curley, 1981).   Moreover, my own
observations in organisations and discussions with managers
suggest that managerial 'mistakes' are being repeated in the
application of the new ITs.   For example, trivial rather than
economically obvious applications are developed first, possibly
in order to learn and at least to achieve technical success,
with more viable applications being discovered later;   top
management support is lacking and DP/IT managers are left to
take the lead; behavioural factors, especially the man machine
interface, are relegated in importance;   and technological
motives   and   drive   outweigh   business,   management   and
organisational understanding.

    So perhaps we do have to learn again for each technology,
and perhaps the role of experienced information managers is to
smooth the learning curve.   The underlying management issues
will be similar but they will manifest themselves differently,
and some of the solutions - the techniques, systems and procedures - will differ.   For example, it is not obvious that small
computing is in need of management controls to the extent that
mainframe DP was.   It is clear that for some of the technologies, the balance between centralisation and decentralisation will be quite different - the hardware costs and development skills are not so influential - but some central overall
coordination will still be desirable (Ein-Dor and Segev, 1982)
and a charter for the information processing function will be
required, even if it is fluid.   Nevertheless, the 'meta-truths'
discovered from management of DP in the past will be just as
relevant - IT must be business-driven, must have top management support and must have user involvement, but the methods
developed to pursue these truths will be organisation-specific,

rather than universal.

Behavioural Factors

'Behavioural factors' can mean all things to all people. I
will use the term to cover the relationship between IT and
human behaviour – at the societal, organisational, group and
individual levels. I want to select only four issues amongst
many.

First, there is growing evidence that, as in DP in the
past, managements are ignoring, relegating or postponing attention to behavioural matters. Two of the new ITs are illustrative. It is becoming clear that robotics all too easily de-
skill work (apart from any effect on employment levels).
Rosenbrock (1982) documents how man is frequently relegated to
machine so that, for example, the robot does the skilled tasks
and the man sweeps up the swarf. Likewise, employers in the US
are reported to be seeking mentally retarded workers to operate
numerically controlled tools[3]. In office automation, we
see experiments and developments commissioned for technical and
economic reasons with little thought, or after-thought, for the
effect on work practices, job design or social behaviour. The
following extracts from an article describing such a project
may demonstrate the point. The emphases are mine.

> 'It is important to remember that our experiment at Conti-
> nental concerns itself chiefly with the equipment and an
> overall technological test of the system. Obviously,
> working at home suits some but not others; however at
> this stage of the program we are not actively trying to
> determine how people adapt to a home work environment...
> The social implications of permanent home work stations
> will be many; however we know only a few at this
> time... Although our development of information systems
> technology at Continental is only a few years old, we have
> gone well beyond the point of no return.' (Mertes, 1981)

Second, there seems to be a new era of technological
determinism dawning. We talk of the impact of IT, we are sold
the economic benefits or imperatives of IT by governments and
their agencies, and we consider the 'behavioural implications'.
Yet, it may be that for reasons of the long term economic and
technical viability of IT applications, as much as for social
desirability, we should aggressively consider how to elevate
social or behavioural criteria and develop and apply IT for the
betterment of man at all levels of society – for example,
seeking to relegate the machine to man, still in the pursuit of
economic gain, as Rosenbrock is trying to do, or seeking to
apply IT to improve job satisfaction as well as to satisfy more
obvious economic goals, as Mumford (1983) continues to
facilitate.

Third, it is likely that protection of social goals and

achievement of wider organisational goals will be more feasible if users are involved in not only the operation and development of IT applications, but in their planning. The need for user participation has been stressed earlier, but the later the participation the more that design alternatives are closed off and the more likely is resistance to change. Participation is not an easy process, but we do have some good research knowledge on the pitfalls and possibilities (Neergaard, 1977). At the procedural level it is clear that in CAD/CAM and robotics, as well as in mainstream DP, lack of early consultation with employees and trade unions is one impediment to adoption of new ITs[4]. Indeed, one study reports that managements prefer to automate first and hammer out any new agreements later, from the position of strength afforded them by the economic climate[5]. Technology agreements are one form of procedure available and there are over one hundred in existence in the UK (Williams and Moseley, 1982). Other approaches include technology conferences and IT awareness and education programmes. Indeed, from all perspectives, one necessary priority may be the enhancement of computer literacy throughout organisations - and not necessarily tackled by management alone, but by trade unions, state education and other interested parties.

Fourth, we do need more research into these matters. Academics have done useful research on IT in the past - as demonstrated by other contributors to this volume - and new research projects are underway. Yet even here, there is some determinism evident. The UK Government, through the Department of Trade and Industry, has invited the SSRC to handle a programme of research on the acceptability of new technology. The principle objective of the programme is:

> 'the formulation of generalizable lessons for industry and government of how to secure greater acceptance of new technologies by developing their positive aspects, and minimizing their negative aspects, from an enhanced understanding of the cultural and organisational determinants of public attitudes.'[6]

To minimise deleterious effects and to maximise benefits is one thing; to minimise negative aspects in terms of attitudes and their determinants is quite another. However, it is not just the academic community which has a responsibility for research. We need action research of an experimental kind in organisations by organisations on the relationships between IT and behaviour, plus monitoring of the behavioural as well as economic and technical outcomes of new IT projects.

MANAGEMENT AGENDA

To synthesise the previous sections, an agenda is offered for the management of new ITs. It has six items or imperatives:

1. <u>Information Management must be 'normalised'</u>. The need
for formal management of IT is becoming well recognised, but it
must also be appreciated that essentially it involves much the
same tasks - planning, organising, controlling - as in any
other function, and it involves user management and general
management as well as the technologists. IT, of course, brings
its own expertise and challenges, but so do other resources.
Certainly each IT in turn may pose novel problems, and IT may
be 'different' because it is new, rapidly changing and growing
- but if we oversell the differences, managements may never
begin to manage it. IT must become a normal focus of management attention.
2. <u>IT strategies must be formulated.</u> The strategic
importance of IT must be recognised, the implications addressed
and a strategy developed. However, the importance of IT strategy will vary amongst organisations, as will the methods of
formulation - and any strategy will have to be flexible, in
order to respond to technological change as much as to business
uncertainty. Nevertheless today corporate strategy is not
complete without an IT strategy.
3. <u>IT infrastructures must be constructed.</u> These include
hardware, software and data. The hardware infrastructure will
comprise the disposition of DP equipment, data communications
networks and the interfaces between multiple ITs. The software
infrastructure will comprise database management systems,
modelling, enquiry and other high level language facilities for
end-users, protocol and other standard interface languages, as
well as mainstream applications and system software. The data
infrastructure will be concerned with the organisation, access
and security of data, which increasingly are a crucial
resource.
4. <u>The IT executive must be elevated.</u> The strategic
nature of IT demands a good business knowledge, a top level
locus, and both communication and political skills for the senior information executive. The importance of fostering a coalition between user managers, general management and information management may well argue that IT managers should have
general and line management experience. This has been found
beneficial in conventional DP management (McKaskill, 1977), and
in 50 per cent of the survey organisations the top DP manager
had line management experience. Equally, the need for IT
infrastructures demands that the information executive is also
an architect. Seventy-nine per cent of the survey DP managers
had previous experience of IT and this also would seem a desirable qualification. All these requirements point to appoint-
ment of broadly experienced executives at the level where they
have both the status of, and real contact with, general
managers. In 30 per cent of the survey organisations there is
an IT executive on the main board.
5. <u>There must be greater attention to, and explication
of, behavioural factors.</u> This is not only required to satisfy

social goals, but in the long run is likely to assist the pursuit of economic and technological goals. There may be, of course, incremental costs in the short run.

6.   Realities must be recognised. The technological trends identified at the outset are a reality, which may necessitate unlearning some of our past experience, before we learn how to cope. More important, organisations change more slowly than does technology. Whilst high expectations are necessary, mistakes will be made. If we recognise this, the 'normalisation' of managing IT will have begun.

NOTES

1. The data presented here are extracted from a pilot survey of 44 executives, namely participants in 'management of IT' courses run at the Oxford Centre for Management Studies. The survey was conducted in late 1982 and early 1983.

2. Data provided by Nolan, Norton & Company, DP Management Consultants.

3. Reported in Computing, 12 May 1983.

4. Results of a NEDO survey reported in the Guardian, 27 July 1983.

5. Results of a study by the Trade Union Unit at Ruskin College reported in Computing, 12 May 1983.

6. As reported in The Times Higher Educational Supplement, 26 August 1983.

REFERENCES

Alloway, R.M. and Quillard, J.A. (1983) 'User Managers' Systems Needs', MIS Quarterly, June, 27–43

Alter, S. (1976) 'How Effective Managers Use Information Systems', Harvard Business Review, Nov–Dec, 97–105

Curley, K. (1981) Word Processing: First Step To The Office of the Future? An Examination of the Evolving Technology And Its Use in Organisations, Unpublished doctoral thesis, Harvard Business School

Down, P.J. and Taylor, F.G. (1976) Why Distributed Computing?, National Computing Centre, Manchester

Drury, D.H. (1983) 'An Empirical Assessment of the Stages of DP Growth', MIS Quarterly, June, 59–71

Ein-Dor, P. and Segev, E. (1982) 'Information Systems: Emergence of a New Organizational Function', Information and Management, 5, 279–87

Gibson, C.F. and Nolan, R.L. (1974) 'Managing the Four Stages of EDP Growth', Harvard Business Review, Jan–Feb, 76–89

Greiner, L. (1972) 'Evolution and Revolution As Organizations Grow', Harvard Business Review, July–Aug, 37–47

Hedberg, B. and Mumford, E. (1975) 'The Design of Computer Systems: Man's Vision Of Man As An Integral Part of the System Design Process', in Mumford, E. and Sackman, H. (eds.), Human Choice and Computers, North Holland, Amsterdam

Keen, P.G.W. and Scott-Morton, M.S. (1978) Decision Support Systems: An Organizational Perspective, Addison-Wesley, Reading, Mass.

King, W.R. (1978) 'Strategic Planning for Management Information Systems', MIS Quarterly, March, 27–39

Lucas, H.C. (1975) Why Information Systems Fail, Columbia University Press, New York

Lucas, H.C. and Sutton, J.A. (1977) 'The Stage Hypothesis and S-Curve: Some Contradictory Evidence', Communications of the ACM, 20(4), 254–9

McCosh, A.M., Rahman, M. and Earl, M.J. (1981) Developing Managerial Information Systems, Macmillan, London

McFarlan, F.W., McKenny, J.L. and Pyburn, P. (1983) The Information Archipelago - Plotting a Course', Harvard Business Review, Jan-Feb, 145-57

McKaskill, T. (1977) Effective Computer-Based Information Systems Operations: A Comparative Organisational Study. Unpublished Ph.D thesis, London Business School

McKenny, J.L. and McFarlan, F.W. (1982) 'The Information Archipelago - Maps and Bridges', Harvard Busines Review, Sept-Oct, 109-120

McLean, E.R. and Soden, J.V. (1976) Strategic Planning for MIS, Wiley, New York

McLean, E.R. (1983) Strategic Planning for MIS: An Update, Information Systems Working Paper 4-83, Graduate School of Management, UCLA

Mendelson, L. (1983) 'Micros for the Class of 83', Computing, 11 Aug, 21

Mertes, L.H. (1981) 'Doing Your Office Over - Electronically', Harvard Business Review, March - April, 127-136

Michael, D.N. (1973) On Learning To Plan - And Planning to Learn, Jossey-Bass, San Francisco

MORI (1982) Opinion Survey On Impact Of Information Technology Year, December

Mumford, E. (1983) Designing Secretaries: The Participative Design of a Word Processing System. Manchester Business School

Neergaard, P. (1977) Some Research Results on Participative Design, European Institute for Advanced Studies in Management Workshop paper

Nolan, R.L. (1979) 'Managing The Crises in Data Processing', Harvard Business Review, March-April, 115-27

Pyburn, P.J. (1983) 'Linking the MIS Plan with Corporate Strategy: An Exploratory Study', MIS Quarterly, June, 1-15

Read, C. (1983) 'Information Technology in Banking', Long Range Planning, 16(4), 21-30

Rosenbrock, H.H. (1982), 'Technology Policies and Options', in Bjorn-Andersen, N., Earl, M., Holst, O. and Mumford, E. (eds.) Information Society: For Richer, For Poorer, North Holland, Amsterdam

Schein, E.H. (1961) 'Management Development As a Process of Influence', Industrial Management Review, 2, 59-69

Swanson, E.B. (1974) 'MIS: Appreciation and Involvement', Management Science, 21(2), 178-88

Tricker, R.I. (1982) Effective Information Management. Beaumont Executive Press, Oxford

Urwick, (1983) 'Quarterly Survey of UK Data Processing Managers', Computing, 14 July, 14-15

Whisler, T.L. (1970) The Impact of Computers on Organizations, Praeger, New York

Williams, R. and Moseley, R. (1982) 'The Trade Union Response to Information Technology - Technology Agreements: Consensus, Control and Technical Change In the Workplace', in Bjorn-Andersen, N., Earl, M., Holst, O. and Mumford, E. (eds.), Information Society: For Richer, For Poorer, North Holland, Amsterdam

Chapter 12

CHANGES IN INFORMATION TECHNOLOGY, ORGANISATIONAL
DESIGN AND MANAGERIAL CONTROL

Roger Mansfield

INTRODUCTION

Throughout history, progress in technological endeavour whether
based on intuition, trial and error or scientific discoveries
has had profound social significance. Perhaps its implications
have been most clearly evidenced in the structure, conduct and
in many cases the very existence of work organisations.
Although observers are united in their belief that technology
and technological change have been intimately and significantly
related to changes in the nature and functioning of work organisations, the particular patterning of such interactions
remains, in large measure, problematic. Despite the inconclusive and often contradictory nature of the evidence, it is
clear that managerial decisions regarding the design of organisational systems have been both inspired and constrained by the
varieties of technology employed. In this chapter the main
focus will be on the linkages between some of the latest developments in information technology and organisational design and
managerial control. In addition to a brief examination of
relationships between the use of the new technology in production processes, offices and accounting systems, consideration
will be given to the structural implications of the utilisation
of information technology in the areas of organisation related
most closely to organisational administration and policy formulation.

NEW INFORMATION TECHNOLOGY

Information technology is not generally used as a precisely
defined concept, but rather its employment is generally taken
to cover a broad category of technological developments relating to the creation, transmission, manipulation and presentation of data. These developments are largely based on silicon
chip microelectronic circuitry and are mainly directed towards
communication, computation and control. One of the characteristics of the latest technological advances is the apparently
enormous flexibility of the underlying technical systems and

ideas, and hence the tremendous variety of hardware manifested in the latest advances of information technology, and the even greater diversity of software designed to accompany them. At the heart of most recent developments in hardware is the microprocessor, usually based on a silicon chip. Chips allied to other developments in technology have allowed such diverse developments as robots, word processors and computer numerically controlled machine tools. The possibilities would seem to be almost endless and already electronic development has progressed a huge distance beyond the achievements embodied in the early computers.

There can be no doubt that the impact of new information technology viewed in the broad terms suggested above depends on where and how it is used (Francis and Willman, 1980). As Sorge et al argue most cogently in the introductory chapter to their book Microelectronics and Manpower in Manufacturing:

> 'it is therefore advisable to exercise great caution when reading accounts or predictions of the effects of information technology.... The wide range of applications leads to a similarly wide range of effects, many of which may be in different directions.' (Sorge et al, 1983, p.4)

The whole issue is further substantially complicated when it is noted that in many instances new information technology is not employed as a new way of carrying out activities which were performed previously in other ways. Rather, it is very often the case that the new technology is employed in remodelled organisational systems, where not just the internal functioning of organisations has been modified, but their strategic objectives and relationships with environmental systems have also evolved into new configurations.

From the foregoing it is clear that it is not possible to formulate general arguments and conclusions concerning the impact on organisational design and managerial control of new information technology as a general phenomenon; at least, not in simple cause and effect terms. In order to determine the relationships involved it is necessary to examine the entire socio-technical system, taking full account of the interactions involved between the technology employed and the social system of the organisation employing it. Obviously in a single short discussion it is only possible to attempt to consider a limited number of applications of new information technology, even in broad categories. Hence, as noted earlier, the main thrust of the analysis will be devoted to a consideration of the role of new information technology in areas linked to strategic and administrative decision-making and associated systems of control. However, before moving on to these issues the general factors involved in organisational design will be considered, followed by a very brief review of the structural implications of operating and office technologies with particular reference to recent developments relating to microelectronics.

ORGANISATIONAL DESIGN

It is clear that organisational structures and control systems do not just happen, nor are they the consequence of impersonal causal patterns set in motion by the adoption of particular technological systems, or the institution of technological change. On the contrary, organisational design, like the choice of technological systems themselves, is a consequence of human decision-making. In the main, such decisions are taken by the senior managers of the organisations in question. More accurately, in most cases the decision-making processes involved are dominated by such senior managers. As Mansfield (1984) has suggested, the structural blueprints stemming from organisational design decisions may be viewed, in large part, in terms of attempted answers to the general organisational problems which management confronts. He suggests that these problems may essentially be viewed under three headings. The first problem relates closely to the goals or strategic objectives the organisation is designed to achieve and may be regarded as the problem of task accomplishment, or in its simplest terms, that of getting things done. The second problem is that of organisational or managerial control and the third that of cost. Clearly these three problems are typically closely interlinked, but the pattern of relationships between them will vary substantially depending on the type of organisation involved.

The characterisation of the varieties of organisational structures, ensuing from the process of organisational design, has been complicated by the wide variety of approaches, concepts and nomenclature that have been employed. In terms of the basic logic of organisations, the different parameters of structure examined by most writers may be considered in terms of the way they influence and regulate the division of labour in organisations, or the processes of coordination.

One of the basic reasons for the existence of organisations would seem to be that they allow a coordinated division of labour between functions and between persons carrying out those functions. Indeed, this seems so fundamental that some writers (e.g. Porter et al, 1975) have incorporated the idea into their definition of organisations. The nature of the division of labour within organisations, both between individuals and between departments or sections, is clearly of importance both for task accomplishment and for the maintenance of organisational control. One critical aspect of this is the basic logic by which such a division of labour proceeds. Most commonly this logic is based on functional differences, but divisions based on products, geography or types of customer are also frequently found. Indeed, in some of the largest companies all the methods mentioned are employed simultaneously in a complex mixture. The logic implied in the division of labour is quite simply that by sub-dividing tasks, those tasks can be carried out more effectively, by being done better, or faster or cheaper.

The division of labour in organisations is not just between different parts of the basic productive tasks which need to be carried out. In addition, there is a division of labour between the carrying out of tasks and the control of those tasks. This further aspect of the division of labour takes two rather different forms. Most obviously in any organisation there is some division between operatives and supervisors and managers, that is between those that basically carry out the directly productive work of the organisation, and those who are their hierarchical superiors who plan, coordinate and control these directly productive activities. However, in many organisations, and in virtually all large ones, there is also a lateral division of labour between those functions, such as production and sales, which contribute directly to the task accomplishment of the organisation and those functions, such as inspection and accounting, which together with management help to coordinate and control these former activities.

The concepts and terms which are most frequently used to describe aspects of the division of labour or its organisational manifestations are functional and role specialisation, differentiation, departmentalisation, divisionalisation and number of hierarchical levels or vertical span.

In addition to structural arrangements for the division of labour in organisations, there are also structural mechanisms for coordination. Clearly, some such mechanisms must be designed into organisations if they are in any real sense to be organised and hence survive as social systems. Broadly, in social systems, two generic types of mechanism have been identified. One depends on exchange relationships regulated by some sort of market forces, and the other depends on some kind of authority system epitomised in the concept of hierarchy (Williamson, 1975). In the organisational setting both are relevant, and both would seem to be employed by all organisations. However, in the main, market transactions characterise the dealings of organisations with their environments, whilst authority relationships characterise the internal workings of organisations.

The authority system is essentially bureaucratic in form in any modern organisation. It depends on the rules and procedures of the organisation, and is most clearly institutionalised in the hierarchical arrangement of organisational positions or offices into levels of subordination or superordination. The characteristics of the system of coordination, stemming from bureaucratic authority, have been assessed by organisational researchers using a range of concepts and terminology. It would seem that the most critical elements can be subsumed under three broad headings, namely bureaucracy, centralisation and integration.

In the Weberian description of the ideal type bureaucracy the two prime characteristics are impersonal standardised rules and procedures, covering most contingencies, and a system of record-keeping and files to act as a sort of collective memory of organisational actions. These two structural dimensions are often referred to as standardisation and formalisation (Pugh et al, 1968).

In terms of the three basic problems for administration suggested above (i.e. task accomplishment, control and cost), it is clear that decisions regarding the extent of bureaucratisation and centralisation in any given organisation are made particularly in order to solve the second problem of control. In addition, integration may be enhanced by such structural mechanisms as ad hoc meetings, formal committees, liaison officers and whole coordinating departments, forming a sequence of higher levels of integration than pure reliance on hierarchy and procedure.

OPERATING TECHNOLOGY AND STRUCTURE

The implications of the operating technology employed and of technological change for the design of organisational structures and systems of control have been the subject of a large amount of research and theoretical dispute. In the main, the results of this extensive work have not led to many clear conclusions. However, there would seem to be the beginnings of consensus that the operating technology employed does cause certain constraints on organisational design decisions. It would seem to be the case that the implications are most heavily felt in those parts of organisations which are functionally closely linked to the technology in question, and that the effects of technology on organisational structures are most noticeable in smaller rather than larger organisations (Hickson et al, 1969; Child and Mansfield, 1972).

Child and Mansfield (1972, p.388) suggested that the results of the Aston and National studies, considered together, suggested the following conclusions with regard to relationships between technology and structural variables:

1. Role and functional specialisation are moderately related to technology independently of size, such that more technologically integrated workflows tended to be accompanied by higher levels of specialisation.

2. Technology is related particularly to the organisation of functional areas such as maintenance and workflow control, which are closely linked to the technology used itself.

3. Different aspects of technology relate differently to structural variables.

They did point out that when comparisons are made with the results of other studies 'the discrepancies....seem to be at least as great as the commonalities' (Child and Mansfield, 1972, p. 389).

The studies mentioned above, like the large majority of research in this area, were carried out before what is now described as new information technology was introduced on a significant scale in organisations. However, in the operations or production areas of organisational activities, recent technological developments would seem to be, in the main, extensions of earlier advances which have added automation to the previous processes of mechanisation. Thus such developments as robots, automatic control, computer numerically controlled machine tools, closed circuit television and automatic inspection, spectacular as they may be in particular applications, can be seen essentially as a continuation of a long term trend.

Although the results of particular studies relating operations technology to structural parameters are often contradictory, as has already been noted, a clearer picture seems to emerge when a broad view of the evolution of technology and associated organisational, social and economic processes, as applied to work organisations, is considered. Following the work of Sorge et al (1983), it is possible to suggest a number of general trends which have been widely observed in work organisations. Thus there has tended to be an increase in:

1. Mechanisation of work leading to the replacement of human effort by machines and technical systems.

2. Automation of work leading to the replacement of human thinking and control by machines and technical systems.

3. Capital intensity leading to a partial replacement of labour costs by investment in machines and technical systems, and more obviously by a shift in the balance of expenditure, thus decreasing the percentage spent on wages and salaries.

4. Division of labour between different functional activities. This is seen both between different personnel involved directly in the production process, and between production activities and control, support and other staff activities.

5. Polarisation of skills leading to a very sharp and significant gap in the skills, experience and qualifications between largely semi-skilled operatives and the frequently highly technically skilled design, control and maintenance personnel.

6. Centralisation of decision-making relating to operating decisions, as increasingly the discretion of operatives has been removed to higher levels or to specialist support staff.

7. Bureaucratisation of production with increasing use of plans and schedules.

These trends can, in large measure, be explained in terms of dealing with the problems of task accomplishment and cost control or reduction in a competitive market situation. In this context it would seem that the problem of maintaining managerial control is largely a secondary one, the solution to which is instrumental in finding satisfactory solutions to the other two problems. Of course, the general patterns of change suggested above have not occurred uniformly in all organisations, and indeed there are clearly cases where developments have gone against the prevailing trend. Such apparent aberrations can typically be easily explained by reference to the particular market and technological circumstances in which such organisations operate, and their strategic response to these. Thus, only by examination of the particular task to be accomplished, and the balance of costs and revenues associated with it, can predictions be made in a particular case.

OFFICE TECHNOLOGY AND STRUCTURE

Until relatively recently office work was not greatly affected by technological change, although it would be unwise to underestimate the implications of the introduction of such technological developments as the typewriter and adding machine. The first really significant changes were brought about by the introduction into commercial situations of the digital computer. As Khandwalla (1977) has reported, in the early days of computer applications in business and industry a large number of diverse and often contradictory predictions were made about the likely impact of computers on organisations. However, in the main, the utilisation of computers led to highly predictable consequences in many accounting and clerical operations. The problematic areas which will be considered in the next section were those surrounding effects on decision-making and control at higher organisational levels, and particularly the implications for middle management.

Given the large costs involved in the purchase and operation of early generations of computers, they tended in the main to be used by larger organisations, where their computational power was widely used in functional areas which required the storage and manipulation of large amounts of quantitative information. This led to three main structural effects. First there was a reworking of the division of labour with the introduction of new types of specialists in electronic data processing, the further sub-division of many highly routine clerical tasks, and the introduction of a substantial division of labour between the designers of systems and programmers, operatives who input data and the managers and staff specialists who used the computer output. The second main structural effect was a further increase in bureaucracy as computer systems required very high levels of standardisation of data preparation and use. The third structural implication of the computer was a centralisation of some record keeping and data processing operations, as a consequence of the high cost of computer installations and the specialised skill required to operate them, in order to gain economic efficiency. Typically as a result of this, companies had few computers (often only one) and needed to keep them fully employed, thus necessitating central data processing departments.

Later developments have substantially changed the situation once again. In particular, the following recent advances and changes have had a profound influence on the office use of electronic technology:

1. The relative price reductions in electronic equipment compared to most other organisational costs; and indeed the absolute price reductions in a very large number of cases.

2. The increasing speed and power of electronic computing and communications equipment.

3. The reducing size of electronic equipment, such that small desk top computers are now commonly available with similar computing power to those that occupied whole rooms in the 1950s and 1960s.

4. The ever-increasing range and sophistication of available software to match computer and microcomputer based systems. Much of this software is now available in off-the-shelf package form with sufficient versatility to fit a wide variety of situations.

5. The increasing ability of computer systems to deal with non-numerical information.

6. The general trend towards user-friendliness in computer and communication systems, making it easier for a wide range of personnel with only limited training to use such systems.

Taken together it is clear that these recent developments constitute a significant shift and widening in technological possibilities from the early days of electronic data processing. Obviously such technology is widely, cheaply and easily available. At the same time significant changes have taken place with regard to the place of computers and associated equipment in society in general with even primary school children having experience of computer use.

There can be no doubt that the various developments noted above have led to a dramatic increase in the adoption of information technology hardware in a very wide variety of organisations, including some of the smallest. Indeed, perhaps the area in which the recent changes have been the most obvious is in the modern office with word processors, electronic sorting and filing, and immediate input and output of quantitative data through VDU terminals. This has led to differences in the quantity and type of jobs involved, but the implications for organisational design have in the main not been that dramatic and have largely been predictable. The widespread use of new systems has to an extent made offices more rigid and bureaucratic in their procedures, as secretarial and clerical staff are not typically trained to use the full flexibility of the latest systems.

Perhaps the most significant changes related to the shift

from large scale computer installations, typically operated as a centralised operation supported by centralised data preparation, operating and development staff, to a much more decentralised system based on microprocessors or remote terminals. Edwards (1982, p. 2) suggests that 'the days of the large centralized computer...are numbered'. He goes on to suggest that the decentralisation of computing using microcomputers 'is effectively moving information processing back to the control of individual department managers - just where it was thirty years ago.' (Edwards, 1982, p. 14).

The implications of such shifts will clearly affect the overall organisational administration and lead to a substantial shift in certain responsibilities, and possibly erode the power position of EDP departments. The structural implications, as they affect offices, however, are usually somewhat limited.

Generally it can be concluded, as Khandwalla (1977) suggests, that, at least as it affects offices and office management:

'information technology bears a close resemblance to operations technology. It incorporates a substantial mechanical component. Like operations technology, it embodies a input-throughput (or process)-output cycle, but with information as the input and output.' (Khandwalla, 1977, p.469)

This being the case, the new technological advances applied to office workers are likely to set in motion organisational design trends, which are in general terms similar to those listed above, under the heading of operating technology and structure. However, as will be considered in the next section, the analogy between the implications of information technology and operating technology for organisational design breaks down when the former is applied in overall organisational systems.

NEW TECHNOLOGY, ADMINISTRATION AND POLICY MAKING

As has already been suggested, it is the possible influence of new information technology on organisational administration and policy making decisions which is the most problematic area of study, and also possibly in the long run the area which will undergo the most profound changes. As long ago as 1960, Simon suggested that in a few years it would be possible to computerise virtually all non-manual organisational operations including all types of decision-making. He cautioned, however, that just because such things became possible it did not follow that they would happen. Certainly in the case of large computer installations, the evidence of empirical research studies suggested that top general managers did not use computers in any significant way in the actual decision-making process, but they did use them in order to obtain more complete background statistics to problems. At the

senior levels of functional management, the computer was used
to a significant extent in functions such as accounting, which
dealt with largely quantitative information, with some
decisions programmed for computer decision-making (Hofer,
1970). It should also be noted that predictions of the effect
of computers on middle management suggested that computer
systems would tend to structure, or in some cases do away with,
the middle management role (Leavitt and Whisler, 1958).
However, empirical research did not bear out these predictions,
suggesting rather that such middle management roles could
increase and become more varied (Shaul, 1964).

The recent developments in information technology have not
only increased the computational power available to organisations, but also in many cases reduced the cost of input for
certain sorts of information, improved the ability to
communicate large quantities of data from place to place, made
the accessing of computer held information by non-computer
staff very much easier, and via networking made it possible to
interlink a variety of information systems:

> 'The suggestion is to distribute processing power to user
> locations and when necessary to allow these smaller compu-
> ters either to pass data to other microcomputers, or to
> despatch data to a central data bank for forwarding to
> other micros. Each user could draw data from a pool of
> basic data as required to avoid excessive duplication of
> data files.' (Edwards, 1982)

Such systems, if appropriately designed and coupled to
well-developed computer models of organisational functioning,
could theoretically provide a system making almost all higher
level organisational decisions, whilst providing dramatically
more rapid feedback of a variety of sorts for control
purposes.

The extent to which such systems will be developed in
organisations, and if developed the extent to which they would
be used, probably depends more on economic and behavioural
considerations than on technical ones. Already, in terms of
hardware, the technology has been developed which would allow
most, if not all, policy and administrative decision-making to
be automated – the development of software follows well behind.
The more obvious factors which will effect whether such systems
will be adopted may be listed as follows:

1. The ability of organisations to develop suitable computer models of organisational functioning, environmental conditions and organisation-environment interactions. So far,
such developments have lagged a long way behind the
developments of models of technical systems. This is partly
a consequence of the complexity of organisational systems and
partly due to a lack of preparedness to expend the same amount
of money and manpower in this direction.

2. The ability to further substantially develop ways of handling essentially non-quantitative data.

3. The accuracy and reliability of the information inputs to such computer-based systems.

4. The preparedness of top management in organisations to rely on computer outputs in the same way as they rely on human decisions, particularly in areas that they believe require judgement as opposed to calculation. This in turn may depend on managers being prepared to examine critically the assumptions and logic which currently underlie organisational decision-making.

5. The relative costs of current systems and the sorts of computer-based systems which might replace them, taking account of the very considerable development costs involved in the latter.

6. The preparedness of lower level personnel in organisations to accept impersonal control signals emanating from computer-based information systems, as opposed to instructions and supervision from human superiors. The evidence from studies of reactions to machine control and pacing in earlier generations of technology suggests that this may be highly problematic (e.g. Blauner, 1964).

It can be seen that many of these effects depend not just on the nature of particular organisational situations and the personnel involved, but on general cultural values concerning the relationship of human beings to machines, and on general attitudes to computers and information technology.

As was suggested at the beginning of this chapter, the implementation of such an approach will involve not just the modification and development of technology, but also a reworking of the whole organisational socio-technical system. Such a reworking would inevitably involve increases in bureaucratic procedures, particularly in the higher levels of organisational systems. This would tend to increase the extent to which integration between different functional areas, product groups or geographic areas was based on bureaucratic computer-based procedures. Such changes would also have considerable implications for the division of labour between functional areas, with a tendency for some staff specialist functions to disappear.

Perhaps more pronounced, however, would be the implications for the division of labour between hierarchical levels, with a possibility of earlier predictions concerning the diminution of the role of middle managers belatedly coming true.

It must be remembered in all these considerations that the control of information is a significant source of power in organisations (Pettigrew, 1973). This would be particularly true where the information is subsequently used automatically to influence organisational policy decisions. A consequence of this is that as any information technology system for managerial control of top level decision-making becomes more all-encompassing, so the potential power of all parties responsible for the input of information to any part of the system will increase. This will necessitate a powerful supervisory function controlling information inputs. The security of the system and the information stored in it will also be a serious problem, necessitating not just elaborate software, but calling for highly sophisticated central specialist personnel. As applications of computer systems to the control of financial information and transactions have already demonstrated, sophisticated systems can make the detection of certain sorts of mistakes and frauds very difficult. The widening of the information base to include non-financial data would tend to exacerbate this problem.

The somewhat limited available empirical data suggest that very few of the changes suggested above have actually taken place, and it must be anticipated that the transition to the use of such systems in organisations, if it occurs at all, will be a gradual evolutionary process.

The complexity of most high level decision-making taken in conjunction with the potentially serious consequences of incorrect decisions will no doubt be given as a reason for the non-adoption of computer-based decision-making systems. Yet, appropriately programmed, the advantage of the computer over the human tends to be greater with increased complexity in the problem to be solved. It will also be argued that human judgement cannot be replaced by technology, although it has already been in many areas. The resistance to this sort of change will be very strong hence it is worth considering the potential advantages and disadvantages which could accrue from such a wholesale adoption of new information technology in work organisations, some of which have been touched on already.

Assuming appropriate choice and configuration of new information technology, and the use of appropriate software, the more obvious potential advantages may be listed as follows:

1. Faster communication and retrieval of information.
2. Faster decision-making.
3. Higher quality decision-making, if appropriate computer models could be developed.
4. Faster assessment of progress to date by automatic checking against targets and budgets.
5. Faster signalling of errors and failures to meet targets.
6. Reduction of costs due to reduction of certain sorts of manpower.

Taken in broad terms such systems could lead to better and faster task accomplishment, and to faster and more accurate control and cost reduction. However, as with the introduction of most sorts of new technological systems, the human element may not fit easily the demands of mechanical systems, leading to theoretical machine efficiencies not being realised. In particular the following potential disadvantages may be associated with such systems:

1. Lack of confidence at top management levels in information and decisions which are provided automatically by computer systems, leading to manual reworking of decisions with incomplete information.

2. Lack of commitment to decision outcomes leading to poor implementation, as personnel may not feel involved in decision-making processes.

3. Vulnerability of the whole organisation to malfunctions in limited areas, due to the high level of system integration.

4. Lack of commitment and motivation amongst lower level personnel due to the impersonality of the system.

5. Vulnerability of the overall system to local industrial disputes.

6. Vulnerability of the system to poor or misleading information inputs arising from accidental errors or deliberate manipulation.

Clearly then, overall, many of the potential advantages may be vitiated due to the need for increased supervision of certain information input operations, and the need to employ relatively large numbers of specialist personnel to ensure the security of the information system and to update the computer models and associated programmes.

When account is taken of these potential advantages and disadvantages, and even allowing the substantial resistance to change that will inevitably occur, it seems certain that the new information technology will inevitably be increasingly utilised for actual decision-making, even in the crucial areas of policy making and administration. For this reason it seems worthwhile to attempt to sketch out the broad outline of possible organisations of the future which have adopted the new technology as a basis for overall system functioning.

ORGANISATIONS OF THE FUTURE?

Obviously predicting the shape of the organisations of the future is a hazardous business. The best interpretation of the results of organisational research up to the present should caution one against predictions of over-dramatic change. After all, although there have been changes in the structure and functioning of work organisations documented by research over the last fifty years, they do not seem very large when compared to the changes in society and particularly in technology over the same period.

Clearly, in the operations area of manufacturing organisations, it is likely that there will be a very high level of automation. This is likely to mean the increasing replacement of the human operator in the actual production process as well as the automation of the processes of scheduling, production control, and inspection leading to better task accomplishment, more efficient and effective control, higher quality, and further reductions in manpower. In the sales function, it would seem likely that the present arrangements, or others very like them, would continue with regard to the actual selling process, but that the various sales suppport activities would be further automated giving faster and more complete information, more rapid access to information regarding the status of orders and availability of capacity in production and more rapid translation of orders into production and despatch schedules.

In the design and development areas there would be an increasing reliance on computers with some parts of the process, including preparation of tenders, cost figures and design modifications, being automated. In other staff support areas there would be an increase in the speed and efficiency of information handling with high levels of automation, particularly when dealing with quantitative information. In corporate planning and related intelligence functions there would be a very high reliance on information inputs via computer networks from other parts of the system and the use of computer models. Overall then, very large numbers of personnel in all functions would spend much of their time linked to computer systems via terminals, micros and word processors.

Except for the top management, the managerial function would have to develop greater skills in the supervision of information inputs and, most of all, enhanced leadership skills to counteract the potentially demotivating affects of automated systems and machine-based instruction and control. Paradoxically, outside the specialist technical functions, managers will have little enhanced need for technological knowledge. Rather, there would tend to be a greater emphasis on personnel and industrial relations skills amongst managers in all departments, as well as a considerable reliance on specialist personnel departments.

Top management's role would develop in two main directions. The first would involve developing greater conceptual skills relating to overall organisational systems and the development of the corporate mission. At the same time top management would become even more important in terms of external relations, and hence would need to develop greater political skills. In order to make all this possible, top management would be supported by a sizeable central systems department which would be responsible for the development and security of the overall information system.

In total then, there would be an almost complete reworking of virtually all organisational roles and sub-systems with many new skills needing to be developed. The changes would be most profound in the area of middle management, and in the short term would put the greatest stress on the functions of system design, staff training and development, and personnel.

REFERENCES

Blauner, R. (1964) Alienation and Freedom, University of Chicago Press, Chicago

Child, J. and Mansfield, R. (1972) 'Technology, Size and Organization Structure', Sociology, 6, 369-393

Edwards, C. (1982) Developing Microcomputer-Based Business Systems, Prentice Hall, Englewood Cliffs N.J.

Francis, A. and Willman, P. (1980) 'Microprocessors: Impact and Response', Personnel Review, 9, 9-16

Hickson, D.J. Pugh, D.S. and Pheysey, D.C. (1969) 'Operation Technology and Organizational Structure: An Empirical Reappraisal', Administrative Science Quarterly, 16, 370-397

Hofer, C. (1970) 'Emerging EDP Pattern', Harvard Business Review, 48, March-April, 16-31

Khandwalla, P.N. (1977) The Design of Organizations, Harcourt Brace Jovanovich, New York

Leavitt, H. and Whisler, T. (1958) 'Management in the 1980's', Harvard Business Review, 36, November-December, 41-48

Mansfield, R. (1984) 'Formal and Informal Structure" in M. Grunenburg and T. Wall (eds.), Social Psychology and Organizational Behaviour, Wiley, New York, 119-147

Pettigrew, A. (1973) The Politics of Organizational Decision-Making, Tavistock, London

Porter, L.W., Lawler, E.E. and Hackman, J.R. (1975) Behavior in Organizations, McGraw Hill, New York

Pugh, D.S., Hickson, D.J., Hinings, C.R., and Turner, C. (1968) 'Dimensions of Organization Structure', Administrative Science Quarterly, 13, 65-105

Shaul, D. (1964) 'What's Really Ahead for Middle Management?', Personnel, 41, November-December, 8-16

Simon, H. (1960) The New Science of Management Decision, Harper and Row, New York

Sorge, A., Hartmann, G., Warner, M. and Nicholas, I. (1983) Microelectronics and Manpower in Manufacturing, Gower, Aldershot

Williamson, O. (1975) Markets and Hierarchies, Free Press, New York

Chapter 13

CONTROL, STRUCTURE AND IDENTITY: MANAGERIAL
PROBLEMS IN TECHNOLOGICAL INNOVATION

Ian Nicholas

INTRODUCTION

This paper is concerned with three organisational and managerial questions, which are seen as important in the process of
technological innovation within manufacturing industry.   The
scope of the discussion may be summarised as follows.   Economic, competitive and strategic circumstances interact with
technological developments and reinforce the need for compatible organisational structures and relevant managerial control
philosophies.   Both of these issues are examined against a
series of new manufacturing demands and a corresponding and
increasing requirement that employee working patterns become
more flexible.   A third consideration is advanced more speculatively;   production and industry life cycles are briefly discussed and some of the implications for technological innovation that appear to be relevant from such a study are examined.
       However, to begin, it is interesting that several months
ago, in response to a question I commented that probably the
two most important elements associated with new technology in
the organisational setting were control and structure.   If I
were asked the same question again, I think I would add a third
dimension - one that is rather less specific than the other two
factors - and which, for the time being, I have called
identity.
       In the remainder of this paper I want to explain what I
mean by control and structure and to speculate, again in the
organisational context, about the nature of identity.   Further,
rather than talking in a general sense about concepts, I intend
to discuss these issues against a manufacturing background, and
one in which the dominant production technology is numerical
control (NC) or computer numerical control (CNC) equipment
(Sorge et al, 1981).

BACKGROUND

There is increasing evidence that, because of strategic and

competitive pressures, companies are being obliged to move away from standardised mass-produced manufacture and to concentrate more and more on products designed and manufactured to meet specialised customer needs. Batch sizes, for example, have had to be reduced from, say, 20,000 to two or three hundred items, although the total number of products might remain somewhere near the same. This change, of itself, does not constitute a particularly difficult technical problem. A modern machining centre (assuming adequate programming capacity) is ideally suited, indeed has been specifically designed, to handle quickly and effectively such production demands. This overall tendency towards product specialisation, however, has far-reaching effects in terms of control and structure within the organisation and this can be reflected, sometimes dramatically, in such departments as, among others, design engineering, production scheduling, work-in-progress, purchasing, inventory control, and so on.

CONTROL

Scheduling and Machine Utilisation

Scheduling, in one of these functional ancilliary departments, is an important form of production control. In essence, it is the job of determining which components are needed; when they are needed; and when, where, and by whom they are to be made; and, at the same time, ensuring that a sensible balance is maintained between machine utilisation and reasonable stock levels.

Machine utilisation and machine reliability are obviously very closely related. Machine downtime, the obverse of machine utilisation, can be the result of any number of difficulties, but generally speaking, the major sources are two-fold. The first of these is machine delays, involving control system or tape-reader malfunction, or mechanical problems, such as faulty motors, bearings, hydraulics, and so on. The second type of difficulty is somewhat different. It is frequently operator-inspired - incorrect operation causing 'smash-ups', such as wrong tool sequencing, failure to re-index the machine, incorrect grade of tool, and the like. Some of the machine-based difficulties can be seen as the result of 'design problems which simply should not have occurred'. Similarly, some of the operating mistakes can be judged to have been 'elementary' and, in one particular study (Sorge et al, 1981), this problem of inexperience was summarised succinctly in terms of 'practices that might be all right on an 8 HP capstan lathe are not all right on a 40 HP CNC machining centre'. This apprehension was not completely one-sided. In the same study, operators quite frequently expressed a certain concern about the capabilities of the machines and, on occasions, were somewhat overawed by the responsibility for their operation.

As has been mentioned above, with the greater emphasis on

product specialisation, batch sizes have fallen dramatically. This tendency has been made all the more likely by the demonstrated flexibility of NC and CNC machines, and further, it has been accentuated by the need to reduce work-in-progress and to maintain low levels of inventory.

Apart from a series of implications concerning the job of the operator (see below), these new operating conditions result in increased preparation and setting time, and greater demands are imposed on scheduling and on achieving and maintaining high machine utilisation. These changes have been of such magnitude that production scheduling has taken on a new significance - in many cases, companies have found that almost their entire production schedule consists of arrears and components 'that (they) did not make yesterday'. Machine production capacity and enhanced manufacturing flexibility are 'outstripping' the rate at which the scheduling department can react, and this is causing quite a number of companies to re-examine this element of their production control procedures as a matter of urgency.

The Job of the Operator

Other considerations which are related to the central issue of control also need to be addressed. As the capacity for increased manufacturing flexibility is more effectively utilised, the question of downtime for setting, preparation, tape-proving, and so on, also takes on a new importance. This not only has implications for the nature of the operator job content, but also requires closer cooperation between various groups of workers on the shopfloor - for example, setters - and also between the shopfloor and ancilliary services, such as programmers, the toolroom, material handlers, inspectors, and so on. This extends to such elementary considerations as the operators having, for example, the same lunchbreaks, starting times, etc.

The question of the adequacy of operator training has been raised above. This is a difficult area, particularly when it is compounded by the question of the necessary level of skill that should be attained. Initially, one of the main justifications for the introduction of NC and CNC equipment was the belief that semi-skilled operators could be used. This proposition is currently subject to increasing scepticism and, if anything, doubt is being expressed about the adequacy of the operator's knowledge of fundamental 'metal removal techniques' and his 'feel' for feeds and speeds, product finish, and overall machining technology. There appears to be a general feeling that, although some of the 'old' tradesmen's skills may be, to some extent, superseded, 'new' skills, including increased vigilance, attention to detail and the elusive 'feel' - that comes only with skill - are essential if effective machine utilisation and operation are to be achieved. To this end, there appears to be a tendency towards the use of skilled personnel on the machines, who can not only operate the machines more efficiently, but who are also capable of performing their own preparation and setting work.

Programming

Coupled with this question of operator skill is the vexed issue of programming and tape editing. At one end of the spectrum, there are those cases where the 'CNC unit' is responsible for its own programming, setting and manufacture of the finished component. The unit can be a single individual or a group of people who work together on a series of machines. At the other end of the spectrum, and usually the practice in the larger companies, is the situation where the operator simply operates, and programming is performed by a separate, and invariably physically remote, service group. In some of these cases, the editing facilities are 'locked', and only nominal machine alterations, such as feed and speed reductions, indexing operations, etc., are permitted. There are, of course, many operating procedures that fall between the two extremes. The reasons given for these restrictions imposed on the machine operators are generally as follows:

1. For large, complex, and hence expensive, castings, the risk of 'mistakes' in the machining process is too high. Standardisation is essential, particularly where the final assembly might take place at an overseas location.

2. 'Short cuts' in the manufacturing process could be detrimental to product quality and specification, and could also lead to damage to machines and personal injury. As a corollary, particularly where the bonus system is linked to output, bonus payments are likely to increase.

3. The operators lack the capacity, the training, the experience, or the willingness, to perform programming activities.

4. Management would lose a substantial element of control over shopfloor activities. In one instance, the programmers claimed that, by issuing complete manufacturing instructions including the relevant tape, production sequencing, tooling lists, jig and fixture requirements, etc., they were, in fact, exercising surrogate supervision over the shopfloor. It was further suggested that if such information were to be diluted in any way, the result would be an unacceptably low level of control, that is, existing supervisors and foremen did not have the will or the capacity to perform their job effectively without the 'assistance' of the programming department.

It is interesting, however, that, even within those companies that pursue the above policies, some doubts are being expressed about whether they are in the best interests of the organisation concerned. These considerations usually revolve around questions of machine utilisation and the lost time involved in waiting for programmers to perform minor modifications, especially during night-shifts. The potentially available shopfloor expertise is indicated by: the expressed desire

on the part of operators to learn how to do their own setting
and preparation work;   the dramatic increase in the ease with
which the programming and data input material can now be fed
into some of the newer-generation equipment;   and finally, but
by no means least in significance, the growing awareness that
CNC equipment offers management the opportunity to 'give the
responsibility for machining back to the operator' and represents a means of 'retaining traditional craftsmen skills' and,
at the same time, is able to go some way, particularly on long-
cycle work, towards relieving the boredom and monotony resulting from 'machine-pacing'.

Managerial Control

It can be seen that the above questions refer to control, in
terms of where and how it is to be exercised, the role of management and supervision, and so on.   But, even more fundamentally, these are questions of managerial philosophy relating to
the faith that management has in its employees and the degree
of trust that management is prepared to exhibit, as well as the
amount of responsibility that employees ought to be given.
This said, the question is even further complicated: many companies are introducing computer-aided design (CAD) systems and
more advanced computer-based purchasing, stock control, scheduling, and other procedures, with the ultimate objective of
the automated manufacturing system.   So, apart from any industrial relations, social or societal implications, the organisational implications are enormous.   How is management going to
manage more advanced integrated systems;   is control to be centralised or decentralised;   are employees to be machine-minders
or are they to actively contribute to organisational performance?

Before any attempt is made to come to some conclusion
about these issues, let us have an equally brief look, again in
the same manufacturing context, at structure.

ORGANISATIONAL STRUCTURE

Introduction

Obviously very closely associated with the question of managerial control is that of organisational structure, and again the
same strategic issues are important - the increasing emphasis
upon flexibility, the capacity of the equipment and the workforce to handle smaller batches, increased product complexity,
higher demands for precision, and so on.

The Changing Environment

It is, however, also crucial in this context, to distinguish
between several different phases in the application and
development of computer-based manufacturing technology.   The
first phase of this development, in a decade covering roughly
the late 1960s, to say, the early 1970s - and representing the

impact of 'conventional' electronic information technology – also corresponded with a period which, in economic terms, might be called the 'production-orientation' phase.

There was, in this period, a buoyant, even expanding market, the emphasis of which was on output, and relatively sophisticated manufacturing equipment was readily available on the market. This equipment, however, whilst capable of increasing productivity, had two fundamental characteristics. These characteristics were: first, that the equipment was relatively inflexible – indeed, much of the plant and machinery of the time was 'dedicated', or at least, 'special purpose' automated machines – and second, it was 'hard-wired' and difficult, certainly time-consuming, even for an 'expert' in data processing, to programme.

Organisational Effects

Both of these characteristics, and perhaps particularly the latter, had the effect of polarising skills, centralising data processing procedures and decision-making activities, and generally contributing towards the lateral segmentation or departmentalisation of the organisation. That is, the traditional 'mass production' model was reinforced, and the flight of personnel, away from the shopfloor and related operator functions, to specialised white-collar technician tasks, was emphasised. However, the market never stays still – it moves onwards and the competitive environment changes.

Presently, rather than an expanding economy, there is stagnation, possibly even a declining manufacturing potential and, as has been previously discussed, enterprises are being forced to cater increasingly for small market niches rather than for homogeneous mass markets. It can now be said that the current phase of much of manufacturing industry is predominantly that of 'production-adaptability', where the emphasis is on the production of a large range of different product variants.

Equally, manufacturing processes, and correspondingly, much of the currently available production equipment, have changed. New-generation CNC machinery, for example, is not only capable of providing new standards of quality and precision, improved concepts in design, reduced lead times, decreased stocks and so on, but they are very much easier to programme.

With the new-generation equipment, it is no longer necessary to be an EDP specialist to instruct the machine, even in the manufacture of highly complex components. Microelectronics, certainly in this context, are becoming less distinctive for their intellectually demanding data processing requirements but, more particularly, as tools which are increasingly simple to handle. Another effect, however, is also apparent: as information processing skill becomes more widely diffused, it becomes less demanding in its own right. Correspondingly, it also reduces the need for separate information workers. Programming has become an integral part of the job and a vehicle by which the vocational expertise of its users can be broadened. Thus, and to some extent paradoxically, it is the more demanding aspects of the manufacturing specialities and other production-oriented tasks which are being emphasised by information technology applications. Whilst it may be true that workers are dealing with increasingly sophisticated technology, it is particularly important to recognise that it concerns the tools of their trade only, and does not affect the objectives of what they are doing nor their primary working goals.

Current Implications

What then are the implications for the organisational structure of the enterprise?

It seems very doubtful whether a need for increased flexibility – a greater variety of smaller batches – is best handled bureaucratically through an increase in the division of labour and the degree of specialisation, or by decision-making by functional, and often remote, experts, and by the resultant deskilling of shopfloor activities. Is this the strategy that the current competitive marketing situation would indicate? Rather, is this not an extension of the classical organisational pattern developed many years ago for traditional process and mass production manufacturing? Would it not be more valuable to provide the increased capacity and enhanced flexibility, necessary to handle the new demands of production, at the level of the machine and the operator?

Indeed, it is this premium on production flexibility, and the ease with which product variability can be handled, that is one of the major contributory items in justification of the introduction of CNC equipment. CNC operators are likely to have to deal with a greater and more frequently changing range of jobs, and this increased need for flexibility will lead inevitably to decentralisation of control, as the only means by which the new demands of manufacturing can be achieved. The crucial bottlenecks are not going to be information processing and calculating skills, but the immediate demands of tools, feeds, speeds, materials, faults and breakdowns. Skills in handling such problems result from experience on the machine, and this emphasis towards the maintenance and increase of craft or shop-worker skills needs to be reinforced. Integration, of course, is important, but the emphasis must be on an increased degree of integration between the operator and the system, rather than between the various parts of the system.

IDENTIFICATION

Introduction

Before examining this question, it is important to distinguish between market-led or user-driven innovation, and technology-driven innovation, and to recognise ways in which product and industry growth patterns change and develop.

Studies in this general area of innovation suggest that as much as eighty per cent of major innovations are a response to market need (Utterback, 1980). In these instances, basic research has usually not been directly relevant. Rather, the more 'normal' procedure is for entrepreneurial firms to take existing knowledge and technologies and combine them in new and novel ways.

There remains, however, still the twenty per cent of product innovations that emerge from research and development effort and, although by no means a numerical majority, they nevertheless represent a very important source of technological progress.

Product/Industry Growth Patterns

Quite typically, and irrespective of the developmental process that applies, the first applications of these innovations are in specialised niches, where the existing technology is not completely appropriate. This innovation usually has cost and reliability drawbacks compared with existing products and, because of this, firms in the older industry manufacturing those products are slow to react. The relative crudeness of the newer product is also part of the reason why such ventures often do not receive support from providers of finance or policy-making bodies at government and company board level.

Competition, whether between the old and the new technology, or between contending versions within the new technology, is based on performance, and substantial experimentation occurs. The choice of product and service options available can be very wide and improvements depend, in large measure, upon feedback from suppliers and users. It has been estimated, for example, that between 1944 and 1950, over seventy-five per cent of all computers made during that time were one- or two-off; by 1953, the corresponding figure for one or two-off was fifty per cent and only about ten per cent of the various models were being made even in small volume (Moore and Tushman, 1980).

As a result of this experimentation, a 'dominant design' emerges. It is an 'optimal' configuration which does not normally undergo any major changes for some time. It is also evolutionary in character, that is, its dominant features may have been incorporated in previous models, including those of its competitors and, as an interesting corollary, it need not necessarily be the 'best' product. One or a number of competitors manage, through skill and perhaps good luck, to put together a winning combination of product design features, process technology, price, distribution and outlets, financing arrangements, and so on, that enables that product to grow at the expense of others in the same or competing technologies.

Dominant design is an extremely important event in the product life cycle of an industry, in that it fundamentally changes the nature of innovation, the basis of competition, the nature of the manufacturing process and the relevant marketing strategies that apply to those firms engaged in the struggle for supremacy and/or survival. And, as a direct consequence of considerations of this nature, it becomes clear that, for the firm to continue to prosper, a series of structural and organisational matters need to be re-examined.

During the introductory phase, the major functional areas are marketing and research and development. Marketing, in this context, includes stimulating primary demand, searching for niches where the product has a differential advantage, and determining who the early users and adopters are. Moreover, marketing must try and establish what forms and levels of the various product attributes are seen as the most desirable. Finally, marketing must often undertake the not inconsiderable task of educating the consumer. As the dominant design emerges, end-user needs become more clearly defined, and research and development is focused on technical opportunities, that is, effort is directed towards utilising new and existing knowledge to improve the product's functional performance.

The entrepreneurial emphasis thus changes. Initially, it uses highly-skilled labour and general-purpose equipment to produce relatively expensive experimental models. With the decision to standardise the product – to rationalise the production process in accordance with the dominant design – the transition from product innovation to process innovation begins and the degree of interdependence between the product and the process increases at the expense of the former relationship between marketing and the product.

These circumstances also have other effects; it is during this phase that a 'shake-out' within the industry occurs with small, even medium-sized, firms disappearing and, again at the same time, established companies, in related or other older industries, entering the field. Often also, at this stage of growth of the industry, there are cost and price decreases. Since the product is fairly well-developed and, as mentioned above, 'static' in the sense that the desired features are more or less established, competition tends to become price-based. This direction is reinforced, in part, by the employment and use of professional 'knowledge workers' for example, engineers, scientists, marketing people, etc., who proceed with a vigorous programme of process development.

Thus, the type of innovation has changed: firstly, the emphasis was on product development; then, as the product and industry mature, the emphasis changes to process innovation.

Without pursuing product life cycle theory in too great detail, there is one further issue that is of relevance. As the product moves towards maturity, product innovation again receives a boost as enterprises attempt to defend their market position. This activity is directed towards product improvement and, commonly through the development of model variants, there is a conscious re-orientation towards particular market segments that might have been ignored, or at least not specifically catered for, in the past. It is unusual for these developments to be particularly imaginative – nor are they normally on a bold scale. Typically, they are variants on the old theme, but they are still innovations and a maturing product or industry is capable of providing many such opportunities. Further, however, and probably of greater entrepreneurial significance, similar areas for development exist in the peripheries, that is, for innovation in the provision of products, materials and services supporting the main industry.

Organisational Implications

Let us try and bring this back to the organisational context. Several factors of significance would appear to emerge from the above observations; firstly, there are different sorts of innovation and they occur at different times during the product or industry life cycle; secondly, innovations result from the endeavours and activities of different sorts of people. Is it likely, for example, that a firm in a mature industry – where its skill, in the corporate sense, is represented by accumulated production know-how and experience in the development of relatively sophisticated process techniques – will be completely happy and confident in a market or product situation demanding imagination, specialised knowledge and faith in a specific , but basically untried, idea? And thirdly, and directly because of the quite dramatic changes that occur within the research and development function during this period, the organisational focus of the innovation process changes.

In an earlier section, it was suggested that companies should attempt to adapt their organisational control and structural features so that they are consistent with the strategic and competitive circumstances within which they are obliged to operate. It would not seem to be unreasonable, therefore, to take a similar view concerning the manner in which companies attempt to adopt new technology and technological innovation. As a starting point, for example, among other issues, it might be useful to consider whether current managerial control and organisational design characteristics are consistent with the existing product and industry cycle pattern and further, whether they are compatible with the management, marketing and other priorities as reflected by the form of innovation under consideration.

Thinking along these lines does not rule out intuition; nor does it eliminate the need for entrepreneurial risk taking. Rather, it emphasises the advantage of a firm attempting to identify its technological position and to give some consideration to the following factors: firstly, whether the dominant design has as yet emerged, and whether the standardisation process, and all that it implies, should in fact proceed; and secondly, if the timing is correct, how the firm is going to manage the transition from one phase to another. Further, and probably of equal importance, a critical examination, with this special focus, reinforces the view that technology is accumulated knowledge and owes its derivation not only to those comparatively rare break-throughs in the research laboratory, but is a combination of, indeed a convergence between, scientific knowledge, technological expertise, marketing knowhow and management skill.

And digressing for a moment - it is particularly in failing to understand this critical interrelationship that government policy is falling down. Whilst government would appear to appreciate that the benefits of technology flow to those countries that use it, rather than those in which the derivative technologies were invented or developed, it appears to primarily direct its attention and priorities to the acquisition of scientific knowledge per se, in what might almost be seen as an 'application vacuum'. As a resultant, yet unfortunate, by-product of this reaction, there appears to be insufficient conscious effort directed towards contributing towards, or indeed, encouraging on anywhere near the required scale, those resources necessary in developing the other aspects of technology - the technical expertise, the craft and managerial skills, and so on, which are so important in the vocational chain, if technological 'take-off' is to be achieved.

However, this sort of dilemma is not exclusively the preserve of government. There is, for example, no sound logical reason why the clear-sighted application of the relevant knowledge, together with the necessary related expertise and skills, cannot lead equally to the development of a new telecommunications or, for that matter, a new bio-chemical or genetic engineering industry, or alternatively again, to the highly effective and efficient production of manufactured products. The introduction and use of technology can have the effect of reducing, although perhaps not entirely eliminating, many of the conventional effects of wage differentials and the traditional comparative advantages conferred by international trade, and upsetting previously accepted views concerning economies of scale, and so on. It is a matter of some regret that these features of technological innovation are not more generally regarded as the bases for serious industrial and/or commercial activities.

Irrespective, then, of the relevance or otherwise of these observations, there appears to be little doubt that the combination of scientific knowledge and technological expertise, and the capacity to utilise and employ them effectively, is essential. Further, it is only those firms with the necessary infrastructure - a rational integration of knowledge, skill and

and expertise - that can realistically hope to successfully
translate an idea into a product or a process. Even though an
appropriate market may exist, without this merging of a range
of complementary talents, ideas have a habit of remaining
ideas.

CONCLUDING REMARKS

The organisational structure of an enterprise and the control
procedures, both formal and informal, must be compatible with
the strategic and competitive circumstances of the firm and the
consequent demand on its manufacturing processes.   These
characteristics, however, are also dependent in turn upon an
additional element, namely, the form and maturity of the
industry and/or the product under consideration.   Indeed, it
would seem that this third dimension yields an overriding
influence. For firms to be effective in the general area of
innovation they must ensure, firstly, that their total
managerial strategy is consistent with the form, nature and
circumstances of the innovation under consideration;   and
secondly, the subsequent development of any such innovation
requires that the technological infrastructure of the firm is
sufficiently well-developed and that an appropriate balance is
maintained between scientific knowledge, technical skill and
expertise, and the structural and process features of the
organisation itself.

REFERENCES

Sorge, A., Hartman, G., Warner, M., and Nicholas, I. (1981) Microelectronics and Manpower in Manufacturing: Applications of Computer Numerical Control in Great Britain and West Germany, International Institute of Management, Berlin, October, Research Report IMM/LMP 81-16, Mimeo.*

Utterback, J.M. (1980), 'The Dynamics of Product and Process Innovation in Industry', in Hill, C.T. and Utterback, J.M. (eds.) Technological Innovation for a Dynamic Economy, Pergamon, New York, pp.40-65

Moore, W.L., and Tushman, M.L. (1980) Managing Innovation over the Product Life Cycle, Research Working Paper, No. 380A, November, Columbia University

---

*See also revised versions of this paper:
Sorge et al (1983) Microelectronics and Manpower in Manfacturing: Applications of Computer Numerical Control in Great Britain and West Germany, Gower, Aldershot

Sorge et al (1982) Microelectronik und Arbeit in der Industrie, Campus

Chapter 14

MICROCOMPUTERS IN RETAILING:
A CASE STUDY

Lesley Sawers

INTRODUCTION

While there is an extensive literature on new information technology applications in retail operations; it is largely didac-
tic and, with a few notable exceptions, it is generally lacking
in systematic empirical investigation, and offers little in the
way of solutions to the challenges posed by such developments.

As part of this author's present research, an in-depth
case study was conducted in a small retail firm.   This was
undertaken to explore some of the areas where new technologies
were likely to have the greatest impact, although at the same
time, it was designed to explore the appropriate research
method for a wider study which is proceeding at the time of
writing.

In the pilot study reported here, data were collected from
eight retail outlets using observation techniques over a three
week period.   A diary of observations of those operating or
directly affected by the technology was kept during this period
and provided the key source of information.   This was comple-
mented by a small number of in-depth interviews and the
analysis of company reports.

The main findings of the study were that the introduction
of microprocessing technology within retailing: increased management control;   brought a variety of 'hard' and 'soft' benefits to the innovating firm;   and led to an increase in operational efficiency.

However, it was also found that a large number of problems
emerged in such areas as: relating objectives to evaluation;
overcoming staff resistance, particularly in specific groups;
and fully integrating the technology with work practice.

In this chapter we consider first what is known about the
actual and potential impact of microcomputers in retailing, and
then present the case study of microcomputer innovation in a
small, Scottish, book retailer.

MICROCOMPUTERS IN RETAILING

Major advances are being made in the electronic sophistication of retailing, and the last decade has shown substantial substitution of capital for labour in this traditionally labour -intensive industry. It is generally asserted that this has been stimulated by the need to remain competitive.

The daily business of the vast majority of retailers consists of very large numbers of specific transactions, and the volume of these, plus their relatively routine nature, suggests that this sector may be well suited to the application of new computer-based information processing technologies. At the same time, the retail sector remains one in which people-managed transactions and the role of personal relationships are frequently seen as key features of the customer-trader relationship. It is this apparent conflict which provided the starting point for this present study.

Bearing in mind the typically small size of many retail outlets, like those described here, a recent investigation by NEDO into the impact of information technology in the distributive trades (NEDO, 1982), considered that the rapidly decreasing cost of computer hardware was bringing the benefits of computerisation and data processing to smaller businesses, and it considered that:

> 'the potential for change in the smaller business is perhaps greater than in any other section of the distributive trades. It is now possible for even the smallest business to have available management information equivalent in relation to its needs, to that available to the larger groups.' (NEDO, 1982)

However, there has been little parallel research into customer response to this technology.

The Impact of Microcomputers

The impact of new technology upon the retail sector can be classified into three main areas: that experienced by the customer; that affecting the outlet; and that felt by those actually working with the technology. These may be considered in turn, together with the implications for retail management.

The Consumer Impact. The Office of Fair Trading (1982) has identified the greatest perceived benefit for consumers, both in US and UK pilot stores, as simply the detailed itemised receipt issued by the electronic point-of-sale (EPOS) terminal. On the other hand, the Article Numbering Association (ANA) and the Consumers' Association include among the customer benefits of the new technologies: reduced queuing time, more efficient store operations, lower costs giving lower prices, improved store layout, increased product information, better stock rota tion and hence improved quality standards, and superior price and product information through self-labelling.

In fact, a number of studies have attempted to examine consumer response to, and attitudes towards, point-of-sale scanning in the US. Langrehr and Robinson (1979) in the USA examined a specific introduction, while the Retail Management Development Programme (1982) looked at five UK stores which employed scanning. These studies indicate fairly widespread customer acceptance. For instance, in the US, 39 per cent of shoppers thought scanning gave a more informative till receipt, while in Britain 60 per cent of those interviewed gave a similar response. Both sets of shoppers thought it led to a reduction in queuing time, although more emphasis was placed on this advantage in the US, with 53 per cent compared to 2 per cent in the UK. Seven per cent of UK shoppers thought scanning led to more efficient operations, whilst no differences were noted in the US study.

The main disadvantage noted by both studies was the use of shelf-edge price marking and the removal of item prices, and the Policy Studies Institute suggests that the direct benefit of scanning to consumers is marginal, they believe that:

> 'the greatest benefit to consumers will be as a result of the "hard" and "soft" savings achieved by the retailer and passed on indirectly to consumers.' (Martin and Zeilunger, 1982)

The Impact on the Retail Outlet. A number of benefits of scanning systems for the retailer were indicated by the McKinsey Study for the Standard Product Number Steering Group (McKinsey, 1974). McKinsey estimated that the Standard Product Numbering System with codes could bring a net benefit to the UK grocery industry of £5m per annum at 1974 prices.

The benefits which were thought to accrue to innovating companies were divided into two types: 'hard' benefits, which can be quantified, and 'soft' benefits, which are less quantifiable and generally manifest themselves over a longer period in improved management control.

Over and above this, French (1980) extends the classification to encompass what he considers 'very soft' benefits. Another researcher notes that:

> 'In the view of some US executives, hard savings should pay for an installation, but soft savings will bring the profit on it.' (Phillips, 1980)

The 'hard' benefits identified by the McKinsey (1974) study were:

> 'productivity improvements at the check-out through the more efficient use of labour;

the removal of mis-ring's at the cash register;
savings on cashier training;
speedier reconciliation of cash;
savings through the removal or reduction of labour
for item price-marking and price changes;
the elimination of the cost of the item price
labels.' (McKinsey, 1974)

A study by Cohen (1979) of a store with a turnover of
$150,000 per week revealed a $119,000 saving in direct costs in
the first year of operation with scanning equipment. The main
savings itemised included the following:

reduced under-ring's	$47,000
lower front-end costs	$36,000
reduced marking costs	$22,000
a saving of 18 hours a week in streamlined book-keeping	$6,400
elimination of 7 hours a week in coupon redemption	$2,400
time saved in check authorisation and price checking	$3,500

The 'soft' benefits, in comparison, were mainly described
as management information benefits, as noted:

'improved re-ordering;
tighter stock control;
fewer out of stocks;
improved sales administration and accounting
procedures;
reduced losses due to "shrinkage";
more efficient marketing techniques and store
layout;
customer satisfaction through improved service;
access to detailed information on all aspects of
the business.' (McKinsey, 1974)

To these may be added the 'very soft' benefits identified
by French (1980), which consisted of: the ability to make quick
price changes; and front-end space savings; and gaining better
knowledge of achieved margins (French, 1980). French, however,
adds one important qualification. He emphasises that EPOS
systems are only a technique to aid management in daily
operations and decision-making, and unless account is taken of,
and any necessary adjustments made to, the operational and
systems environment in which they are used, no real benefits
are likely to be achieved.

Impact on Employees. Naturally, the organisation particularly concerned with this aspect of microelectronics in retail

operations is the Union of Shop, Distributive and Allied Workers (USDAW), which had a total membership of 441,500 in 1977 out of a total of 1.8m retail employees. USDAW have generally welcomed technological developments within retailing, but they have expressed some concern, as they are aware that the capacity to improve check-out operations, and remove many tasks presently done manually, may destroy some retail jobs. In response, they have produced an 'Action Pack' (USDAW, 1981) to help employees understand and negotiate any changes with management. Similarly, NEDO (1982) has drawn up thirteen recommendations that urge management to negotiate any job changes and provide retraining for staff, with the introduction of new technology. Studies by Bamber (1981) at Durham University Business School, indicate that 'the introduction of microprocessing technology appears to be intended to increase efficiency and to reduce or re-schedule labour'.

Impact on Management. In addition to improved labour product- ivity and possible labour reductions, a retail organisation, like any organisation, has need of management information of all types and at all levels, in order to effectively manage its business. Previously, the data were theoretically available but the 'enabling technology' did not exist to transform the raw data, e.g. sales records, inventory levels etc., into management information, that is to give historical trends and forecasts. The advent of the new information technologies has enabled computers to capture, store, manipulate and distribute these data and to pass them on to the management information system, at an acceptable cost and without massive dislocation. Thus, control of the organisation by management is directly affected. If we assume that there are essentially three levels of decision that confront management, as illustrated in Table 14.1, then each requires a different type of information on

Table 14.1 : Management Decisions

TYPE OF DECISION	RANGE	EXAMPLE
Strategic	Long-range	Opening a new branch Selling new merchandise
Operational	Short-range	Redress windows Replacing old stock
Managerial	Medium-range	Measuring store performance Personnel responsibility

which to base decisions, as summarised in Table 14.2, based on Jones (1977).

Table 14.2:   Management Information Needs

	STRATEGIC	MANAGERIAL	OPERATIONAL
Source	External	Internal management control	Internal operations
Accuracy	No	Yes	Yes
Scope	Summary	Detail	Detail
Frequency	Periodic (as required)	Frequent/ regular	Real-time
Time–span	Long range	Medium range	Short range
Form	Loose	Structured	Very struc- tured
Update		As required	

Source: Jones (1977)

However, in retail management, information is frequently concerned with mainly short-range problems, since retailers manage in a fast-changing environment, and often run quite efficient information systems at the operational or middle management level, and it is these systems that can be improved most through the introduction of new technology.

The point is that the main concern of a retailer tends to be short term operations (i.e. day-to-day or up to a year), and he therefore needs organised and efficient information systems which deal with daily business.

Consider now the range of technological innovations potentially affecting retailer operations and management information systems.

THE TECHNOLOGICAL REVOLUTION IN RETAILING

Electronic cash registers range from simple electronic cash registers (ECRs), which record data on a cassette tape, to systems incorporating cash register terminals connected to computers. From the literature we can identify four distinguishing features of Electronic Point of Sales Equipment that separate it from the more basic ECR's: (a) the ability of the system to record and store transaction data and print a till receipt that gives an abbreviated description of each item purchased; (b) the ability of the system to carry out data processing; (c) the ability to communicate electronically with other parts of the system; and (d) the existence of a price look-up facility.

To this may be added such possibilities as electronic funds transfer from customer bank accounts, electronic pricing (with computer files of product prices accessed by product codes), and linked portable data entry terminals, for example, for stock checking.

Merchandising Marking Systems

The key to operationalising the EPOS is merchandise marking to input product data. There are a number of methods of data input to an EPOS system, but all depend upon the allocation of a code number to all or part of the product range. These code numbers are then manually or automatically entered at the point-of-sale. There are three systems of automted data input currently available. First, there are various optical systems, including optical mark reading, which uses a simple binary code, and optical character recognition, which uses a limited set of standard typewritten characters. Most significant, though, are product bar codes, using a pattern of black bars of varying thickness, normally in one of the two standard international formats – European Article Numbering (EASN) in Western Europe and Japan, or Universal Product Code (UPC) in the USA. Second, are magnetic systems, which are the most widely used alternative to bar coding, relying on magnetic ink character recognition, where a magnetic stripe on the sales ticket is encoded magnetically and is 'wiped' at the point of payment by a magnetic pen reading and recording the stock code, price information, etc. Third, there are systems using punched cards or tags, such as the familiar Kimball tags, and Dennison tags.

As already noted, such innovations offer improved productivity in operations, but also an important advance in management control in retailing.

Management control may be defined in simple terms as executing procedures in accordance with the plans and policies established, and it has frequently been observed that in retailing, tight management control is essential for efficient and effective trading. Apart from finance, the main areas of control in retailing have been described:

'1. What goods you buy
2. Who to buy from
3. How much to buy
4. How to get the merchandise to the shop
5. How to get the merchandise out of the shop
6. The people who will perform the buying, selling and service functions.' (Ornstein, 1978)

Clearly, microcomputers offer the facility to store, manipulate and distribute the information, upon which to base these decisions, quickly and cheaply.

Given the description of these potential benefits, we may now turn to examine a case study of microcomputer innovation in a small retail firm in Scotland.

CASE STUDY: A GROUP OF BOOK SHOPS

The Company

Company X is a private company, with a long trading history in book retailing, which operates eight retail outlets, with administration for the company and its branches performed by a head office. The company employs some 180 people, made up of sixty in administration and 120 elsewhere in the operation. In 1980, Company X's turnover was just under £5m.

The Company's organisation chart is shown in Figure 14.1.

Figure 14.1:   Company X's Organisation

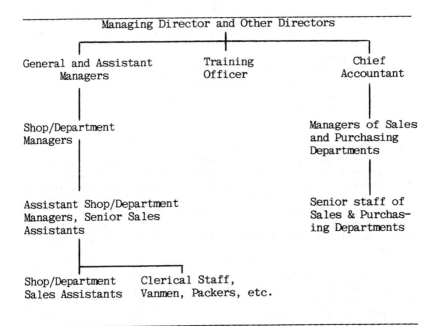

Each department and branch has its own manager, who is responsible for the running of the department/branch, with a certain number of subordinate staff, whose own seniority within the department is usually determined by length of service to the company. Each member of staff is responsible for certain sections within their department.

Department or branch managers usually do all the necessary

buying and ordering, subscribing to new publications, dealing with holiday arrangements, and so on, with the administrative centre coordinating the activities of the different branches and departments.

The Company's Business and the Need for New Technology

One important reason for introducing the computer to this firm was an attempt to rationalise the pattern of decentralised decision-making by different branches, and to routinise department operations, in order to give greater accountability and control to management.

To begin with, stock control is of vital importance generally to the retail trade, where a considerable amount of capital is tied up in stocks. In Company X's business, there are well over 400,000 items, and approximately 30,000 new products appear each year. In 1981 the total was 43,083, including 9,387 reprints and new editions, and the general trend has been steadily upward for 30 years. So the problem common to all retailers of what and how much to stock of a product range is especially acute for the bookseller. A good stock control system is therefore essential, and will aid management decision-making.

The manual stock control system of Company X was well established. The general approach to stock control was that traditional in the book-selling trade, where ordering relied on the buyer's knowledge and experience, and his ability to detect gaps on the shelf. As a stock control system this proved unsatisfactory. The shops needed a method of controlling stock which provided a 'memory', and which could be operated by the most junior members of staff.

The manual stock control employed a card system, where each product in stock had a 'master' card in the main file. The purpose was to provide an accurate record of sales over a period of time, which in turn could be used to maintain stock at the required level. In addition, the manual system was intended to provide product details, a record of orders placed, and to supply information on stock for the use of all members of staff.

The cards were filed under subject matter and further classified into alphabetical order by author. Physical stock checks were carried out periodically, when all the cards for a certain subject were extracted from the file and compared with the books on the shelves. The difference between the numbers of copies on the shelves at the last stock check, plus any orders received, and existing stocks, gave the numbers sold over the intervening period.

Return of goods unsold is critical to book retailing and the firm had devised a system whereby each product or item was coded when it arrived at the warehouse. The code consisted of a letter denoting the year when the goods were received, and a number denoting the quarter. The stock was checked systematically and, in general, if it had remained unsold for more than six months, it was returned to the publisher.

The process of ordering stock was made more efficient by the introduction of a teleordering facility in 1981. The order was still written out manually on a standard order form, but was then passed to teleordering where the international standard book numbers, quantity required and order reference were keyed into the machine. At the end of daily business the machine was linked up to a telephone, and all the information relayed to a central computer, which in turn relayed the information to the individual publishers and distribution houses. The whole process took twelve days from the time when the order was keyed into the machine until the books were received at the company's warehouse.

The stock card system traced the sales history of a product and was intended to aid the manager, acting in his role as buyer. Operated correctly, the manual system, in conjunction with teleordering, should have ensured that each shop would never run out of fast-selling lines. In operating terms this was never achieved.

The two main disadvantages of such a system that had become apparent over the years were, firstly, the human factor: e.g. sales assistants forgetting to write up cards, misfiling cards, etc. which resulted in a loss of confidence in the system as a source of accurate information; and secondly, the physical storage problem of such a system and the loss of sales area that could be used more profitably to display books.

Other disadvantages included: the laborious and time-consuming sales administration and accountancy procedure, involving lengthy manual operations to record department/branch ordering and stock levels; no systematic stock checks could be taken; there was a lengthy customer waiting time for any book requested, since orders had to be physically circulated to other branches as their current stock holdings were not known; there was no centralised merchandise display policy or marketing practice followed; and there was a growing inability to detect and control stock shrinkage.

It appeared that the advantages offered by a computerised system were enormous. By 1980 the company had already gained some experience of computers, having used the services of a computer bureau in many of its administrative functions for a number of years. In addition, in an effort to gain greater control over the ordering process, the teleordering machine described above had been installed, with the result that the ordering process had become more centralised.

The Innovation Decision

There were two principal factors that prompted management to consider the installation of their own computerised equipment. First, the increasing volume of data handled in all aspects of company operation, and second, the problems caused by conventional data collection methods, including: data losses and errors, shortcomings in customer service, and high clerical workload.

The decision to install a microprocessing system took six years from its point of inception to installation, and the project stages consisted of: (a) a feasibility study; (b) equipment selection; (c) pilot implementation; pilot review; and full implementation.

In total, eight equipment suppliers were consulted. The overriding criteria for selection were the compatibility of the new system with existing manual operations, and the size of the capital outlay required. As suggested earlier, the company sought new technology at an acceptable cost, and without massive dislocation. In fact, the company installed an on-line real-time system with the microprocessing unit housed in a central unit.

The company undertook research to assess the extent of the compatibility of their manual system with that of the computer, and to consider any changes in costs, staff time and running expenses, and concluded that the present system of operation would require little or no change.

The main saving envisaged by the company was that of staff time, which they believed would free efforts from 'routine clerical work' to concentrate on other more profitable duties. These gains included time saved in invoicing, in dealing with customer inquiries, in reordering stock, and in checking off orders, with the major advantage that order data need not be physically circulated to all branches, as stock listings were accessible through the system.

The company believed that once staff were used to the system, its own inherent advantages would reduce the amount of time involved to well below present levels. They did envisage an increase of staff time initially of approximately 10-45 per cent, in order to enter data, but believed this could be absorbed by the temporary employment of students.

A five month implementation timing schedule was constructed, so that by the time the company 'went live' the complete stock records for all the branches, customer accounts, suppliers file, purchase ledger, and staff wages file, would all be entered. October 1981 was the deadline, but due to initial technical problems, difficulties encountered by staff, etc., the operation ran behind schedule. Indeed, at the time of the study in May 1982, one branch was still entering stock records.

During the first year, responsibility for running the system was shared between Company X and equipment suppliers, leading up to the complete hand-over to the company.

It was intended that all staff would be involved with the actual day-to-day input, queries, and general use of the system, with four senior members of staff responsible for overall supervision.

Company X's stated principal concerns in installing the computer were efforts to improve: their financial position; their efficiency; and the level of customer service/image. They believed the main advantages behind the introduction of microprocessing equipment would be:

'1. Dealing with customers' enquiries quickly and accurately.
2. Finding stock held elsewhere.
3. Raising invoices quickly and accurately.
4. Better stock control leading to higher stock-turn rate.
5. Added confidence in staff who feel the firm is progressive, and who can feel that they are capable of using sophisticated equipment and are seen to be capable by customers.
6. Having the nominal ledger on the computer, with benefits of speed of entry and control.
7. Removal of the need to circulate order slips physically.
8. Increase in output.'

The company did however anticipate some immediate obstacles to the attainment of these goals.

An increase in overheads was expected through installation costs, telephone rental, electricity charges, and the initial increase in staff time in certain key departments, and additional pressure would also be placed on floor space at head office where the central processing unit was to be located.

However, the company did not believe that the annual costs would be much more than present operational costs, and in the long run there would be suffcient saving in staff time to allow Company X to do the present level of business with four or five fewer full-time staff. Alternatively, it was hoped that present staff levels could be maintained if a real increase in company profit of 10-15 per cent could be achieved.

The initial capital cost of installing the computer, allowing for interest on outstanding capital, was expected to take three years to recover, after the system was fully operational.

One key area highlighted for future development was the introduction of light pens linked to the central processing unit, to record sales and allow automatic stock adjustment and reordering facilities.

The Actual Operational Impact

This may be considered at three levels: the retail outlet, the management decision-making process, and consumer reactions.

The Retail Outlets. The introduction of the computerised stock system did remove the difficulties identified earlier in terms of storage problems at both branch and head office level; the time-consuming ordering process: and the quick availability of information on stock levels.

With the new system, stock is delivered to the warehouse, where it is physically checked against the invoice as before, except now it is listed on the computer, a computerised sales slip made, and then is dispatched to the appropriate branch. The computer maintains a complete stock list on the stock card and an automatic reordering facility, to ensure that the shops never run out of fast-selling lines. When the stock arrives at the branch, it has only to be shelved by the staff. In addition, each branch can determine which other branches hold particular titles.

Shopfloor staff have less responsibility for the stock record cards, as all new entries are now made at the warehouse, and thus the old manual stock control system was theoretically rendered obsolete.

As expected, members of staff in the firm generally welcomed the new developments. They felt that the new technology enhanced their position as sales assistants, and made the company appear more progressive to the general public. No concern was expressed that the ability of the new system to improve stock control and to remove many tasks previously done manually, would lead to redundancies or labour rescheduling. Rather, the computerised system was seen as assisting and alleviating many of the more routine and boring tasks.

As a result of the introduction of the microprocessing equipment, more detailed and accurate information was generated, which enabled management to obtain reports on all essential areas of operations: sales analysis, inventory levels, and trading position – at the department, store and company levels. Stock ordering, sales, purchase, nominal ledger and general accounting procedures were greatly improved.

In total, the effect of the introduction of a computer in Company X resulted in responsibility for stock control being removed from the shopfloor. This formed part of the company's long term aim of reducing operating costs through tighter stock control and staff savings.

However, many of the savings originally envisaged by the company, particularly those concerned with decreases in staffing have never been fully realised. This is mainly due to failure to keep up with the implementation schedule, and minor technical problems. In addition, many departments have kept the old manual system running alongside the computer, thus duplicating work. In some departments, e.g. purchasing and sales, this was seen as an essential double-check, given the volume of data involved, the its importance for the yearly accounts. But in most of the retail outlets this resulted from the manager and staff having more confidence in the manual system, and the perceived need for an historical sales record which was not provided by the computer. It appears that to many staff the computer works 'in addition to' and not 'instead of' the manual system.

Internal company politics also aggravated the situation, with individual managers attempting to gain control over both the equipment and its output, effectively preventing efficient operations, and as a consequence the implementation of training, vetting entries for errors, and consultation with lower managers with respect to any computing problems, have all been neglected.

The company's administrative system – due to the type of operation and previous experience with a computer bureau – appears to be the only part of company operations fully at ease with the new system.

While many of the advantages identified earlier have been achieved, although perhaps not the increased confidence of staff, the shift in control to higher levels in the management hierarchy, and a tightening of procedures, has had the effect of distancing the operators of the new technology from management.

Computerisation has resulted in some deskilling of staff on the shopfloor, and concomitant to this deskilling is a reduction in the degree of knowledge or specialisation required, fewer errors being made, and a noticeable increase in the speed of operations. The introduction of the microprocessing equipment has also resulted in the need for a formalised training programme. Company X did not follow many of the recommendations concerning the introduction of new technology. Rather, the new system was presented as a fait accompli, not subject to negotiation or consultation with the staff on the shopfloor or those required to operate it. For some members of staff, this resulted in a lack of confidence and understanding of the technology, which became apparent through their unwillingness to operate the computer, and preference for consulting the manual system.

Management and the Decision-Making Process. There was no 'technological imperative' for the introduction of the computer that necessitated change in the work of the departments. Rather, the decision to remove ordering, and discretion to decide what stock to return, from the departments was made by senior management in an effort to gain greater control over operations.

This observation reinforces two rules of thumb identified by Boddy and Buchanan (1982), as used by management in organising work around information technologies, that is: where possible to replace people with machines; and improve management control over the workforce to make it more consistent and predictable.

These informal guidelines are compounded by the fact that senior management is often removed from shopfloor practice, losing insight into the day-to-day operations, and as a result fail to correctly identify the response, and all that it encompasses, from the shopfloor. This point can be illustrated through Anthony's model, as shown in Table 14.3.

Table 14.3:   Management Levels and Decision Types

| | MANAGEMENT LEVELS | | |
Decision Type	Top (e.g. Board of Directors	Middle e.g. Office Manager	Lower (e.g. Shop/ Department Manager
STRATEGIC	*	X	
MANAGERIAL	X	*	X
OPERATIONAL		X	

* main involvement   X some involvement

Source: Jones (1977)

As already noted, the introduction of the computer was seen by senior management as a decision of strategic importance to the company, as it formed part of a long term objective to reduce operating costs, and thus improve the company's competitive position. All other outcomes were secondary in importance to that objective. Senior management granted authority for the introduction of the computer, but left its operational aspects to middle management.

Microcomputers offer middle management the opportunity to increase their control over company operations, and middle management consider the ultimate aim of the new technology is to remove all decision-making and initiative from the shopfloor by routinising operations.

On the other hand, lower management consider the new technology as an operational tool to smooth workflow, alleviate shopfloor difficulties, and generally as an aid in pursuing other company objectives. Their main involvement is in the day-to-day operation of the system.

However, operational criteria are now the preserve of the computer, which provides the information upon which middle management can make decisions, and authority is no longer vested in lower management.

This observable shift in control to higher levels in the organisation leads to a widening of the gap between unskilled workers and lower management and the higher qualified skilled managerial level.

This study also suggested that the different levels and functions in management accept and use the new information technology for different reasons. Senior management look for a return on investment and increased sales and productivity (i.e. strategic objectives), while middle management are concerned with consistency and predictability of output for management control purposes, and in contrast lower management are interested mainly in smoother workflow, fewer problems and less pressure (i.e. operational objectives).

With the introduction of the computer in Company X the findings generated by the case study appear to match management expectations.

Senior management had their expectations fulfilled in that an increased workload had been met without the need to employ more staff. In the Goods Inward department, where employment was expected to rise, a decrease in staff of two had been achieved on a non-replacement basis. However, ROI calculations had not yet been undertaken since the system was still at an early stage, and likewise any increase in sales as a direct consequence of the introduction of a computer was difficult to identify at this point.

Middle management appeared the most satisfied group in the management hierarchy, with respect to the fulfilment of expectations. This group had successfully removed operating control and decision-making from lower levels, and in so doing they had made company procedures more centralised, consistent and routine. By incorporating these functions as their own they had effectively enhanced their corporate position.

Likewise, lower management achieved their operational objectives, as daily operations became more systematic throughout the entire company. This group had played the major role in installing the new system - dealing with staff enquiries, complaints and operating difficulties - yet in so doing their previous responsibility and control was transferred to middle managers. The removal of most discretion, initiative and responsibility for decision-making had led to discontentment among some individual department and branch managers, who felt that the more interesting aspects of their job had effectively been removed.

This study would seem to reinforce the earlier findings of Whisler (1970), in that those in the 'boundaries of organisation' and who interact with the public (i.e. in this case, shop assistants), are less affected by computers than those performing 'internal functions' such as problem solving, information transmission and transformation (i.e. lower management functions).

Consumer Reactions. The finding most reinforced by this pilot study was that of the Policy Studies Institute (Martin and Zeilunger, 1982). Few direct benefits were perceived by customers, with the exception of reduced waiting time for personal orders through improved company ordering and office procedures. This said, it is believed that customers of

Company X will benefit in the long run indirectly, from the improved company performance.

CONCLUDING REMARKS

The introduction of new technology within retailing presents the ability to compile, manipulate, retrieve and store information at an acceptable cost and without massive dislocation. Different management levels use this information for different purposes, although many management objectives are never stated and are, therefore, difficult to define. However, the overriding aim generated from both the literature and this pilot study is the concern to increase management control and, as a result, improve the company's operational performance. In the study reported here, this resulted in an upward shift of power in the organisational hierarchy.

The resulting centralisation and augmentation of control functions increased efficiency and the speed of operations in many departments, but had the effect of distancing many operators from management. In addition, unlike the McKinsey study (1974) an increase in staff training time through the introduction of a formalised training programme was noted. In fact, no labour saving or rescheduling was achieved.

The case study suggested that, with the introduction of new technology, retail management consider only the 'soft' to 'very soft' potential benefits that will be generated. No operational criteria or quantitative analyses were ever applied to assess the advantages or disadvantages. Rather a qualitative assessment was used to consider operational impact. The main benefits thought to be realised were of a 'soft' nature as identified by McKinsey, i.e. mainly of a management control nature.

This result is interesting since these particular benefits were assumed by McKinsey to be essentially long term in nature. The case study suggests the reverse. 'Hard' benefits may, in the case of the non-food retailers, be the most difficult to quantify and may therefore require many organisations to readjust management thinking and begin setting quantifiable objectives for retail departments, similar to those techniques used by manufacturing industry.

One important reason why the 'hard' benefits identified by McKinsey may not have been achieved is due to their dependence on the removal of manual pricing operations, and the accompanying labour savings. The products sold by the company in the case study have traditionally been subject to Resale Price Maintenance and, as goods are priced at source, no similar work is required at the point-of-sale, so many direct savings cannot therefore be achieved.

The initial staff response was predicted from the literature – an acceptance of the technology as a relief from the more boring and repetitive tasks. In the short term, work attitudes and performance levels were improved. The long term consequences, however, indicate that the microprocessing equipment may have the effect of distancing its operators and branch managers from upper management levels, and as a result lead to a significant deterioration of communications within the company.

Although improved management control procedures can lead to better implementation of company policy and objectives, in operational terms these gains may never be achieved if lower organisation levels are isolated from the system. Other commentators suggest that this response is a consequence, not of the technology itself, but rather of the way work has been reorganised around it.

Unlike the scanning stores mentioned in the literature, the technology of Company X did not require the removal of item pricing. As a result, many customers were not aware that a new computerised system was in operation. No significant reduction in queuing time was achieved, as no technical alteration had been made at the point-of-sale. The improvement in stock control was indirectly passed on to the consumer in such factors as: improved store layout - placing more popular items at a point of easy access; better stock rotation and stockturn rate, ensuring fewer out-of-stocks; increased product information being available; and an increase in the level of service offered, since staff could offer more assistance to customers with purchases, because the computer had reduced the time previously required for manual operations.

One conclusion is that many of the 'hard' savings that may have been achieved by Company X were not visible, as an accompanying increase in service levels counterbalanced cost reductions.

However, given that the company at the time of the study had been 'live' for less than one year and was still encountering many 'teething' problems, it may be premature to make any judgements on the computer's impact on operations, other than to say that few of the envisaged or expected 'hard' savings had been achieved.

REFERENCES

Bamber, G. (1981) 'The Implications of Technological Innovation', Quarterly Review Trimestrielle Magazin, 40(3)

Boddy, D. and Buchanan, D. (1982) Organization in the Computer Age, Gower, Aldershot

Cohen, B. (1979) 'Say Scanners Pay Off in About a Year', Supermarket News, Feb. 5, 39

French, B. (1980) 'EPOS 80 - Where the Real Benefits Lie', Retail and Distribution Management, Sept/Oct., 25-7

Jones, G. (1977) Data Capture in a Retail Environment, NCC, Manchester

Langrehr, F. and Robinson, R. (1979) Journal of Consumer Affairs, 13(2), 61-76

Martin, J. and Zeilunger, A. (1982) New Technology in Banking and Shopping, Policy Studies Institute, London

McKinsey (1974) Evaluating Feasibility of SPNPS in the UK Grocery Industry, McKinsey & Co., London

NEDO (1982) Technology: The Issues for the Distributive Trades, Distributive Trade Economic Development Council, National Economic Development Office, London

Office of Fair Trading (1982) Microelectronics and Retailing Office of Fair Trading, London

Ornstein, E., (1978) The Retailers, Assoc. Business Programmes, London

Phillips, K. (1980) The Impact of Scanners in the Retail Grocery Industry, MSc Thesis, Durham University

Retail Management Development Programme, (1982) Guide to Retail Data Capture Systems, RMDP, Brighton

USDAW, (1981) New Technology Action Pack, Union of Shop, Distributive and Allied Workers, London

Whisler, T. (1970) The Impact of Computers on Organization Praeger, New York

Chapter 15

NEW INFORMATION TECHNOLOGY AND MARKETING SYSTEMS

Nigel Piercy

INTRODUCTION

Any attempted consideration of the relationship between marketing and new information technology suggests that attention
should be devoted to the observable and overt changes in products and their costs, and the success of marketing management
in researching, launching, promoting and distributing new and
improved products. Indeed, there is some justice in the claim
that recent UK performance in this respect has not been out-
standingly effective, and some commentary is possible on the
nature of the change in market systems, highlighting the difficulties faced. However, the bulk of the paper is concerned not
with these external market changes, but with the more covert
and largely ignored, impact of new technology on corporate
marketing systems. In particular, we examine change in the
administrative systems for marketing relating to information
and to organisational structure.

MARKET SYSTEMS CHANGE

At the strategic level, one implication is that the competitive
structure of many markets becomes unstable with fundamental
technological change and there is a risk that marketing expertise may not transfer easily to new sectors. For instance,
there are various examples of 'innovation by invasion' by firms
entering new product-markets in which they had not previously
been considered competitors (Twiss, 1978), such as Mattel, the
toy manufacturer, launching a home computer, or Sinclair's
moves from pocket calculators to digital watches to home
computers to mini-televisions, or the moves by semi-conductor
producers into end-user products. Texas Instruments has integrated into such product-markets as weighing machines, security
systems, video games, and educational aids, as well as home
computers. Interestingly, it was noted of Texas Instruments'
ill-fated attempts to market electronic watches:

> 'TI managers reckoned that they could compensate for being wet behind the ears on consumer-marketing techniques by producing a steady stream of relatively inexpensive, high-technology products. They were wrong. This lack of marketing nous helps explain TI's dismal showing in personal computers.' (The Economist, 1981)

Diversification and forward integration in market terms offers the opportunity to exploit a technology in more user-applications, but clearly at the higher risk of marketplace failure.

Indeed, even relatively minor strategic moves may meet with a lack of competitive success. Hewlett-Packard, for instance, has achieved spectacular success in the minicomputer market, but has made little impact with its personal computers (Heller, 1983).

Perhaps the most fundamental point is that market diversification, of whatever form, involves a high risk, and that the competitiveness created by faster product obsolescence adds to this risk (Mann and Thornton, 1981).

The need for what has been called 'accelerated marketing', where time-scales for decision-making are reduced, suggests both the need for attention to a strategy of information and intelligence and of structural adjustment in companies, as well as the need to change and adapt marketing techniques. These latter adaptations may vary from simply adopting 'systems selling' - as in marketing word processing systems, rather than simply separate pieces of office equipment (McLean and Rush, 1978) - to more fundamental changes represented by such innovations as 'telemarketing' and the 'electronic channel of distribution'.

The point is, of course, that the impact of new technology in the marketplace can lead to spectacular commercial failures, arguably through a lack of integration of marketing strategy with technology. Consider the following recent examples:

1. The viewdata system 'Prestel' has lost money for the past three years, achieving only a very limited penetration of its market potential (Brooks, 1983). Envisaged by its sponsors as a universal computer data bank for the residential market, British Telecom, having abandoned its test market before results were clear, is considered to have lost touch with the market:

> 'Telecom had thought Prestel would sell itself. The marketing's task was to promote the service's general concept through mass media advertising, to raise general awareness....The effect on Prestel seems to have been a neglect of the market to the cost of design, and quality of service.'
> (Witcher, 1981).

Indeed, currently it is rumoured that if the present campaign aimed at home users does not succeed, British Telecom may end the service (Brooks, 1983).

2. The current excitement over the go-ahead for cable television in the UK and the 'wired-up society' is giving way to scepticism about the market demand for 30-channel cable TV in the light of declining TV audiences, and hence its diminishing attractiveness as an advertising medium. Certainly, existing cable TV experiments fuel this pessimism (Spandler, 1983). Indeed, the longer US experience is far from encouraging, with major losses and closures among cable companies and already signs that the cable technology may quickly become obsolete due to direct broadcast technologies without the need for cabling, and possibly fibre optics replacing the standard coaxial telephone cable (Campbell, 1983).

3. The launch of the Nimslo 3-dimensional camera has been immediately followed by a price reduction of almost a quarter, because of disappointing sales and the withdrawal of the product by some major distributors. This had led to comparisons with successes in the photographic market by the Kodak Disc camera, which was developed specifically to overcome the problems found by family 'snapshot' photographers, and with the success of Polaroid. It is suggested by one source that:

> 'it is difficult to escape the conclusion that Nimslo 3-D photography is a clever invention in search of a market.' (Marketing, 1983).

Indeed, on a broader scale the National Economic Development Council's information technology working party has pointed to growing import penetration, loss of market share, and a failure to match foreign competitors, and one comment is that:

> 'Britain still lacks the skills to pursue the information revolution as keenly as it should. There is no lack of innovation, but much of it fails to realise its potential.' (Brooks and Eglin, 1983)

This said, what does not appear immediately apparent is the availability of theoretical approaches from marketing to structure and facilitate the necessary coping with challenges of such technological innovations. However, while firm conclusions are inappropriate at the present stage of knowledge, there would seem some grounds for questioning strategic factors such as:

1. The need for clearer planning of product-market strat-

egy and the exploitation of corporate resources of all kinds, rather than simply technological innovation. It has been noted, for instance, that 'product design is everybody's business' (Libien, 1979), not the prerogative of the technologist.

Clearly, there have been many advances of new technology in the product offerings made, in the sense of completely new products, the up-dating of existing products with new features, and incorporating new control devices to replace older versions, as demonstrated most obviously in the consumer electronics field.

For example, a recent electronics exhibition in Japan manifested such innovations as miniaturised video systems and audio equipment, household and game-playing robots, and many other gadgets. A report of the exhibition concludes with a particularly apposite comment:

> 'Last word goes to a manufacturer at the show who shall remain anonymous. A smiling assistant touched little dots on a TV screen that emitted musical notes, duly recorded in sequence by a computer. When asked who would use it, the beaming engineer replied "No-one at all that I can think of."' (McGill and Vines, 1982)

The suggestion is that it is all too easy to assume a market need, which may not exist or may not be large enough to be attractive.

2. Reliance on price competitiveness may be dangerous in opening up new technological markets.

One currently urgent problem in marketing new technology lies in the tendency for competition to be dominated by price. For instance, a recent analysis of the consumer electronics industry drew attention to the dramatic price-cutting being used by suppliers to maintain market share (Oliver, 1983). Indeed, it has recently been reported that the cheapest Sinclair home computer has reached a price low of $29 in the USA, providing possibly the first example of the expendable or throwaway computer.

The inevitable danger in price wars is that in spite of economies of scale, experience effects, and more efficient production systems through increased volume, profits disappear.

Further, it has long been recognised that buyers use price as an indicator of quality (Gabor and Granger, 1966), or at least they do in those circumstances where there is no more easily available criterion of judgement. Technological product complexity, wide brand choice, and rapid market change would seem to provide those necessary circumstances, suggesting the potential for non-price competition.

One presently observable implication of the price-orientation of competition in such markets is described by the concept of the price elasticity of expectations (Kotler, 1971). The effect is that rapid decreases in price may actually reduce rather than stimulate demand, as potential buyers withdraw from the market, awaiting further price falls or the launch of the next generation of the product.

3. By implication, one source of business failures of the type discussed above, is the emphasis on technology at the expense of existing or potential market demand in the classic demonstration of 'marketing myopia' (Levitt, 1965). Interestingly, it has been noted, for instance, in the consumer appliance market that successful Japanese firms do not use revolutionary new marketing methods, but are simply better and more thorough in their use of traditional methods.

4. In spite of the above points, it is also apparent that new products may demand new marketing approaches, as for instance, in the Japanese concept of development partnerships, or such innovations as 'telemarketing' and 'teleshopping'.

In the first place, new products and high levels of competition may bring about the need for new channels of distribution.

At one level, these may simply be new channels to the particular company. For instance, in entering the home computer market, IBM has chosen to use High Street retail outlets, while in its more traditional markets the company is testing in the UK the 'box selling' principle pioneered by Ford. By selling a large number of standard units rather than a tailor-made system, IBM is using computer service companies rather than selling directly to computer buyers (Walton, 1982).

At a more fundamental level, channels are changing through new order-taking media, such as terminals in the marketplace; teleshopping - as now pioneered in the West Midlands; and in the most extreme formulation through 'telemarketing'.

Telemarketing is conceived as an electronic channel of distribution, in which telecommunication links between suppliers, distributors and buyers, allow electronic order-taking, advertising and promotion to chosen targets, the immediate pursuit of sales leads and control of marginal accounts, the measurement of advertising effectiveness, and the collection of market research and intelligence (Voorhees and Coppett, 1983).

Further, in the area of marketing communications, taking together the areas of advertising, sales promotion, personal selling and public relations, fundamental changes in this area relate to rapid changes in the media of mass communication, and the impact of such changes on advertisers; as well as their ability to segment markets with greater precision.

Much attention has been devoted to the impact of new technology on mass communications media, in the form of such developments as satellite broadcasting, cable television, videotex with the interactive television receiver, video-recording, and so on.

While on the one hand such media may offer new vehicles

for advertising and promotion, there are already suggestions that more media may simply spread audiences more thinly and reduce access to them for the advertiser, and indeed that more media may mean higher advertising costs. Apart from the media costs themselves, the increasingly difficult problems of media planning and budget allocation, may tend to increase operating costs.

This said, new media do promise the opportunity for more accurate market segmentation to reach specialist target markets. Indeed, allied to this, and already operational, is the computerised ACORN system (A Classification of Residential Neighbourhoods) and the Post Office's related Consumer Location System. This approach is based on the greater similarity within defined neighbourhoods and housing types of demographic and social characteristics and lifestyle, than has been demonstrated by the more traditional socioeconomic and income classifications.

However, even given the significance of the problems of marketing the outputs of new information technology in the form of new and improved products, through new channels and new communications media, perhaps most surprising is the lack of attention devoted to the impact of new information technology on marketing management itself. To some extent, it will be seen that this impact is unavoidably linked to environmental change generated by the new technology, but there appears some merit in examining the issues raised for the corporate role of the marketing function.

THE ADMINISTRATIVE SYSTEMS OF MARKETING: INFORMATION AND ORGANISATION

To begin, two points are worthy of note: first, the prescriptive notion that corporate marketing activities provide the boundary-spanning function which reflects the marketplace within the company; and second, that the internal corporate relationships between marketing and other functional specialisms remain problematic in many situations.

The first of these points is summarised in the prescriptive ideas of 'market orientation', 'customer satisfaction' and the 'marketing concept'. While there is some controversy surrounding the utility of such prescriptions, they remain central to marketing education and training, and provide much of what may be recognised as the developed paradigm of operational marketing.

What is perhaps the best-known statement in this area is:

'The marketing concept is a management orientation that holds the key task of the organization is to determine the needs and wants of target markets and to adapt the organization to delivering the desired satisfactions more effectively and efficiently than its competitors.' (Kotler, 1980)

The central elements of this viewpoint are a focus on the needs of the buyer and the integration of all customer-impinging resources within the firm.

In support of the first element, Levitt's (1965) classic 'marketing myopia' paper blamed business failures on an emphasis on products or technologies rather than more fundamental buyer needs, while management writers like Drucker (1968) have reached such normative conclusions as:

> 'Marketing is so basic that it cannot be considered a separate function... It is the whole business seen from the point of view of its final result, that is from the customer's point of view.' (Drucker, 1968)

While contemporary analysis suggests that there is much in such writing which is simplistic, and the search for a relationship between 'marketing orientation' and commercial success has proved largely fruitless (Davidson, 1975), and while other evidence suggests a very limited application of the marketing concept in British industry (Hayhurst and Wills, 1972), for present purposes it may be seen that there is a distinctive perspective prescriptively associated with the marketing function.

Indeed, it is the nature of this perspective which leads to the second point relating to internal company relationships between marketing and other functional specialisms. It has been suggested for example that:

> 'Marketing, in trying to mobilize the company's resources to develop customer satisfaction, often causes other departments to do a poorer job in their terms ... In some cases the hostility against the marketing concept erupts in costly power struggles and inconsistent departmental policies and actions.' (Kotler, 1965)

Indeed, there have been many detailed commentaries on the conflicts between marketing and other functions, and particularly those with production and research and development.

It is suggested, therefore, that the relationship between marketing and technical management in a firm provides one key to analysing the real impact of new technology on marketing systems.

In many ways it is this potential for goal difference and conflict which suggests the importance of the boundary-spanning function of marketing in what has been analysed as the 'corporate battleground' for marketing (Piercy, 1983b). In particular, it is this function of marketing which highlights the significance of the formal corporate positioning and structuring of marketing, and the related area of the marketing information systems.

The following analysis attempts to explore the impact of

new information technology in these areas: marketing information, and marketing organisation structure.

Marketing Information

It is already clear, from what has gone before, that marketing
information is central to the corporate role and functioning of
the marketing subunit, and that new technology is radically
changing the availability of information. While it is tempting
to regard more and better marketing information as a benefit of
new technology, enough is known already to demonstrate the
strategic significance of such developments and thus in
consequence the need for a strategic response by marketing and
general management.

In each area of marketing information, new technology is
already providing more data, faster and cheaper. Developments
are many and include: private viewdata systems to collect and
manipulate field sales information; computerised on-line
interviewing of respondents; test marketing using cable television advertising; laser scanning in retail outlets to measure sales; and the ability to process, store, and disseminate
large volumes of information.

However, while the technology is largely in-place, what
remains in doubt, for several reasons, is the ability of
marketing managers and organisations to absorb and use these
informational resources.

Macro-Marketing Information Systems. In the first case, in
exploiting new information technology and dealing with the
informational environment, it must be recognised that
information may be controlled and owned by those who do not
wish to share it. For example, in the grocery and packaged
goods field, the bar coding of products and laser scanning
in-store offers the potential of a channel or market
information system to support product, price and advertising
decisions with hard data and market tests.

The potential offered has been described by this writer as
that of a 'macro-marketing information system', involving a
distributed network of information inputs and users of the type
shown in Figure 15.1.

However, the extent to which this potential may actually
be realised remains questionable. The point is that one implication of the new information technology is that the existing
structural power of distributors in the channel is magnified by
the control of informational resources. In fact, there are
already indications that because critical marketing data are
controlled by distributors, not only is free information-
sharing a somewhat optimistic expectation, but suppliers may be
placed at a positive disadvantage because of the increased
decision-making power of distributors.

Figure 15.1:   The Macro-Marketing Information System

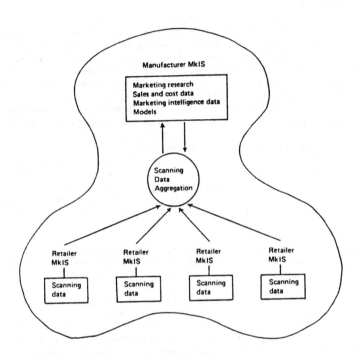

Source: Piercy and Evans (1983)

Possible responses by retailers are summarised in Figure 15.2, varying from outright conflict through competitive and commercial relationships to one of co-operation.   While a co-operative strategy of information-sharing may appear attractive to the supplier in terms of realising 'shared' or 'joint' marketing in the channel (Walters, 1979), and the possibilities of reducing total channel costs through increased logistical and marketing efficiencies, what remains to be seen is the price that will have to be paid to achieve these advantages.

Even accepting the notion of 'quasi-integration' between large distributors and their suppliers, it seems likely that information sharing based on new technology will be bought by suppliers only through such concessions as: information sharing by suppliers in terms of plans and market data;   reduced manufacturer discretion to make independent or unilateral marketing and product development decisions; and increased customisation of brands and communications to distributors' requirements.

To some extent new technology may simply be reinforcing the existing structural power of the distributor (e.g. see Reve and Stern, 1980), and where co-operative marketing does not emerge, for whatever reason, then it seems likely that manufacturer responses will include: greater expenditure on their own information systems to counter the distributor's informational advantage; greater expenditure on 'pull' strategies creating a customer or market franchise to counter the distributor's increased power in the channel; and the exploration of opportunities for co-operative relationships with others at the same level in the channel, again to counter distributor power.

However, the first major implication for management is concerned not with the specific form which tactics will take, but the need for a strategic response to a changed informational environment in the channel and the information sharing product-market, which results from the impact of new technology.

Marketing Information Control in the Organisation. A second issue is that of the control of marketing information in the company, and specifically the impact of new technology on the power of the marketing department, as specialists or experts in the market boundary-spanning position in an organisation.

Following the received theory, to the extent that marketing information is critical to organisational needs, then it should follow that the marketing department is in a powerful position, although this presupposes not merely centrality but also an absence of routinisation and substitutability (Hickson, et al, 1971).

One prediction is that the integrated communication-information system may both routinise certain marketing information handling operations, and also increase substitutability. For instance, if sales forecasting is taken as an example of an uncertainty absorption role frequently performed within the marketing subunit, then the integrated system offers the opportunity for sales and market data to be analysed by the system and model-based extrapolations to be produced without human intervention, or in other words routinised; and those extrapolations will provide a forecasting and planning base open to manipulation by any system user - whether in the marketing, production, finance or other subunit, or by general management.

While the diffusion of information control is by no means inevitable - subsystems may be protected, political games may be played to retain control of information, and routinised information processing may not prove effective in rapidly changing conditions - there is certainly an implication that the power of the marketing subunit may be reduced. Indeed,

Figure 15.2: Distributor Marketing Information Strategies

Strategies of Marketing Information Use	Retailer Advantages	Manufacturer Advantages
Conflict	Power from information control is used to pursue self-interest	–
Competition	Leverage in negotiation and bargaining	–
Commercial	Income from sale of marketing information	Information is available, but at a financial cost
Co-operation	– Reduced total channel – costs through integration	

Source: Piercy (1983a)

there is precedent for such a change – for instance, as advertising expenditures have become heavier in some companies, much control over budgeting seems to have passed to general management, and a response to the dominance of large retailers by some consumer goods firms has been to establish Trade Marketing departments, sometimes leaving the marketing department responsible for no more than a third of total sales (Wills and Kennedy, 1982). The implication is that managerial choices have to be faced. We return to this question in examining the organisational structure for marketing.

Marketing Management Information Needs.   A third issue relates to the effectiveness of upgraded information systems within the marketing subunit itself. In the general literature it is some time since Ackoff (1967) described the characteristics of 'management misinformation systems' which obstruct rather than support decision-making. Similarly, Tricker (1971) has described the 'myths of management information' such as: (a) that more data in reports is the same thing as more information for management; (b) that more frequent reporting means that more useful information is provided; (c) that instant availability increases the usefulness of information; and (d) that accuracy in reporting is of vital importance.

There would seem some considerable danger that the attempted implementation of new information technology within marketing will be prey to just such assumptions. Indeed, this writer has described earlier the risks involved in implementing new technology in the marketing information system as relating, on the one hand, to ignoring the opportunities provided, but also on the other hand to mismanaging implementation to the extent that existing decision-making processes are undermined, and the total effect is that of reduced competitiveness. (Piercy, 1981).

Indeed, more generally, there have been difficulties in linking the development of more sophisticated information systems to improved organisational performance, and more recently one systems analyst has concluded:

'Some management information systems, as well as much of the literature on MIS, rest on a significant misconception...... Very few line managers want more data than they now get, whether historical or projected; most managers are inundated with data, and if they want more they can commonly get it.' (Vyssotsky, 1980)

In the marketing field particularly, great operational difficulties are faced in determining what <u>management information need</u> actually are. This arises partly from the implied need to model decisions to understand information needs, and the increasing difficulty in predicting or meeting information needs as the decisions concerned move from the routine to the strategic level. While there may be clear gains in automating such processes as stock re-ordering, order handling, and logistics, what appears less evident is the extent to which upgraded information systems will improve product-market strategic choices, advertising strategy, or channel management, where much reliance is on 'soft' data and qualitative analysis.

One information systems analyst has concluded that:

'Strategic decisions make or break the enterprise, and these are the decisions the CEO is paid to make. The quality of available information on which such decisions must be based is commonly so poor that extrapolation by pencil and paper will usually yield as much insight as there is to be had. (Vyssotsky, 1980)

Given the nature of marketing variables and the environment in which decisions are made (Piercy, 1983b), it has been suggested that in practical terms, it may not simply be that marketing management information needs are difficult to identify, but that these needs may not be 'knowable' (Piercy and Evans, 1983).

In fact, setting aside this question, then even in the simpler areas of more routine decision-making in marketing, the process of implementing new information technology is further complicated by the existence of idiosyncracies in information use, and the highly individual nature of different managers' decision-making, which implies different information needs (e.g. Hellriegel and Slocum, 1980).

Indeed, there is a considerable danger inherent in assuming rationality and orderliness in decision-making, as the basis for exploiting new information technology in marketing. For example, it has long been recognised that marketing information plays a variety of strictly non-objective functions - such as providing a collective memory, or a stabilising factor, or a source of reassurance, or even as a way of delaying decisions by 'taking the heat off' which arise from the needs of organisations (Channon, 1968).

Over and above this, moreover, the organisational aspects of information suggest the need to recognise politics, where information is liable to manipulation and secrecy, in the context of the power of particular individuals and groups and the conflict found between departments. Researchers at M.I.T. have suggested, for example, that the link between information systems and power arises from the fact that:

> 'Information systems increasingly alter relationships, patterns of communication and perceived influence, authority and control.' (Keen, 1980)

Keen has categorised the 'games' or counterimplementation strategies used by those resisting information systems change into: (a) diverting resources, (b) deflecting goals, and (c) dissipating the energies of those promoting the change, and has developed the notion of 'countercounterimplementation' strategies as a managerial response.

While these points may be regarded as merely illustrative of the practical barriers to be overcome in implementing new information technology in marketing systems, the suggestion here is that they are indicative of something of rather more fundamental managerial importance. The implication drawn is that the times when a piecemeal, ad hoc adoption of new information capabilities, involving no more than the addition of pieces of peripheral equipment have gone. The changes now faced in the organisational role of marketing and in managing new marketing information resources imply the need for an explicit strategic information plan in marketing (see Benjamin, 1980; and Piercy and Evans, 1983).

Marketing Organisational Structure

From what has been said above, it appears almost inevitable that there should be a twin concern with structure and information in marketing, although there has been little or no manifest recognition of that relationship in the marketing literature.

At one level, a certain amount of attention has been devoted to the structural requirements for innovation in products and in marketing methods. Given the very high failure rate in new product development, attention has focused on such devices as product management, new product departments, venture groups and matrix structures, as ways of coping with the demands of innovation, as opposed to managing existing products, through greater product-market specialisation and decentralisation.

For example, it was noted earlier that Hewlett-Packard has met little success in the personal/microcomputer market, in spite of the company's strength in minicomputers. Because of the substantial market differences between the two areas, the company's response has been to create a Personal Computer Group as a coordination mechanism, to operate in a different way to the rest of the company (Heller, 1983).

Similarly, there has been empirical evidence suggesting that increasingly product and market diversity and change lead towards the matrix or programme/resource structure in the marketing operations of large American corporations (Corey and Star, 1971).

However, more fundamentally, new information technology has a number of other, less overt and certainly less well understood, implications for the structure of marketing.

There is, to begin with, an argument that upgrading information systems may to some extent be an alternative to restructuring the organisation (as well as itself causing the need for organisational change).

For instance, Galbraith (1972) put the case that a structure represents an information processing capacity, while the environment poses information processing burdens. With increasing environmental complexity, a choice may exist between either reducing the burden of information processing (through reduced performance standards or structural realignment) or increasing information processing capacity (through information systems development or structural change).

To pursue these points separately:

1. Structural self-containment to reduce information processing needs involves fewer specialised roles and units, duplication, and reduced economies of scale. The reduced interdependence between units lessens the total information processing need, because smaller autonomous units require less coordination than does a large integrated unit. In the marketing area such realignments are manifested, for example by market groups or area management, each with its own marketing specialists. Similarly, the emergence of the Trade Marketing department mentioned earlier may represent this type of change. In product management, the pattern of change would seem more complex. Given that the 'little general manager' concept of product management has never been widespread in practice (Wills and Hayhurst, 1972), the 'flattening pyramid' would seem more to take the form of replacing product managers with category

managers or business segment managers with typically broader responsibilities, than of an enhanced product management role.

2. Increasing the capacity to handle information may involve increased computerisation (with the implications already discussed) or it may involve structural change, in the form of additional 'staff' posts. In this case, it may be that the result is more clerical staff in marketing, more 'assistants-to', and more low-level product managers rather than fewer.

3. Increasing the capacity to handle information through lateral relations and joint decision-making, is described by Galbraith (1972) as involving mechanisms such as committees, project teams, new product groups, and ultimately the matrix organisation of programme management. One prediction is that the impact of complex, overlap structures of this kind is that the role and power of the marketing subunit is reduced, because strategic decisions are pushed higher in the structure and the managerial emphasis is on portfolios rather than individual products (Doyle, 1979). Indeed, the centralisation/ decentralisation debate may imply in some cases the disintegration of the marketing subunit altogether, following its relatively recent emergence through the integration of advertising and sales (Weigand, 1961).

The implication of these points will be made explicit shortly, but returning first to the informational issue discussed under 2. above, if the choice made is to use new technology to collect, process, store, and disseminate more marketing information, then similarly this of itself has further organisational implications for marketing.

First, the nature of the marketing manager's job is likely to change, since much of the information handling role may be delegated further down the organisation and there may, in any case, be fewer levels in the hierarchy. The impact of the integrated communication/information system on middle management has been associated with lowered morale on the one hand, and with resistance to change on the other (Conrath and du Roure, 1977).

Second, there have been a number of predictions that information technology has the effect of centralising control and becoming part of the control structure (e.g. Whisler, 1970). To the extent that these predictions are true, then the role of the marketing subunit will inevitably change. To some extent this change is implicit in the current suggestions for a division between operational, routinised aspects of marketing, and marketing planning and development (Wills, 1980), though a more pessimistic view is that:

'The new structures have diffused marketing decisions and curtailed the autonomy of marketing management' (Doyle, 1979).

Doyle's view is essentially that organisational change of the type discussed above, implies that: the focus of management will shift to integration; emphasis will be on portfolio rather than product management, with more use of teams and venture groups; and that the product manager role will become obsolete.

Third, as already implied above, more generally the present status of the marketing department is threatened by new technology, simply because power flows to those who control the technology, and thus the information, so that it is anticipated that the power of the Information Systems department will increase (Bariff and Galbraith, 1978).

Clearly, each of the issues highlighted above is worthy of more detailed analysis, but for the moment enough has been said to demonstrate the less overt, but more pervasive impact of new information technology on marketing. The implication to be drawn at this stage parallels that in the previous section: the impact of new technology is not merely upon information systems in marketing, it is on the structuring of marketing activities, and the task faced by analysts and managers in marketing is the design of a strategic organisational plan to cope with the demands of new information technology (Piercy, 1984).

CONCLUSION

It was seen that the most overt impact of new information technology on marketing was in the problems imposed by the need to develop and launch new and improved products in turbulent markets, and to cope with new media of communications and distribution. These issues are demonstrably of current practical significance, and it was seen that there are grounds for highlighting the need for strategic planning to cope with technological change and to avoid technical/marketing failures of the type illustrated.

However, most of the attention here has been devoted to the less overt, but arguably more fundamental impact of new information technology on the administrative systems for marketing in companies. This is related to the first section in two ways: because a lack of technology/marketing integration and a failure to successfully perform the boundary-spanning role may lie at the centre of marketplace failures with new technology; and because the existence of goal differences and conflicts and commercial failures may accentuate the perceived need for change in internal marketing systems.

The focus here was firstly on marketing information, and secondly on the related area of organisational structures for marketing.

In the relationship between the corporate marketing information system and the environment it was seen that the potential was for a 'macro-marketing information system' based on new technology, in the channel and product-market. However, it was equally the case that there are considerable practical obstacles to information-sharing and 'joint marketing', which call for a strategic response from marketing management.

It was also seen that information sharing within the company may alter the standing of the marketing subunit in terms of expertise and the ability to act as the point of uncertainty absorption relating to the marketplace.

A further issue relates to the difficulties of implementing new information technology in the marketing information system. The conceptual and practical problems inherent in identifying and meeting marketing managers' information needs remain problematic, and the danger identified is that of reducing decision-making effectiveness through new technology, rather than increasing it.

The implication drawn from this is that management is faced with the need to construct and implement a strategic information plan for marketing, which sets appropriate goals in the light of competitive needs and the practical barriers to technology.

Secondly, the impact of new information technology on marketing structure was examined, albeit somewhat speculatively. Over and above the question of designing appropriate organisational mechanisms to develop and launch new products, there is some need to make explicit the structural choices implied and, indeed, the potential trade-off between upgrading marketing information systems with new technology and making structural changes.

In the same way that direct information systems change influences the corporate functioning of marketing, then so do changes in organisational structures within and outwith the marketing subunit.

The implication drawn, therefore, is that hand-in-hand with the need for an information strategy and plan, is the need for this to be integrated with an organisational strategy and plan for marketing, to make explicit the choices faced and the changes necessary for the future.

Returning to the initial point made, perhaps the most fundamental implication of new information technology for marketing is that in external and internal systems the pressures for change are simultaneous, and call for strategic, rather than piecemeal, managerial responses in both areas.

REFERENCES

Ackoff, R.L. (1967) 'Management Misinformation Systems', Management Science, 14(4), 147-156

Bariff, M.L. and Galbraith, J.R. (1978) 'Intraorganizational Power Considerations for Designing Information Systems', Accounting Organizations and Society, 3, 15-27

Benjamin, R.I. (1983), 'Information Technology in the 1990s: A Long Range Scenario', Management Information Systems Quarterly, 6(2), 11-31

Brooks, R. (1983) 'Prestel's Gamble: Is There No Place Like Home?', Sunday Times, 27 March, 65

Brooks, R. and Eglin, R. (1983) 'Who Will Nurture Our Infant-Industries?', Sunday Times, 20 February, 57

Campbell, S. (1983) 'Cable TV Teeters on the High Wire', Sunday Times, 6 March, 62

Channon, C. (1968) 'The Role of Advertising Research in Management Decision Making', Proceedings: Market Research Society Conference

Connell, S., Morris, A. and Whittens, P. (1982) 'The Challenge of Change', Journal of the Market Research Society, 24(3), 180-210

Conrath, D.W. and du Roure, G. (1977) Organizational Implications of Comprehensive Communication-Information Systems, Working Paper, Centre d'Etude et de Recherche sur les Organisations et la Gestion, Aix-en-Provence

Corey, E.R. and Star, S. (1971) Organization Strategy: A Marketing Approach, Harvard University, Boston, Mass.

Davidson, J.H. (1975) Offensive Marketing, Penguin, Harmondsworth

Doyle, P. (1979) 'Management Structures and Marketing Strategies in UK Industry', European Journal of Marketing, 13(5), 319-331

Drucker, P. (1968) The Practice of Management, Pan, London

Gabor, A. and Granger, C.W.J. (1966) 'Price as an Indicator of Quality', Economica, 33, 43-70

Galbraith, J.R. (1972) 'Organization Design: an Information Processing View' in J.W. Lorsch and P.R. Lawrence (eds.), Organization Planning: Cases and Concepts, Irwin, Homewood, Illinois

Hayhurst, R. and Wills, G. (1972) Organizational Design for Marketing Futures, Allen and Unwin, London

Heller, M. (1983) 'HP's Micro Gamble', Marketing, 2 June, 28-32

Hellriegel, D., and Slocum, J.W. (1980) 'Preferred Organizational Design and Problem Solving Styles: Interesting Comparisons', Human Systems Management, 1, 151-8

Hickson, D.J., Hinings, C.R., Lee, C.A., Scheck, R.E. and Pennings, J. (1971), 'A Structural Contingencies Theory of Intraorganizational Power', Administrative Science Quarterly, 16, 216-29

Keen, P.G.W. (1980) Information Systems and Organizational Change, Working Paper, Center for Information Systems Research, Massachusetts Institute of Technology

Kotler, P. (1965) 'Diagnosing the Marketing Takeover', Harvard Business Review, November/December, 70-72

Kotler, P. (1971) Marketing Decision Making: A Model Building Approach, Holt Rinehart and Winston, New York

Kotler, P. (1980) Marketing Management: Analysis, Planning and Control, 4th ed., Prentice-Hall International, London

Levitt, T. (1965) 'Marketing Myopia', Harvard Business Review, September/October, 173-81

Libien, M.A. (1977) 'Product Design is Everybody's Business', Managerial Planning, January/February, 30-33

McGill, P. And Vines, S. (1982) 'Computers That Close Curtains', Observer, 27 October, 21

McLean, J.M. and Rush, H.J. (1978) The Impact of Microelectronics on the UK, Science Policy Research Unit, University of Sussex

Oliver, B. (1983) 'Computers: Is the Price Right?', Marketing, 8 September, 2-4

Piercy, N. (1981) 'Marketing Information: Bridging the Quicksand Between Technology and Decision Making', Quarterly Review of Marketing, Autumn, 1-15

Piercy, N. (1983a) 'Retailer Information Power - The Channel Marketing Information System', Marketing Intelligence and Planning, 1(1), 40-55

Piercy, N. (1983b) 'A Social Psychology of Marketing Information', Journal of the Market Research Society, 25(2), 103-119

Piercy, N. (1984) Marketing Organisation - An Information Processing Perspective, Allen and Unwin, London

Piercy, N. and Evans, M.J. (1983) Managing Marketing Information, Croom Helm, Beckenham

Reve, T. and Stern, L.W. (1980) 'Inter-Organizational Relationships in Marketing Channels', Academy of Management Review, 4(3), 405-16

Spandler, R. (1983) 'Cable Gets the Go-Ahead - But Who Pays for Wiring Up the UK?', Marketing, 5 May, 12

Stonier, T.T. (1978) Materials Production and Labour Requirements in Post-Industrial Society, CPRS, London

Twiss, B. (1978) Managing Technological Innovation, London, Longman

Tricker, R. (1971) 'Ten Myths of Management Information', Management Accounting, 49(8), 231-3

Vorhees, R. and Coppett, J. (1983) 'Telemarketing in Distribution Channels', Industrial Marketing Management, 12, 105-13

Vyssotsky, V.A. (1980) 'Computer Systems: More Evolution than Revolution', Journal of Systems Management, 31(2), 21-7

Walters, D.L. (1979) 'Manufacturer-Retailer Relationships', European Journal of Marketing, 13(7), 179-222

Walton, P. (1982) 'IBM Tests New Sales Route in the UK', Marketing, 2 September, 12

Weigand, R.E. (1961) Changes in Marketing Industries in Selected Industries, Ph.D Thesis, University of Illinois

'Why Nimslo Had to Slash its Prices', Marketing, 16 June, 1

Wills, G. (1980) 'Sweeping Marketing Overboard', European Journal of Marketing, 14(4), 1

Wills, G. and Hayhurst, R. (1972) Organizational Design for Marketing Futures, Allen and Unwin, London

Wills, G. and Kennedy, S. (1982) 'How to Budget Marketing', Management Today, February, 58-61

Witcher, B. (1981), 'Public Service Videotex, Prestel, Innovation and Marketing', Proceedings: Marketing Education Group Conference

AUTHOR INDEX

Abegglan 148, 158,
Ackoff 273, 280
Allen 25, 44
Alloway 196, 199, 213
Alter 203, 213
Ansoff 6, 12
Argyris 100, 118
Armstrong 177, 185
Arnold 76, 83, 92
Ashworth 25, 44
Atkinson 25, 44

Bamber 248, 262
Bariff 278, 280
Barras 105, 108, 118
Barron 124, 137
Batchelor 8, 39, 44
Benjamin 275, 280
Bennett 27, 28, 44
Best 131, 135, 137
Betwick 15, 16, 44
Bird 86, 92, 113, 118
Blackaby 123, 137
Blatt 124, 126, 137
Blauner 145, 158, 226, 230
Blois 3, 12
Blyton 9, 130, 137
Boddy 112, 114, 118, 257, 262
Bodington 161, 166, 167, 168, 171
Bollinger, 36, 44
Boon 34, 44
Booth 105, 120
Botkin 27, 28, 44

Braverman 85, 92, 145, 146, 148, 158, 163, 171
Brighton Labour Process Group 145, 158
British Computer Society 83, 92
Brittan 82, 92, 149, 158
Brooks 264, 265, 280
Brophy 104, 105, 118
Brown 156, 158
Brunet 109, 118
Buchanan 2, 12, 112, 114, 118, 257, 262
Bullers 22, 44
Burbridge 32, 44
Burns 30, 46

Campbell 265, 280
Channon 275, 280
Chartered Mechanical Engineer 64, 72
Chernier 109, 118
Child 101, 118, 220, 221, 230
Chubb 26, 44
Clark 130, 137
Clegg 179, 185
Clocksin 57, 72
Cohen 247, 262
Cole 147 158
Conrath 277, 280
Cooley 169, 171
Coombe 15, 47
Cooper 135, 138
Confederation of British Industry (CBI) 131, 137
Coppett 267, 282

Corey 276, 280
Cotter 8, 44
Coulon 39, 44
Cresswell, 18, 19, 45
Crouch, 156, 158
CSE Microelectronics Group
    168, 171
Curley 207, 213
Curnow 123, 137
Cutler 145, 158

Dabney 43, 44
Damordaran 79, 92
Davidson 269, 280
Davies, A. 9
Davies, B. 124, 125, 133, 138
Davies, D.S. 122, 137
Davis 174, 185
Dehning 75, 92
Deis 19, 45
Dellenbach 27, 34, 45
DeMatteo 109,, 118
Department of
    Communications, Canada
    109, 115, 118
Department of Employment
    131, 132, 137
Department of Industry 1, 12
Dew 82, 92
Doeringer 146, 148, 158
Doll 5, 12
Dore 147, 158
Dorf 39, 45
Dover 106, 118
Down 194, 213
Doyle 277, 278, 280
Drazan 7, 30, 44
Drucker 269, 280
Drury 203, 204, 207, 213
Duffle 36, 44
Dupont-Gatelmand 32, 45

Earl 7, 9
Eason 109, 114, 118
Edghill 18, 19, 45
Edwards, C., 224, 225, 230
Edwards, R.K., 156, 158
Eglin 265, 280
Ein-Dor 207, 213
Elger 145
Ellul 144, 158

European Trade Union
    Confederation 128, 137
Evans 271, 274, 275

Fitter 83, 92
Forester 122, 137, 154, 158
Forrester 20, 21, 23, 29, 45
Francis 217, 230
Freeman 149, 158
French 246, 247, 262
Friedman 145, 158
Friedmann 144, 158
Fry 144, 158

Gabor 266, 280
Gaines 16, 45
Galbraith 276, 277, 278, 280,
    281
Gee 82, 92
Gerwin 144, 159
Gevarter 22, 45
Gibson 199, 203, 213
Gordon 146, 147, 159
Gower 109, 114, 118
Graham 18, 45
Granger 266, 280
Greenberg 105, 119
Gregory 133, 138
Greiner 207, 213
Groover 29, 30, 34, 45

Halal, 5, 12
Handy 3, 4, 12
Hanlon 32, 45
Hayhurst 269, 276, 280, 283
Hedberg 80, 81, 82, 92, 199,
    213
Heginbothan 34, 45
Heller 264, 276, 281
Hellriegel 275, 281
Hennestad 162, 163, 164, 171
Henshall 81, 93
Heywood 64, 72
Hickson 220, 230, 272
Hill 146, 159
Hiltz 99, 119
Hirschheim 87, 92, 99 119
Hofer 6, 12, 225, 230
Holloway 20, 45

Stonier 123, 139, 282
Storey 145, 146, 160
Sumiya 148, 160
Sutton 207, 213
Swann 105, 108, 118
Swanson 203, 215

Tapscott 96, 120
Taylor, F.G. 194, 213
Taylor, I. 40, 42, 47
Taylor, J.R. 98, 102, 120, 121
Thomas 20, 37, 38, 46, 47
Time 111, 121
Touraine 145, 160
Towill 7, 22, 25, 44, 47
Tracy 181, 185
Trades Union Congress (TUC) 128, 129, 139
Treurniet 111, 121
Tricker 202, 215, 273, 282
Turoff 99, 119
Tushman 238, 243
Twiss 263, 282

Union of Shop, Distributive and Allied Workers (USDAW) 248, 262
Urwick 194, 199, 215
Utterback 238, 243

Vater 128, 139
Verba 133, 138
Villers 30, 31, 39 47
Vines 266, 281
Vorhees 267, 282
Vyssotsky 274, 282

Wall 182, 185
Walters 271, 282
Walton, P. 267, 282
Walton, R. 173, 181, 185
Wang 25, 26, 47
Warner 9, 85, 94, 154, 160, 162, 171, 243
Webb, B. 127, 139
Webb, S. 127, 139
Weber 144, 160
Weigand 277, 282
Werneke 125, 139
Weston 32, 45

Whisler 194, 215, 225, 230, 259, 262, 277
White 133, 139
Whybrew 133, 139
Wieslander 25, 47
Wilensky 155, 160
Wilkinson, B. 154, 160
Williams, J.E. 29, 46
Williams, J.H. 43, 47
Williams, R. 88, 89, 94, 168, 169, 171, 173, 175, 185, 209, 215
Williamson 219, 230
Willman 217, 230
Wills 269, 273, 276, 277, 281, 283
Wilson 175, 182, 185
Winkler 183, 185
Witcher 264, 283
Wood 145, 160
Woodward 145, 160
Work Research Unit 113, 116, 121
Wynne 84, 94

Yeoh 19, 20, 47
Younger 88, 94

Zeilunger 246, 259, 262
Zorkoczy 15, 47

SUBJECT INDEX

jobs, pattern of 2, 155
  see also new information
  technology, and employment
  see also new information
  technology, and work
  structure
  see also work, structure of

Kodak 265
knowledge workers 96, 105,
  107, 117

labour displacement 4, 10,
  52, 78, 122, 124, 135,
  174, 256, 259
  see also new information
  technology, and employment
labour displacement, and work
  sharing 9, 127-136
  see also new technology,
  and employment
  see also work sharing
  see also working hours
  reduction
labour market segmentation
  146-8, 149
labour shedding 4, 84, 123
  see also new information
  technology, and employment
  see also labour
  displacement

machine intelligence 56
machine intelligence, and
  speech recognition 57,
  60-61
machine intelligence, and
  speech synthesis 57
machine vision 8, 62-66
macro-marketing information
  system 11, 270-272, 279
management, choices with new
  technology
  see new information technology, management choices
management control 2, 4, 7,
  9, 10, 86, 101
  see also new information
  technology, and management
  control

management information
  systems,
  see new information
  technology, and
  information systems
management strategy 3, 5,
  6, 7
  see also new informa-
  tion technology,
  strategy for
management strategy,
  definition 5
management style 5, 86,
  114, 191, 206
manufacturing management
  see new informa-
  tion technology, in
  production systems
market environment 2, 238-
  240, 263-268
market segmentation 267,
  268
marketing, information
  strategy for 11, 270-
  275
marketing, organisational
  strategy for 11, 275-
  278
marketing systems 7, 11,
  263-279
Mattel 263
microcomputers 3, 32, 36,
  49-51, 75, 83, 95, 96,
  9,195, 245-49
microcomputers, for
  on-line control 51-52
microtechnological
  change, phases in 3, 8,
  95-96
microelectronics, in the
  office
  see electronic office
  technology
  see new information
  technology, in the
  office
motivation 2, 18, 228,
  see also demotivation

National Bureau of
  Standards Automated
  Manufacturing Research
  Facility 40-41

networking
    see information networks
networks
    see information networks
new information technology,
    and careers 76
new information technology,
    and centralisation
    see centralisation
new information technology,
    and co-determination 89,
    90, 161-184
    see also industrial
    democracy
    see also new information
    technology, and employee
    consultation
new information technology,
    and communications 8, 29,
    95, 98-102, 165, 202, 205,
    261, 267-8, 272, 277
new information technology,
    and competition 52, 67,
    176, 201, 237-240, 239-40,
    242, 258, 263, 274
new information technology,
    and conflict,
    see conclict
new information technology,
    and data base access 102-3
    102-3
new information technology,
    and decentralisation
    see decentralisation
new information technology,
    and deskilling 76, 105,
    108, 112, 113, 146, 163,
    165, 182, 208, 257
new information technology,
    and distributed
    intelligence 98
new information technology,
    and economic growth 54-55,
    122, 123, 126, 150
new information technology,
    and education 2, 196,
    197, 223
new information technology,
    and employee consultation
    115, 116, 155, 168

new information tech-
    nology, and employee
    health 8, 77, 78, 89,
    95, 98, 109, 110-111,
    135, 169, 174, 175
new information tech-
    nology, employee
    resistance to 76, 78,
    169, 244, 277
new information tech-
    nology, and employment
    7, 8, 9, 77, 78, 95,
    109, 116, 122, 124,
    135-6, 154, 163, 174,
    178-9, 183, 208, 247-
    48
new information tech-
    nology, and identity
    10, 231, 237-242
new information tech-
    nology, and industrial
    democracy
    see industrial
    democracy
new information tech-
    nology, and
    industrial life cycles
    238-40
new information tech-
    nology, and industrial
    relations 9, 143, 153-
    4, 163, 229, 235
    see also new informa-
    tion technology, and
    trade unions
new information tech-
    nology, and information
    access 102-103, 166
new information techno-
    logy, and information
    manipulation 229
new information techno-
    logy, and information
    suppression 101
new information technolo-
    gy, and information
    systems 6, 17, 57-62,
    189, 191, 205, 248-9,
    263, 273-5

.